Free Food

Other books by the author:

The Wilderness Cure

Free Food

WILD PLANTS
AND HOW TO
EAT THEM

Mo Wilde

With illustrations by Talya Baldwin

**SIMON &
SCHUSTER**

London · New York · Amsterdam/Antwerp · Sydney · Toronto · New Delhi

1 3 5 7 9 10 8 6 4 2

Simon & Schuster UK Ltd
1st Floor
222 Gray's Inn Road
London WC1X 8HB

www.simonandschuster.co.uk
www.simonandschuster.com.au
www.simonandschuster.co.in

Simon & Schuster Australia, Sydney
Simon & Schuster India, New Delhi

The authorised representative in the EEA is Simon & Schuster Netherlands BV,
Herculesplein 96, 3584 AA Utrecht, Netherlands. info@simonandschuster.nl

The author and publishers have made all reasonable
efforts to contact copyright-holders for permission,
and apologise for any omissions or errors in the form of
credits given. Corrections may be made to future printings.

A CIP catalogue record for this book is available
from the British Library

Hardback ISBN: 978-1-3985-0866-8
eBook ISBN: 978-1-3985-0867-5

Pages designed by Studio Doug

Printed and Bound in the UK
using 100% Renewable Electricity at CPI Group (UK) Ltd

MIX
Paper | Supporting
responsible forestry
FSC® C013604

Contents

To Matthew,
who notices the important little details
when identifying plants and fungi,
and who taught me that pedantry
is a virtue to help you stay alive!

Introduction

"My love affair with nature is so deep that I am not satisfied with being a mere onlooker, or nature tourist. I crave a more real and meaningful relationship. The spicy teas and tasty delicacies I prepare from wild ingredients are the bread and wine in which I have communion and fellowship with nature."
EUELL GIBBONS, *STALKING THE HEALTHFUL HERBS*

My fascination with plants and the natural world began at an early age, during a childhood spent outdoors in the Kikuyu uplands of Kenya. Even when I was sent away to school in Britain, I was lucky to be nurtured by Mima, an adopted granny, who taught me the ways of the plants in the woodlands and hedgerows. Neither foraging nor herbalism was on the careers curriculum at school so I did the most rebellious thing I could think of and went to art college, where I quickly realised that my aspiration was greater than my talent. It wasn't until I was fifty that I studied for a Master's degree in herbal medicine. It just goes to show that it's never too late to pursue your passion.

As a young adult, raising three children on my own, I worked hard at multiple jobs, always scraping for a way to make money. In 2008, a friend who was leading a children's outdoor art project for the Forestry Commission asked me to come up with something to teach the adults as I 'know about plants'. That was the first time that I ever 'taught' foraging as a profession. It felt strange at first to be paid for sharing the little knowledge that I had. But it was serendipitous, as I adore what I do. I feel so lucky to be able to introduce the ever-growing number of people seeking reconnection with nature to this wonderful world.

While teaching foraging these past two decades, I've often been asked the ultimate post-apocalypse survival question, 'Could you live *only* on wild food?' During the Coronavirus lockdowns in 2020 and 2021, I decided to do just that. For a year, I stopped buying food and ate a hunter-gatherer diet that consisted solely of wild plants, fungi, seaweeds, game and seafood. I wrote about that life-changing journey in my book *The Wilderness Cure*. It was an experience that challenged many of my preconceptions about food, changing my body and enriching my soul.

Introducing foraging into your life and diet doesn't have to be as extreme as my year of exclusive wild eating. In this book, I want to share with you some of the wisdom I gathered, and explain how you, too, can become an expert forager on whatever scale suits your lifestyle. I am not going to cover hunting or fishing, just the plants and seaweeds that you can easily gather yourself.

To educate myself on how to survive only on what I could glean from the wild, I scoured antique books and research papers on hunter-gatherer tribes and on lost dietary traditions. Importantly, I spent huge amounts of time outside, opening my eyes (and my mouth) to the world around me – even eating my way through all of the grass seeds that grew on the lawn. Whilst much of what I know comes from tradition and communal experience, my experiments in living wild have also given me some unique and deeply personal insights. This book introduces you to the plants and seaweeds that I love, and many aspects of my foraging life. I hope it will inspire you to enrich your diet with wild foods and perhaps, in the process, to improve your health, deepen your connection with nature and find sustainable alternatives to consumer culture.

Though I am an optimist by nature, I recognise that, over the next century, we face uncertain times. Climate breakdown has the potential to trigger economic meltdown. Already, the gap between the rich and poor is the largest in the history of humanity. At the time of writing, the cost-of-living crisis is affecting a huge swathe of the UK population.

The pressure of migration is at a boiling point as people displaced by fire, floods, famine, earthquakes and poverty attempt to build new lives elsewhere. Even in this, the twenty-first century, citizens in, or fleeing from, countries at war find themselves foraging for survival. There are compelling reasons for everyone to know how to survive outside of the supermarket system, if needed.

Whether you're after a survival manual in the wake of the apocalypse, or just want to make small changes to your day-to-day diet – perhaps adding a little bit of wilderness into an urban life – this book is for you. We have been foragers since the dawn of humankind. We're hard-wired to be foragers in the most ancient part of our brains. Be open again to that knowledge, one plant at a time.

PART ONE

GETTING STARTED

CHAPTER 1

First Steps

"The problem, then, is how to bring about a striving for harmony with land among a people many of whom have forgotten there is any such thing as land, among whom education and culture have become almost synonymous with landlessness. This is the problem of conservation education."
ALDO LEOPOLD, *A SAND COUNTY ALMANAC*

Reasons for foraging

All over the world, nearly 2 billion people gather and depend on wild food for their survival. Wild fruits and vegetables – added to rice, wheat, corn, maize or other farmed starchy calories – are what make the difference between malnutrition and well-being for many, even those in wealthy cities. But in the Western world, where, for the most part, food is readily available to us in the supermarkets, just what is the point of foraging? And yet, in recent years, we've seen a dramatic rise in the number of people doing just that. The reason foraging is enjoying a resurgence is that it's not just about food. Foraging brings a host of benefits.

Physical health: Adding wild foods improves the health of our gut microbiome and nourishes us with many more micronutrients than supermarket veg. Dandelion leaves, for example, have three times the vitamin A levels of spinach, while nettle is high in iron, calcium and other important minerals. During my wild food year, my gut microbes became super-responders to the foods that I ate, and the composition of my gut microbiome changed significantly (for the better). I lost weight without trying, and my friend Matt, who accompanied me in my year-long experiment, reversed his diabetes. Time spent walking outdoors looking for food is also physical activity that exercises and strengthens the body without the tedium of the treadmill.

Then there is the simple fact that foraged food tastes great and often unlike any supermarket fruit, vegetables or fungi. Many plants have unique tastes that are great as snacks, flavour enhancers or a complete meal.

Finances: Foraging also saves money – it offers a way to make interesting, nourishing meals for free. Knowing how and what to forage can be the difference between food poverty and food security. Superfoods, like nettles, charge you nothing to supercharge your meals.

Mental health: There is growing evidence that activities like foraging are good for our mental and spiritual as well as our physical health – the 'green prescription'. Many of us live in a highly technological world, often under high levels of stress. Spending time in nature is scientifically proven to reduce stress and enhance health and well-being, especially mental health. In 2020, the NHS included 'green social prescribing' in the NHS Long Term Plan and the Environment Secretary allocated £5.5 million for projects 'preventing and tackling mental ill health through green social prescribing'.[1]

For children, nature-based activities have been shown to improve happiness and self-confidence and can help those with conditions such as attention-deficit disorder to flourish. Foraging provides a focus and a reason for being outside,[2] as well as enhancing a sense of self-reliance. Knowing that you can survive and are blessed by nature teaches you about yourself and encourages a mindset of abundance and gratitude.

Enjoyment: Foraging is also fun. What better way of spending a few hours on a fresh or sunny day than ambling through the woods or hedgerows, or along a seashore, looking for wild food? You lose track of time, forget to check your phone, get exercise, enjoy learning and discovering, and you fall deeply in love with the countryside.

Environmental health: Learning about the nature of food and where it comes from leads to a deeper awareness and love of the natural world. Even if you live in a city, knowing the names and habits of the non-human species that surround you creates a host of friendly faces. Nature is not our enemy, fierce in tooth and claw. She is our beloved, who takes care of us by offering up food, air and water.

Having a connection to nature through foraging and the ability to identify plants and fungi creates conscientious stewards. It increases our respect for the plants, fungi, algae and creatures that inhabit the shared ecosystems of our planet, and our appreciation of the resilient food systems that are available when we manage the land and its resources sustainably. Well-taught enthusiasts become more aware of and sensitive to the natural environment. If you foster a love of nature in a child, they will love and respect her for life. Humanity and the planet need that attitude.

Mindful foraging plays an increasingly important role in supporting, promoting and defending the health of all plants, fungi, algae, animals (including humans) and the habitats or environments in which they live. Humans are a part of nature rather than apart from nature. As the artist and environmentalist Andy Goldsworthy writes, 'We often forget that WE ARE NATURE. Nature is not something separate from us. So when we say we have lost connection with nature, we have lost connection with ourselves.'[3] Only through engaging with nature in practical and meaningful ways can we truly experience this all-important connection to who we are.

Inclusivity: One of the best things about foraging is that it requires no course, no diploma, no degree, no certificate, and no formal qualification. You can't be a Foragist or a Foragologist and there is no Foragism. Of course, it does require some study, but you can do this at your own pace and in a way that suits you.

Foraging is yours, regardless of race, culture, creed or political belief. Nature shows us that diversity exists on a scale that we humans haven't even dreamt of. Neurodiverse? A relationship with nature embraces all of us and in foraging the 'autism advantage' often shines. Many of my friends who teach foraging around the world find it a struggle to fit in with conventional society, yet, having found their niche in wider nature, they thrive. In fact, some traits that modern society considers a disadvantage may be present in our genes because they had a use in our older tribal structures. Colour-blindness, for example. One in twelve men are colour-blind (compared to one in two hundred women). There is a theory that those who are colour-blind may be better at finding camouflaged prey or detecting predators (especially at night) while those with full colour vision can spot red-ripe, edible berries more easily.

Age is also no barrier, as even a two-year-old can catalogue the species in your lawn given the right encouragement. In today's hunter-gatherer tribes (the few that remain), children aged six can identify hundreds of species with the same level of accuracy as the adults. Sadly, in the UK, many children are told that all wild berries, plants and mushrooms are poisonous and grow up distrustful of nature and of their own identification ability.

I'm often asked if foraging is hard to learn. 'With so many plants and fungi out there, will I remember them all? Could I poison myself?' Yes, there are toxic plants and fungi, but there are very few records of people poisoning themselves. Most people are sensibly cautious. There are species that can be confused with poisonous plants but you can easily learn how to identify the few harmful ones. While learning to forage can feel a little daunting, if you can tell the difference between a lettuce and a cabbage, you have the brainpower to do this. It is just a question of methodical learning. Like everything in life, what matters is taking the first step. The 'doing' quickly becomes the 'being'.

Remember, though, that you must not eat or drink – nor teach other people about – any plants or fungi that you are not 100 per cent confident you can identify and that you know to be safe. Never be afraid to say that you don't know. Make identifying an unknown species part of the process of teaching children to research and look things up for themselves.

How to start foraging

While books and manuals are a great starting point and will be a lifelong reference, learning from books teaches you only so much. Home study can't impart touch, texture, smell, taste, aura, mood; these you only learn by being there. Go out with others who know plants. Sign up to a foraging walk. Adopt an elder. Take time to hang out with each plant. If your resources allow, consider taking a course with an established teacher; you could start by looking up classes run by members of the Association of Foragers (**foragers-association.org**).

Be wary when learning from informal blogs, websites and social media groups – they can be helpful but they are also sources of misinformation. Chat GPT failed all the foraging tests I set it! Look for an identifiable author of the online content you have found, then look up who they are and what their expertise actually is. Plenty of people regurgitate information without checking its accuracy, and marketing companies often publish error-filled articles just to build online communities centred around popular topics, from which they later harvest data. So take your time to verify the source of the information you find. Trust that slowly and steadily you will deepen your knowledge. It is a lifelong journey, not a race to win.

Ideally, you need access to land where plants grow in abundance. However, many edible weeds thrive in urban areas or on the edge of cultivation. So even in the centre of a city, once you know how to look, you will find generous plants waiting for you.

If you're a complete beginner, it's a good idea to start with the familiar garden weeds – nettle, dandelion, daisy – and build up your knowledge over time. One species per week is a great way to begin and grow your repertoire; by the end of the year, you'll have learnt about fifty different plants. In the week dedicated to each plant, learn everything about it – including any possible dangerous lookalikes. Pick it, press it, draw it, smell, feel, touch and taste it (if edible). Learn where it likes to grow and look for it there. Take notes, make drawings or stick pressed samples into a notebook – record anything that strikes you about a plant's smell or texture.

Nature Table

When I was a child, our primary school set up a nature table each morning. We were encouraged to find something on the way to school – a leaf, a flower, a berry, a feather or a pebble – and put it on the table. The teacher would then tell us what it was and label it. This helped me to learn the names of trees and plants and their uses.

Today, when teaching both adults and children, I find it is helpful to gather a single specimen of each plant found on a foraging walk, and you might too. At the end of the walk, roll out some lining paper or brown parcel paper on a table, or the ground, and lay out each plant. Write the names of each one, then photograph them or perhaps draw around the leaves. Roll it up to take away afterwards. This helps you to remember the plants and the walk later. If you write the date on the roll, it will let you see what you found at different times of the year. Eventually the rolls can be used as wallpaper for your shed or as kindling.

As you learn each new plant, you'll find that your eye for detail improves. You start to see shape and colour, serrated or plain edges, succulence, delicacy, the feel of the square stem of those in the mint family, the dry taste of tannins. Your learning speed will start to increase. Review your notes when you're back from your walk and look up each species in a plant identification book while it's still fresh in your mind.

Soon the plants will start to teach you. Your tuned senses will begin to tell you about the world around you in a way that you just don't know right now. You will experience a sense of harmony with nature that not only finds you food but also revives your spirit and lifts your heart.

Some of my favourite edible flowers:

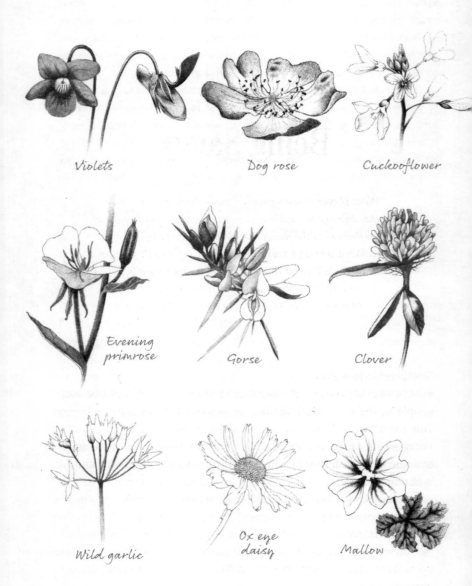

Violets

Dog rose

Cuckooflower

Evening primrose

Gorse

Clover

Wild garlic

Ox eye daisy

Mallow

CHAPTER 2

Being Savvy

"What if every time an ecosystem or forest is damaged a similar damage immediately appears inside human beings? A reflection of the macro appearing in the mirror of our micro. What if things are not nearly so simple as they've been made out to be? What if there is no real separation between us and the landscape of which we are a part?"
STEPHEN HARROD BUHNER, *EARTH GRIEF*

Sustainable foraging

Remember that you're not foraging in isolation. There might be other people in the community gathering wild species, and the resources you are drawing from are also food for animals, birds and insects. Foraging should *never* compromise future species populations nor the biological communities of which they are a part. With that in mind, it is also important to:

Be considerate: The land and its bounty are a shared resource. Be respectful, encouraging and supportive of other community members who practise foraging or nature-based activities. If you regularly share resources with the same community, consider developing a shared harvesting plan to support sustainable foraging and equal division amongst everyone.

Do no harm: Don't use harvesting methods that cause permanent damage to plants or to the environments in which they exist. For example, don't cut down or ring-bark trees, or dig up swathes of bulbs.

Be aware: Different species require different approaches to sustainability. Familiarise yourself with each species you forage and its location, learning all you can about them. Some species may be abundant, while others may be rare in your location, even if they are abundant in other places. While there's generally no problem with picking several kilos of wild bramble berries or wild raspberries, for example, it could be harmful to the plant population if you picked all the wild sea kale in one of the few places along the Scottish coast where there is little shingle habitat – although it is more prevalent on some stretches of the English shingle shore.

Be observant: Note how different species in your area respond to harvesting. If a particular harvesting technique proves detrimental to a species and/or location, share that knowledge among interested local parties.

Be sparing: Harvest only as much as you know you'll be able to use; never waste resources. If a plant is not abundant, appreciate it but take nothing more than photos.

The above guidelines are the foundation for living in harmony with plants, people and planet.

Pollution and hygiene

If you're able to, choose areas to forage that are away from pollution. This means avoiding routes along main roads that may be contaminated by car exhausts, dog-walking paths and posts where they pee. If harvesting near a path, step away from it by a metre to avoid obvious dog fouling zones.

If the only areas that you can forage from are roadsides, wash any leaves before you eat them. A study done on urban wild weeds in San Francisco showed that washing them makes them as free from pollution as supermarket lettuce.[4] This is not the same for roots, which pull up minerals from subsoils; flowers which are too delicate to wash; or thin-skinned berries. So washed leafy vegetation is fine, but avoid picking other parts from roadsides, contaminated brownfield sites, or places with high levels of industrial or agricultural chemical pollution.

When harvesting roots from clean soils, wash and scrub them in plain water before eating – this lets you appreciate their flavour without traces of earth muddying the taste. When you wash berries, you need to eat them all pretty quickly, as rinsing them encourages a humid microclimate, perfect for mould and bacteria to thrive in.

If you're foraging from clean, unpolluted areas, there's no need to wash the leaves, berries, nuts or flowers you collect. At least 57 per cent of our bodies is made up of bacteria, viruses and fungi – organisms other than ourselves. Like us, plants also host microbial communities, and the species that make up their rhizobiome (the ecosystem of microbes around their roots) is similar to our gut microbiome. Modern hunter-gatherers (such as the Hadza or Aché peoples) have two-thirds more gut microbe diversity than the average Western city dweller. By foraging we are increasing our gut diversity in a healthful way. Some of the main bacteria in soil – like *Mycobacterium vaccae* – can also boost dopamine levels, enhancing our happiness. Washing your food is a personal preference so follow your heart on this one. I only pick in areas that I know to be clean, so I'm much more relaxed on this subject than others.

Staying safe outdoors

As with any outdoor activity, there are some risks involved in foraging. If you're foraging close to where you live, in a park or populated area, you're unlikely to run into trouble. But if you're venturing into the wilderness, be aware of the following:

Getting lost: Stay on established paths if you don't know the area, and keep together if you're in a group. Carry a fully charged mobile phone and a battery pack with its charging cable, and if you're going deep into wild or mountainous areas, consider installing the what3words app on your phone so you could tell a rescue team where you are. Take a paper map and compass, as mobile phones can lose their signal and GPS can stop navigating. Don't just rely on other people and technology – learn how to tell what direction you're facing without a compass. You can do this by becoming more aware of your surroundings. Where is the sun? What direction do the trees grow shown by the prevailing wind? You can practise orienting yourself in a landscape by emulating the Australian Guugu Yimithirr tribe and replacing the words for *left, right, in front of* and *behind* with the compass directions *north, south, east* and *west.*

Dehydration: Always carry water. Ideally, two litres of water per person per full day out. Warm weather can dehydrate you quickly, but heavy physical effort does too. Wear layers that can be removed so you don't overheat.

Exposure or hypothermia: This can happen in poor weather but also at high altitudes or after getting wet. Take extra layers of clothing to keep warm, as well as waterproofs. If the weather is exceptionally poor, reconsider going out.

Accidents: Even when taking the best precautions, accidents sometimes happen. Being mentally prepared makes a big difference to the outcome. Make a note of the contact telephone numbers for emergency services, know where the nearest doctor's surgery and hospital are, and think about the route you'd use to get casualties out in an emergency. Take a first-aid kit that you know how to use (including tick tweezers). A first-aid course can save lives. I particularly enjoy wilderness first-aid courses and like to do a refresher every three years. In very remote locations I carry a personal SOS satellite tracker.

Fitness: Foraging usually happens at a slow amble, but you can still trip or fall. Make sure you, and anyone you're foraging with, are capable of moderate exercise on uneven ground. Be conscious of distance travelled, as it's easy to walk far on the trip out and misjudge how you'll feel on the return leg, when your energy is depleted. Wear suitable footwear. (Yes, it sounds like a no-brainer but I am often surprised at the flimsy or non-waterproof shoes that people think are suitable for a hike – or for paddling to get seaweed.) Keep to paths and use hiking poles if helpful.

Workplace hazards: Remember that outdoor areas are also workplaces. In forests you can be seriously injured from falling timber in the woods. Look out for signs signalling forestry work and listen for the sound of chainsaws or machinery. You can often check with rangers that there are no harvesting operations in the area. Keep an eye on weather forecasts and don't go out in a gale where winds exceed 40 mph – over 8 on the Beaufort scale – as there could be falling trees or branches. In some forests and in army areas, people may be shooting. Military zones are usually well signposted, with red flags on active days. In agricultural areas you may need to watch out for farm machinery, crop spraying, or herds of large animals that may not take kindly to a canine companion. And, speaking from personal experience, do watch out for electric livestock fences! Areas near old quarries and mines sometimes have unstable or contaminated ground. Always consider the history of a place as you get to know the land.

Poisoning: Take a zero-risk attitude to eating wild foods by making sure you can identify anything you pick before eating it. Have a separate container for any unknown plants or berries you collect for identification and don't mix them in with edible finds. The risk from merely touching poisonous species is generally low – they have to be ingested to cause harm – but one or two species, such as Monkshood (*Aconitum* spp.) can be dangerous to touch.

Allergies: Very occasionally, someone has an allergic or medical reaction to a new, wild ingredient. If you have known allergies (for example, to celery, nuts, fungi, penicillin, perfume, essential oils), just try a small amount of a new ingredient first. Any new food (wild or not) can potentially cause an adverse reaction. Some medicines or medical conditions can make you more likely to have a side effect; for example, if you take medication for high blood pressure and get drunk on hawthorn gin, you might lower your blood pressure too much.

There might be other risks according to your location: busy traffic for urban foragers, or the tide coming in and slippery rocks for seaweed foragers – so just be mindful, think through the risks and how you would react if the worst happened. Having done your preparation, go out and enjoy yourself.

The law across the UK

It's perfectly legal to forage wild plants, mushrooms and seaweeds for your personal use. This is stated in the Wildlife and Countryside Act (1981). However, it is illegal to *uproot* plants, or to pick for commercial purposes, without the landowner's permission. You also cannot harvest if specifically forbidden by a public by-law, or take specified plants in a restricted area such as a site of special scientific interest (SSSI).

The few species that are specially protected against picking are listed at the back of the Wildlife and Countryside Act (1981) in Schedule 8. Do check both the English name and the botanical species, as there are some internal errors and inconsistencies, and ask a more experienced forager if you're not sure. For example, 'Fungus, Hedgehog' is listed as *Hericium erinaceum* and is prohibited. Most foragers, however, know *Hedgehog Fungus* as *Hydnum repandum* (not

---

Further reading

To improve your navigation through the landscape, read Gooley, Tristan (2020), *The Natural Navigator* (Random House). Or Gooley, Tristan (2014), *The Walker's Guide to Outdoor Clues and Signs: Their Meaning and the Art of Making Predictions and Deductions* (Hachette UK).

To improve your first-aid skills, read Isaac, J. (2013), *Outward Bound Wilderness First-Aid Handbook* (Rowman & Littlefield, Chicago). Or Backer, H. D.; Bowman, W. D.; Thygerson, A. L.; Paton, B. C.; Thygerson, S. M. and Steele, P. (2008), *Wilderness First Aid: Emergency Care for Remote Locations* (Jones & Bartlett Learning).

For wilderness survival, read Canterbury, D. (2015), *Advanced Bushcraft: An Expert Field Guide to the Art of Wilderness Survival* (Simon & Schuster).

prohibited) and call *Hericium erinaceus* (which is the correct spelling) the Lion's Mane mushroom (prohibited).

Seaweeds are not governed by the Act as technically the foreshore all belongs to the Crown Estate, although this is usually administered by local councils. Seaweed collected for personal use, in small quantities, does not require a licence.

Access and trespass

In England, Wales and Northern Ireland, the law of trespass can block your access to many good sites for foraging. Under the law, landowners have the right to exclude anyone from their land, whether they have one acre or a thousand acres, and they can use 'reasonable force' to make you leave. Unless you have their explicit permission, you are trespassing. You have some public rights of way over some land, but only for passage across it, and by law you should stick to the path. However, any wild plant you pick belongs to you and not the landowner.

In Scotland, the right to roam is enshrined in the Scottish Outdoor Access Code, which tells you what areas you have the right to access. You're allowed to forage wild plants for personal use in these areas. If you are foraging in a large group, it is both polite and improves community relations to let the landowner know, where possible. It's courteous to ask, but know your rights and stand your ground.

Further reading
There is an excellent book about land access rights in England by Hayes, Nick (2020), *The Book of Trespass: Crossing the Lines that Divide Us* (Bloomsbury).
Schedule 8 of the Wildlife and Countryside Act (1981) can be read online at: **legislation.gov.uk/ukpga/1981/69/schedule/8**
You can read up on the Scottish Access Code online and download the full code at: **outdooraccess-scotland.scot**
Details of seaweed harvest licences from the Crown Estate are at: **thecrownestate.co.uk/en-gb/what-we-do/on-the-seabed/coastal/seaweed-harvesting**

PART TWO

THE
PLANTS

CHAPTER 3

Learning
Identification Skills

There are around 3,445 species of plants in Britain and Ireland, of which 1,692 are natives. I have eaten well over three hundred of them because they are delicious, nutritious, edible vegetables and fruits. When you start foraging you'll probably try a few, well-known ones first: wild garlic, watercress, blackberries, wild strawberries, bird cherries or samphire, for example. You'll notice how much flavour is packed into them. Their supermarket relatives taste insipid by comparison. Once you can recognise and enjoy a few, you will want to try more.

I have not used a calendar-based approach in this book to give you foraging information. It isn't always helpful. Some plants are in leaf all year and fruiting times vary across regions. Microclimates, soil type and habitat all make a difference to when you can harvest something.

Simply listing species from A to Z doesn't help either. Learning plant species one by one, without a coherent understanding of the relationships between them, can make it harder to remember them and see the big picture. Similarly, using ID apps doesn't help you to retain information long term.

Here I focus on explaining the plants' relationships with each other. By understanding how they are visually related through family traits, you will quickly learn to recognise them and identify them with confidence. For example, did you know that all members of the mint family have square-edged stems?

The Kingdoms of Life

Species classification is a hierarchical system developed by the botanist Carl Linnaeus (1707–78) from which our modern system evolved.

All living things belong to one of five generally accepted *kingdoms* (although some biologists would argue for six, seven or even eight). Although Carl originally put fungi and seaweeds together with plants in one large 'Kingdom Vegetabilia', nowadays plants are in their own Kingdom Plantae. There is also Kingdom Fungi that produce mushrooms, Kingdom Protista where seaweeds and algae live, and Kingdom Animalia for mammals, reptiles, birds, fish, crustaceans, insects, etc. Kingdom Monera, the fifth, is home to bacteria and archaea but, for the forager, all our needs are met in four.

Kingdom Plantae includes all types of plants. A plant is defined as an organism that photosynthesises using the green pigment, chlorophyll, to create nutrients in their leaves and that stays in one place with roots to take up water and minerals. Sometimes the boundaries move. For example, some phycologists (seaweed scientists) include green seaweeds (algae) with plants as they are distantly related and also use chlorophyll to photosynthesise. For our purposes, 'plants' mean trees, shrubs, herbs, grasses, ferns and mosses.

Within *kingdoms* you have *orders* and below orders you have *families*. Just as human families belong to tribes (or regions), tribes belong to nations, and nations belong to continents. Within families you have a *genus* (pl. genera), and in each genus you have the *species*.

Plant families

Knowing that *all* plants belong to *families* and *genera* helps us to break down the mass of greenery into logical groups. All plants within a genus will have the same 'surname' – the first word in their binomial (species) name – and they will share common traits, just like human parents, siblings, cousins. Key family characteristics help us to narrow down the search for a new plant's identity. Once you can identify a plant as far as its family, then you will find it easier to understand how they all fit together in the landscape, in relation to each other, and in their gifts to us.

I will be grouping all the plants by their family and describing their common characteristics as well as their unique features.

Using botanical keys

While this book will introduce you to many new species, my focus is on which parts you can eat and how to prepare them. It will not give a long description of each species and you will need to use field guides and botanical keys for identification purposes.

Dichotomous keys known simply as 'keys' are a system of narrowing down the distinctive features of a plant, to help distinguish it from similar-looking plants. Keys help you to structure your questions to narrow down the choices quickly. Each key starts with a multiple-choice question. The answer leads you to the next question, and then the next, until eventually you end up with the identity of the plant you are looking for.

Some people are put off using keys because most use botanical language as a shortcut. Many of these terms are shortcuts for describing shape and form, which I've illustrated on pages 28 and 29. Once you're familiar with these terms the rest becomes much easier. So persevere!

Further reading

Elpel, Thomas (2013), *Botany in a Day: The Patterns Method of Plant Identification* (HOPS Press; 6th ed.)

Bayton, Ross and Maughan, Simon (2017), *Plant Families: A Guide for Gardeners and Botanists* (University of Chicago Press).

Foraging apps

Using reference books may feel very low-tech. There are many apps around that will have a go at instantly identifying different plants (and fungi) with greater or lesser degrees of success. The trouble with apps is that information learned this way doesn't 'stick' in your head, whereas the 'slow method' makes sure the information stays in your memory for good. Take a plant home with you, examine it closely, touch, feel and smell it, and work out what it is through books and keys. This way what you learn will be retained.

At the risk of sounding ancient... when I was a child, I had an entire bank of phone numbers in my head. Now the only number that I know is my own, because the phone does it for me when I click on a name. So my brain just doesn't bother to store phone numbers anymore. In my experience, this is the same with plant and fungi identification apps. The more you rely on them, the less likely you are to build a powerful library of information stored inside your own brain. This wouldn't necessarily be a problem if we could guarantee that there will always be electricity, network coverage and access to the internet. While I am not a prepper, we do live in increasingly uncertain times. There may come a time when there is no internet cover and your phone battery is dead, but you still need to know what you're about to put in your mouth!

Further reading

Poland, John and Clement, Eric (2020), *The Vegetative Key to the British Flora: A New Approach to Plant Identification (Second edition)*, (published by John Poland, available from Summerfield Books). This book of keys helps you to identify nearly 3,000 native and alien plants without flowers or fruit, using nothing more than a hand lens. As most field guides depend on flowers or fruit for identification characteristics, this is a vital tool for identifying plants all year round.

Rose, Francis and O'Reilly, Claire (2006), *The Wild Flower Key: How to Identify Wild Flowers, Trees and Shrubs in Britain and Ireland* (Penguin). A colour-illustrated field guide with keys to more than 1,600 wild plants found in Britain and Ireland, including keys to plants when not in flower.

If you prefer a more interactive approach, colouring books can be a helpful way of learning. One of my favourites is: Paul Young (1999), *The Botany Coloring Book (Coloring Concepts)* (Collins Reference).

Useful botanical terms

The challenge – whether you are reading about plants here, in field guides or using botanical keys – comes in learning the botany vocabulary that is used as shorthand to describe the parts of a plant. In every walk of life, people develop their own terminology – words that act as shortcuts to longer descriptions – and plant identification for foraging is no exception. Unless you only intend to eat a few easily recognisable species, you need to know these terms.

Learning new words may seem frustrating at first but it is unavoidable so stick with it. The advantage is that a single botanical word can replace the need for many other words. For example, a *hastate* leaf means a leaf that has a *narrow triangular shape with sharp basal lobes spreading away from the base of the petiole*. Most people can visualise the toothed leaf of a dandelion. Its entry in *The Vegetative Key to the British Flora* by John Poland and Eric Clement ends with the following key:

> Petiole hollow > Lvs (±) hairless, often shiny green above, the lateral lobes often triangular, midrib often reddish nr base. Per. All yr.

This translates as:

> Hollow leaf stalk > The leaves are sometimes, but not always, without hairs, shiny green on the upper surface, with triangular shaped projections along the side or the stem in the middle (that is often a bit red near the bottom). Perennial – meaning it grows again every year from the same root. Flowers all year round.

You need to think about leaf shape, texture, leaf arrangement, veins, edges and so on. This is called plant morphology. *Morpho-* means form, structure (in Ancient Greek) while *-ology* is the study of something. The right vocabulary will speed this process. That said, a picture is worth a thousand words, so on the following pages I've shown a number of key botanical terms accompanied by diagrams, which will help you to memorise them. Perhaps get some index cards and crayons and make yourself some test flash cards from the diagrams, if you learn better that way.

Parts of a plant:

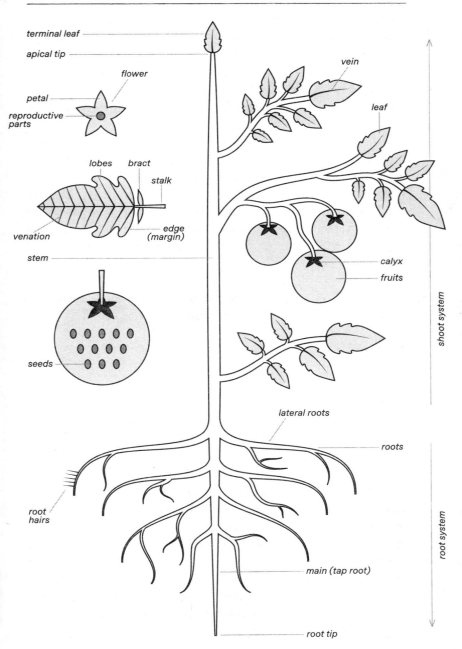

Leaf shape:

LEAF TIPS

  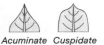

Acute   Acuminate   Cuspidate   Obtuse   Emarginate

LEAF ARRANGEMENT

Alternate   Opposite   Whorlet

LEAF ATTACHMENT

Stalked   Sessile   Perfoliate   Rosette

LEAF VENATION

Parallel   Palmate   Pinnate

LEAF SHAPES

Needle   Linear   Oblong   Elliptic   Ovate   Obovate   Lanceolate

Oblanceolate   Spatulate   Orbicular   Rhomboidal   Deltoid   Reniform

LEAF BASES

Attenuate   Acute   Obtuse   Truncate   Oblique   Auriculate   Cordate

     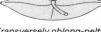 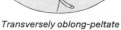

Sagittate   Hastate   Transversely oblong-peltate   Orbicular-peltate   Sagittate-peltate

LEAF MARGINS

Entire   Undulate   Crenate   Dentate   Serrate   Lobed   Pinnatifid   Pinnate-trifoliate   Pinnate   Bipinnate

Plamately lobed   Pedately lobed   Palmate-trifoliate   Palmately compound   Peltate-palmate   Tendrils   Stipulate

Flower arrangement:

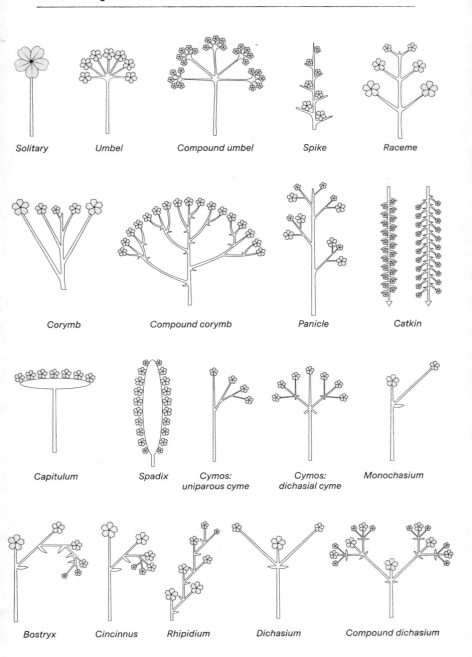

Solitary Umbel Compound umbel Spike Raceme

Corymb Compound corymb Panicle Catkin

Capitulum Spadix Cymos: uniparous cyme Cymos: dichasial cyme Monochasium

Bostryx Cincinnus Rhipidium Dichasium Compound dichasium

A foraging glossary

In the diagrams on the previous pages, I have tried to illustrate most of the common botanical words, so do look there for them. In this table, I have defined some useful words that are not illustrated.

achene	A small, dry, single-seeded fruit that does not split open. The fruit of the London Plane is a dense ball of achenes.
alkaloid	A natural bitter-tasting compound containing at least one nitrogen atom, such as caffeine or quinine. Some of them are toxic.
angiosperm	A plant classification. An angiosperm produces its seeds inside a vessel, e.g. the nuts of broadleaf trees.
annual	A plant that only lives one year and grows again from seeds.
antioxidant	A natural molecule, such as vitamin C, that inhibits the oxidation that damages and ages our bodies.
basal rosette	A group of leaves that form at ground level from which a flowering stalk rises. See example on page 28.
biennial	A plant that grows over two years from seed to dying off. It only flowers and produces seed in the second year.
binomial	The official scientific name of a species. Often derived from Latin or Greek, it has two parts. E.g. Rosa canina.
blanching	Dipping into boiling water for a few minutes to tenderise, then plunging into cold water to stop the cooking process.
bletting	When fruit it left to ripen on trees until almost rotten.
botanical key	A deductive system of identifying a plant.
bract	A modified or specialised leaf-like part that grows from the stem below a flowerhead.
bulb	A swollen, often round or oval, underground basal stem from which roots and shoots grow.
bulbil	A tiny secondary bulb, often in a group, that forms in the axil of a leaf or in place of flowers, e.g. few-flowered leek.
calyx	The collective name for the sepals at the back of a flower. Usually green and often fused together.
chaff	The unwanted husks surrounding grain that is removed by threshing and winnowing.
corolla	The collective name for the petals of a flower.
dioecius	A plant that is either male or female and needs another plant of a different sex to reproduce.
disc	The inner circle of a composite flower.
disc floret	The tiny flowers packed inside the disc of a composite flower.
drupe	A fleshy fruit with a thin skin and stone, or nut, in the middle that contains a seed.
fermenting	(fermentation) A method of preserving food that uses salt or brine.
field guide	A reference guide for identifying plants or fungi with species-specific detail.
gravadlax	A cold curing technique for raw fish or meat.
hips	The name for the fruit of the wild rose.

in vitro	An experiment done in a laboratory petri dish or test tube.
in vivo	An experiment done on a living organism.
inflorescence	A technical name for a group of flowers, or flower cluster, arranged on a stem or stems. See examples on page 29.
leaflets	The leaf-life parts of a compound or pinnate leaf that look like mini leaves, e.g. wild carrot leaf.
microclimate	A climatic variation that affects a specific habitat or region.
monoecious	A plant that contains both male and female parts but in separate places.
nodes	Joints on a grass stem, twig or shoot from where new stems or leaves grow.
nutlets	A small nut; thick-walled achene or small seed inside the stony shell of a drupe.
oxalate	A natural anion compound found in plants, e.g. in spinach and sorrel, that can form oxalic acid.
pectin	A natural soluble fibre and polysaccharide compound, found in apples, berries, etc., used to set jam.
perennial	A plant that lives more than a year and regrows after winter from an ongoing root or bulb system.
petal	The colourful parts of a flower that attract pollinators, arranged around the reproductive parts.
petiole	The stalk that attaches the leaf blade to the stem.
pistil	A flower's female reproductive organ, including a stigma, style, and ovary.
plumes	A plant part that looks like a feather or cluster of feathers, e.g. pampas grass.
pseudocereal	A plant whose starchy grains are used as a cereal but is not in the Poaceae family of grasses.
ray petals	The petals that form the outer circle of a composite flower, arranged around the disc and disc florets.
rennet	An enzyme used to turn milk into curds and whey, when making cheese.
runner	A shoot that grows out of a plant and runs across the ground, to take root at points along its length.
sepal	The outermost whorl of flower parts that protect the bud and form the calyx. Usually green and leaf-like.
stamen	A flower's male reproductive organs, including a filament and pollen-producing anther.
stipule	A small leaf-like appendage at the base of a leaf stalk.
succulent	A fleshy plant, such as aloe or cactus, that stores water in its leaves and stems.
terminal leaf	The final 'end' leaf at the end of a twig.
thresh	The beating of cereal plant heads, to help separate the grain and the husk or chaff.
twining	Climbing by winding around a support, such as a pea plant climbing on a stick.
winnow	To remove something, like chaff, by blowing or moving a current of air through it.

A word about names

Common name: Usually a common name, for instance, dandelion, is not spelt with a capital letter. But this can be confusing. If I mention a small-flowered willowherb, do I mean 'a willowherb with small flowers' or is there a specific species called 'small-flowered willowherb'? It is the latter. Is 'green alkanet' simply any 'alkanet with green leaves' (e.g. *Alkanna tinctoria*) or specifically the species 'green alkanet' (*Pentaglottis sempervirens*), which also has green leaves?

You can see the problem. So in this book I have chosen to use capital letters when talking about the name of a specific plant or seaweed, keeping the lower case for adjectives rather than the parts of a name. So for the two examples above I will put Small-flowered Willowherb and Green Alkanet. The exception to this is if I am talking about a group, or a family name, which contains a mixture of species. The individual species will be capitalised but the group name won't be. For example: 'The goosefoot family contains Fat Hen' or 'Watch out for the leaves of daffodils' as daffodils describes a group of many different *Narcissus* species. I will also stick to lower case when I refer to a plant in the name of a recipe – such as wild garlic and nettle soup – to avoid the excessive use of capitals in Wild Garlic and Nettle Soup.

This will annoy purists while pleasing those who think plants deserve proper names but ultimately makes it perfectly clear what species I am talking about.

Binomial or Scientific name: Where two words appear in italics just after a common name, for example, Japanese Rose *Rosa rugosa*, it refers to the species' botanical name. Importantly, the plant's surname *Rosa* comes before the personal name *rugosa* – unlike in English but just like Hungarian. The genus name always has a capital letter to start it off. The second word – the species (individual) name – is written without a capital letter. While a plant can have many common or local names, they have only one scientific name (well, when DNA scientists don't change them). For instance, what I call Common Hogweed my American friends call Cow Parsnip and my French friends call Berce Commune. But we all know it as *Heracleum sphondylium*.

Where sp. occurs after a plant's name, e.g. *Rosa* sp., it means an unnamed particular rose species. If it's spp. it means all species (plural) within that genus (in this case of roses).

If a plant is mentioned just after a close relative, it is common to abbreviate the surname. For example, I might talk about Dog Rose (*Rosa canina*) and compare it to the Japanese Rose (*R. rugosa*) and Sweet-briar (*R. rubiginosa*). Here, in the second and third instance *Rosa* is shortened to *R.*

Some people are quite resistant to learning the scientific names of plants. If you ever had to learn Latin or Greek at school, I can understand your reluctance as I also baulked at Latin, 'a dead language' that I thought would never be useful in adult life. It seemed remote, pointless and hard to pronounce. However, we now live in a multicultural society and are far more used to a wide variety of names than our grandparents' generation. *Veronica beccabunga* is no harder to say than Monica Wilde and more amusing than 'brook-lime' while *beccabunga* comes from the old Swedish word 'bäckebunga' which means 'brook bunch'. *Veronica* is the family name because some of the wild species' flowers have dark lines on them, radiating out from the centre. These were thought to resemble the rivulets of sweat and blood on the face of Jesus, when St. Veronica wiped it, leaving an impression on her veil. *Achillea millefolium* is as easy to say as Rupram Chakrabarty (a noted Bengali poet) and it tells you so much about the plant. It has *mille* (a thousand) *folium* (leaves) and belongs to the family *Achillea* – named after the great hero Achilles, who used it as a wound healer in battle.

Once you know the stories behind the names, it makes them unforgettable and even more valuable. It also means you can travel worldwide and talk to others with the same interests as you, without confusion. Persuaded?

CHAPTER 4

The Main Plant Families

The first question to ask yourself when you have found a plant is whether it is *herbaceous* or *woody*. In other words, is it a soft, fleshy plant (like a herb) which dies back after flowering or does it have persistent woody stems above the ground like a tree?

Plants that don't have woody stems are called *herbaceous*. This includes herbs, small bushes, grasses and ferns, but excludes trees and woody shrubs. There are many more herbaceous plants than tree species.

Herbaceous plants provide an exciting range of edible plants to forage. Many are annuals, meaning they flower and set seed in a single year and don't last beyond that. Biennials sprout and grow leaves in the first year, but don't flower and set seed until their second year. Some are perennials, arising from their root base every year, and can grow for many years. We'll look at the herbaceous families first.

All herbaceous plants are *angiosperms*, the largest group of plants on Earth. This means they are plants that produce flowers and seeds, and their seeds are enclosed in a fruit, which protects them and helps them spread to new places. *Gymnosperms* – the other class – are plants that produce seeds, but unlike angiosperms, their seeds are not enclosed in a fruit (e.g. pines, spruce and fir with cones). Angiosperms are found almost everywhere, from forests and grasslands to deserts and even underwater. What makes them important to us is that they include most of the plants we use for food, like fruits, vegetables, grains and nuts.

Angiosperms then break down into two further divisions. Monocots and dicots, the two main types of flowering plants. These are the main external ways that they differ.

Seed structure: Monocots have seeds of one part which produces a single seedling leaf (*cotyledon*), while dicots have seeds with two parts producing a seedling with two leaves.

Leaf veins: The leaves of monocots have veins that run in straight lines (*parallel venation*), while dicot leaves have veins that spread out like a net (*reticulate venation*).

Root system: Monocots have a *fibrous root system* or thin, branching roots. Plants that grow from bulbs are monocots. For example, Wild Garlic. Dicots usually have a *taproot system* of one main root with smaller branches. For example, a Dandelion.

Flower parts: Flowers of monocots usually have petals in groups of three, while dicot flowers have petals in groups of four or five. Knowing these differences is helpful because it is another characteristic to help you identify plants.

On the next pages I've shared information on the main *herbaceous* plant families you need to know as a forager. Major families make up most of the entries, but where there are only one or two useful species in a family, I've just focused on the species.

To see if a plant might grow near you, enter its name (preferably the botanical name) into the BSBI search box at: **database.bsbi.org/maps**

BSBI stands for the Botanical Society of Britain and Ireland and the map data is submitted by county recorders, local groups and taxonomic experts. This might give you a clue as to whether the plant you're looking for has already been found in your area.

Allioideae – the onion subfamily

This large family – the home of Wild Garlic – is a foraging favourite. It contains the Allium species of wild garlics, leeks and onions. This is one of the easiest plant families to identify thanks to the strong garlicky smell of the leaves and bulbs. *Allioideae* is a subfamily of the family *Amaryllidaceae*, which also includes daffodils and snowdrops. Alliums are often mentioned in reports of wild food poisoning. Although they are easy to correctly identify, sometimes concentration or hand–eye coordination fails and poisonous daffodil, bluebell or snowdrop leaves from nearby clumps are accidentally added to a foraging basket, whose leaves and bulbs will produce stomach cramps, diarrhoea or worse symptoms. So make sure you are paying attention when picking – especially if you're also chatting to friends or keeping an eye on children or dogs – and know your onions.

Many of the flowers develop bulbils that are also edible.

Key features

The plants have bulbs with a strong onion or garlic smell. The tall linear leaves grow up from the bulb on fleshy stems and, when crushed, also smell distinctly of onions or garlic. Small flowers are grouped into umbels. Flowers of the wild species are usually white, sometimes pink and occasionally purple. Some also have aerial bulbs, called bulbils, next to the flowers. All parts – leaves, stems, flowers, bulbils and bulbs – are edible.

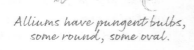

Alliums have pungent bulbs, some round, some oval.

MAIN FORAGING SPECIES

Wild Garlic ✳ *Allium ursinum*

This is our very popular native wild garlic species. It is very common along riverbanks and in damp woodlands in the spring, usually found between late February and the end of May. Wild Garlic, also known as Bear's Garlic, is a darker green than the wild leeks with a wider leaf and stronger flavour. It also has an erect flower head. All parts are edible, but if you want to harvest the bulbs (rather than just the leaves) you'll need to seek permission. You can add Wild Garlic fresh to salads, turn it into a brilliant pesto that can be canned or frozen, powder it to make a garlicky seasoning and use it to make a wild garlic salt. Or, follow a centuries-old tradition and make a wild garlic and nettle soup. The leaves are the tastiest in the spring but the juicy flower stems that follow are a real treat and lend themselves to fermenting. The potent fruits are great in spicy pickles like achar.

Few-flowered Leek ✳ *Allium paradoxum*

The wild Few-flowered Leek likes the same damp woodlands as Wild Garlic, often crowding it out as it often sprouts a week or two earlier. It is sometimes mistaken for its more famous cousin by people who aren't aware there are multiple *Allium* species. It is also very common along verges next to ditches. Few-flowered Leek has a thinner leaf, of a lighter green, and a milder, slightly sweeter onion taste than the wider-leaved Wild Garlic. Of particular note is its triangular stem and rather pathetic attempt at a flower. Only one or two flowers per stem branch out from a small cluster of tiny green aerial bulbs. These bulbils are particularly nice preserved as pickles later in the year. You can use the leaves in exactly the same way as Wild Garlic.

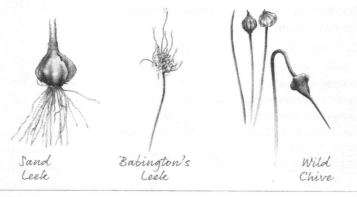

Three-cornered Leek ❋ *Allium triquetrum*
This has similar foliage to Few-flowered Leek but has
several drooping flowers. It also has a distinct triangular
(think Toblerone) profile to the flower stalk. I often find
Three-cornered Leek as an introduced species in formal
parkland or cultivated woodlands, especially in the south of the
country as it seems to prefer a bit of warmth, even sprouting in
December in mild, protected spots. It is invasive and the round
bulbs cram together in large quantities that are very satisfying to
harvest and make perfect mini 'pickled onions'. Sometimes thinning
overcrowded plants in this way can improve the health of the colony
but only dig bulbs with the landowner's permission, of course.

You may also occasionally find other *Allium* species. Other wild
garlics include: Crow Garlic *Allium vineale*, Rosy Garlic *Allium roseum*,
Field Garlic *Allium oleraceum*, Hairy Garlic *Allium subhirsutum*, Honey
(Sicilian) Garlic *Allium siculum*, Keeled Garlic *Allium carinatum*,
White (Neapolitan) Garlic *Allium neapolitanum,* and Pale Garlic
Allium paniculatum. In Poland I have tasted the Victory Onion *Allium
victorialis*, which unlike Wild Garlic, doesn't die back in the summer.

Other wild leeks include: Leek *Allium porrum*, Babbington's Leek
Allium ampeloprassum var. *babingtonii*, Round-headed Leek *Allium
sphaerocephalon*, Sand Leek *Allium scorodoprasum* and Wild Leek
Allium ampeloprasum.

Sand
Leek

Babington's
Leek

Wild
Chive

Further reading

Block, Eric (2010), *Garlic and Other Alliums: The lore and the science* (RSC Publications).

You can also sometimes find Wild Chive *Allium schoenoprasum*. 'Wild Chive', which refers to naturally occurring, uncultivated plants found in the wild, is essentially the same species as 'garden chives' but has thinner leaves and a more variable flavour.

Lacto-fermentation: Fermenting is a great way of preserving the flavours of spring, especially if you don't have a lot of room in your freezer for frozen pesto. The basic process is to finely chop green leaves, then pound with 3 per cent salt by weight – for each 100 grams of plant add 3 grams salt. Massage the leaves by hand, then pound with a mortar or rolling pin, until the leaves start to break down and exude liquid. Pack all into clean jars and press down to remove air gaps. If the liquid does not cover everything, top the jar up with 3 per cent brine (30 grams of salt to 1 litre of water) until 1 cm below the brim. Cover loosely and leave for at least two to three weeks before eating. They should be bubbling nicely and have a sour, sharp flavour. Store the jars in a cold room or fridge, if you want to keep them for months. All the garlic and leek family can be fermented to preserve the leaf stalks – either plain or mixed with spices (like garlic, ginger and chili) to make kimchi, a fiery Korean-style pickle.

Herb salts: The heat of Wild Garlic dissipates a bit on drying, so making a wild garlic seasoning salt really locks in the flavour for later. I find that a ratio of 4:1 works best. So use 40 grams of finely chopped Wild Garlic leaves to 10 grams of rock salt. Pound them together or put them in a food processor, then dehydrate the paste. Once fully dry, crumble it up again and keep it in a dark glass jar. (Sunlight makes the vivid, green colour fade.)

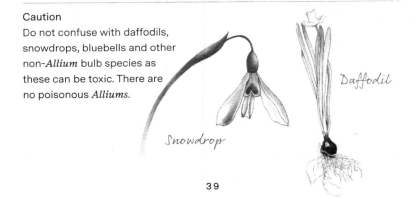

Caution
Do not confuse with daffodils, snowdrops, bluebells and other non-*Allium* bulb species as these can be toxic. There are no poisonous *Alliums*.

Snowdrop

Daffodil

Amaranthaceae – the amaranth or goosefoot family

This family contains the subfamily Chenopodioideae. *Cheno-* is Greek for goose, *podia-* for foot – leading to its common nickname 'goosefoot' due to the triangular-shaped leaves of many of its members. The goosefoot family provides a lot of food plants around the world. Sea Beet *Beta vulgaris* subsp. *maritima* (as per page 45) has been eaten since the Stone Age. Species such as Spinach *Spinacia oleracea* or forms of beet *Beta vulgaris* (e.g. Beetroot and Chard), are used as modern vegetables, for animal feed (Mangelwurzel), and sugar (Sugar Beet). In other countries, the edible seeds of Quinoa *Chenopodium quinoa*, Amaranth *Amaranthus* spp., Pitseed Goosefoot *Chenopodium berlandieri* and Kañiwa *Chenopodium pallidicaule* are used as pseudo-cereals. This family also includes the genus *Salicornia* (the glassworts), of which Marsh Samphire *Salicornia europaea* is the best known.

Goosefoots are especially common in estuarine and sandy habitats. Most are found in poor-alkaline soils and many taste salty. They're generally high in calcium, salts and even nitrates if the soil is over-fertilised. If you're a keen gardener you are also bound to have weeded out Fat Hen or Lamb's Quarters.

A classic 'goosefoot' leaf shape.

Key features

A key characteristic of Amaranthaceae is an absence of stipules. (Remember the botanical terms diagram on page 27.) The inflorescences are usually densely clustered small flowers, often in plumes, and there is no difference between the sepals and petals (nicknamed 'tepals' in plant biology) – or some have sepals but no petals. The seeds of many goosefoots develop inside tiny, lidded capsules, each called a pyxis. (A pyx is a small round container used in Christian churches to carry around consecrated hosts.) In the *Chenopodium* subspecies some seeds are nutlets. Most of the seeds are edible and the only toxic amaranths I know of are tropical species. Those that grow in temperate climates are all edible as salad and pot herbs.

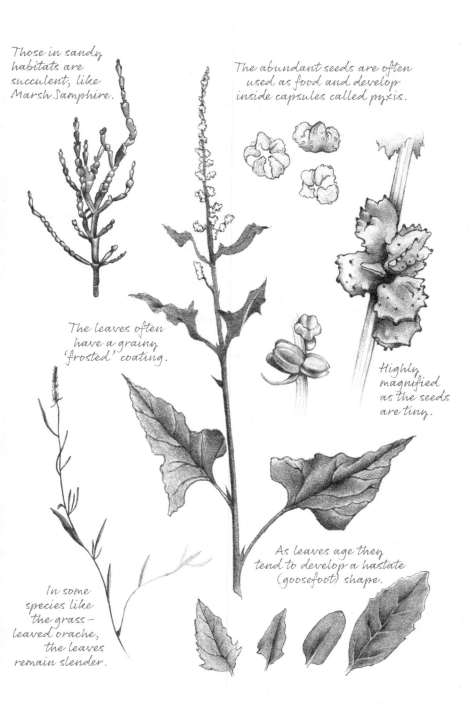

Those in sandy habitats are succulent, like Marsh Samphire.

The abundant seeds are often used as food and develop inside capsules called pyxis.

The leaves often have a grainy 'frosted' coating.

Highly magnified as the seeds are tiny.

In some species like the grass-leaved orache, the leaves remain slender.

As leaves age they tend to develop a hastate (goosefoot) shape.

MAIN FORAGING SPECIES

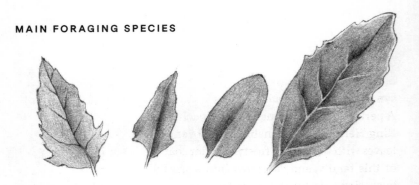

Fat Hen (Lamb's Quarters) ✳ *Chenopodium album*

Fat Hen is easy to identify with goosefoot-shaped leaves and a slightly powdery surface. The leaves vary in shape but are distinctively green on top and silvery white underneath, covered in a mealy bloom. Fat Hen has a lot of protein for a vegetable (203g per kg of leaves has been recorded) with balanced amino acids.[5] Packed with nutrients, it is extremely high in calcium as well as vitamins A, C, B2, iron, carotenoids and fibre, plus nitrogen, phosphorus, potassium, magnesium and manganese.

This versatile wild edible plant was cultivated as a vegetable in Europe and Asia in ancient times and was even found in the stomachs of prehistoric mummies. During times of scarcity and famine, it served as a critical food source due to its availability and nutritional value. Nowadays Fat Hen is a common agricultural weed found growing among wheat, barley, mustard, gram and other crops around the British Isles and Ireland. It is also fond of gardens, as it likes disturbed, manure-rich soils, such as the edges of fields or allotments. Fat Hen is best eaten in the spring when it has the best flavour and is full of antioxidants.

Pick young, tender leaves or shoots before the plant starts to flower, as older leaves can become tough and bitter. The leaves have a spinach-like flavour, making them excellent for cooking or eating raw in salads. It's a delicious vegetable either steamed or sautéed and served with a little butter or oil, salt and pepper. Alternatively add it to soups and stews. The leaves can be dehydrated and, in India, dried leaves are sometimes incorporated into green gram dal and paratha recipes. The fleshy seeds of Fat Hen are prolific, and you can use them as a 'no-food miles' polenta or native grain, but it does require careful processing to remove saponins, which can give them a bitter taste (see page 237).

Good King Henry ✳
Blitum bonus-henricus
syn. *Chenopodium bonus-henricus*

A perfectly good alternative to spinach, Good King Henry has reasonably large, triangular leaves with the typical frosty-powder coating of this family, and can grow into a sizeable bush. However, the leaves are best pre-soaked as they can be bitter. Soak the leaves in brine (a concentration of 3 per cent sea salt dissolved in fresh water) for half an hour before rinsing it off and steaming the leaves for about five minutes until tender. In April, the young shoots can be harvested at 15–20 centimetres high and steamed (without brining) just like asparagus. In fact, in some parts of the country, it is called Poor Man's Asparagus. Although Good King Henry is high in oxalates – the large leaves much more so than small ones – boiling for 2 minutes significantly reduces levels.[6] For more about oxalates, see Wood Sorrel on page 111. Unopened flower buds of Good King Henry make a tasty substitute for broccoli.

Marsh Samphire ✳ *Salicornia europaea*

Marsh Samphire is a well-known vegetable with a distinctive shape (it looks like miniature spineless saguaro cacti) that is commonly steamed and served with fish. It's traditionally been harvested from the summer solstice onwards, as it is too small before then. Despite the fact that it grows on vast mud flats in Britain, the samphire we buy in shops is almost entirely grown in and imported from Israel, Morocco and Mexico. Even more puzzling is the question of why this is the only estuarine plant we eat regularly. Samphire's close relative Annual Seablite *Suaeda maritima* is also delicious and has a far longer cropping season. Fresh Marsh Samphire will keep up to three weeks in the fridge, so it is a useful vegetable to gather on a trip to the coast. It can also be pickled and will keep for a year, although the texture is crunchier when eaten the same winter that it is bottled. Cut the tops of the samphire rather than uprooting the plants. Best picked in July and August, I never harvest it before the summer solstice.

There are two other plants with the common name 'samphire' but they are not related. Rock Samphire is in the Apiaceae family with Carrot and Fennel, while Golden Samphire is in the Asteraceae family with Daisy and Lettuce. Both of these pungent samphires are used as seasoning herbs, being particularly delicious in egg tarts and quiches.

Orache (many species) ❋ *Atriplex* spp.

The oraches are a large family and it can be hard to tell one species from another but they are all edible. My favourites that grow along the coastal shoreline are Spear-leaved Orache *Atriplex prostrata*, Babington's Orache *A. glabriuscula* (also known as Scottish Orache), Frosted Orache *A. laciniata* and Grass-leaved (narrow-leaf) Orache *A. littoralis*. They are also an alternative to spinach – they don't require pre-soaking – and many prefer them as they don't have spinach's iron overtones. Eaten from July onwards when it reaches a decent size but still has tender leaves.

Sea Beet ❋ *Beta vulgaris* subsp. *maritima*

Sea Beet is one of my absolute favourites out of all the coastal vegetables. Although it doesn't have a swollen edible root like cultivated Beetroot – the result of an early horticultural experiment by the ancient Romans – it grows with a thick mass of glossy, dark green leaves that have an infinitely better flavour than spinach, with less metallic overtones. The young leaves can be eaten raw in salads, layered into savoury spanakopita with filo pastry, or baked into a quiche. Older leaves – which can get mildly leathery with age – are steamed or sautéed and served with olive oil or melted butter. Both make excellent soups and additions to stews. Harvest it sustainably by only taking a quarter of the leaves from each Sea Beet plant and they will reward you by growing vigorously and supplying a fresh, supply of green leafy vegetables for several months. It's available in most seasons except the depths of winter.

Prickly Saltwort ❋ *Kali turgidum*

Salsola kali, now *Kali turgidum*, is a saltwort (also sold as Land Seaweed) and known as *agretti* or *roscano* in Italian. It is a slightly salty, slightly grassy, crunchy seaside vegetable. It grows all around the coast of the UK except in the far north of Scotland.

Apiaceae – the parsley/carrot family

Once called Umbelliferae, this is a large family that contains many of our most treasured vegetables, herbs and spices, including Carrot, Parsley, Celery, Fennel, Dill, Cumin and Caraway. However, this is the trickiest family when it comes to identification, as there are some fatally unpleasant relatives. It is extremely important to learn to identify them with 100 per cent accuracy as these are the most common dangerous plants in Britain. It's worth the effort, though, as some of the tastiest plants also belong to this family. If you can differentiate between Flat Parsley, Curled Parsley, Fennel, Dill and Celery leaf in the supermarket, you can master this group.

Many have swollen edible roots or tubers.

Key features

The flowers are borne on umbels, with individual flowers on separate stalks that radiate from a central point like umbrella spokes. Some are compound umbels, each group mounted onto another umbel spoke.

Many umbelliferous flowers are flat-topped or only slightly rounded. In the first year each plant produces a basal rosette. In the second, it flowers on tall, often branched, hollow stems. The leaves are very divided – often fernlike – in forms called pinnate and bipinnate (see diagram on page 28). The leaves and seeds are highly aromatic.

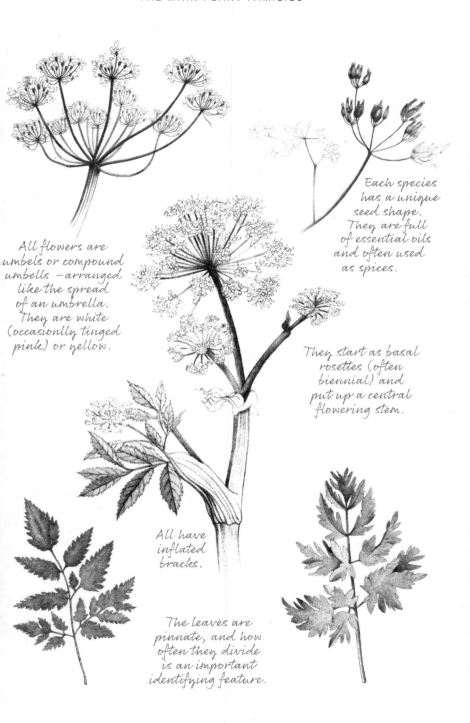

Each species has a unique seed shape. They are full of essential oils and often used as spices.

All flowers are umbels or compound umbells – arranged like the spread of an umbrella. They are white (occasionlly tinged pink) or yellow.

They start as basal rosettes (often biennial) and put up a central flowering stem.

All have inflated bracts.

The leaves are pinnate, and how often they divide is an important identifying feature.

MAIN FORAGING SPECIES

Common Hogweed ❋ *Heracleum spondylium*
From April, the young shoots from the base of
Common Hogweed and the pouches on the
flower stem are particularly good when fried.
I adore hogweed shoot tempura – it's the
only reason I own a deep-fat fryer. The seeds are
widely used as a spice – they taste like coriander
infused with orange oil – excellent in curries
and chutneys. In Persian the seed is called
golpar and it's a popular Asian spice. You can
pick seeds green in late summer or ready-dried
brown on the seed heads in autumn. In Ukraine
and Poland, the leaves, flowers and young stems were traditionally
fermented to make a soup called *borscht* (now mainly replaced with
beetroot). The Slavic word *borschevik* means hogweed. Do not handle
Common Hogweed roughly as, if attacked (such as strimming), it can
cause burns in self-defence like Wild Parsnip *Pastinaca sativa*. And do
not confuse it with its nasty relative Giant Hogweed, which is very
dangerous to touch (see page 53).

Hogweed has a flat-topped umbel.

Cow Parsley ❋ *Anthriscus sylvestris*
Cow Parsley, sometimes called Wild Chervil, is a very common ditch
plant in country lanes. It is extremely similar in appearance to its
(mainly coastal) relative Poison Hemlock. Unlike Hemlock, the basal
leaves have a U-shaped profile and tiny hairs along the stem that give
it a sandpapery texture. Hemlock has an O-shaped profile and feels
smooth as it is hairless. Nor does Cow Parsley have purple spots on
the base of the stems as it matures. I like to chop Cow Parsley fronds
finely and use it as a herb (on glazed carrots, for example). The young
flowering stems are also delicious. Picked and peeled before they
flower and get fibrous, they make a
fabulous alternative to Celery sticks
in a dip. Why not give the dip a spicy
twist by adding ground, toasted Cow
Parsley seed as well?

Cow Parsley   *Poison Hemlock*

Ground Elder ❋ *Aegopodium podagraria*
Highly invasive and the bane of many
gardeners, Ground Elder nevertheless
tastes delicious and can be used plentifully.
Introduced by the Romans as a kitchen
herb, the bright green baby leaves
are especially pleasant with the best
flavour, tasting like a cross between
parsley and celery leaf. They make a
great base for a salad. I use big handfuls to
flavour soups and stews in place of Parsley. You can
chop it finely and add it to a wide range of dishes
from omelettes to mashed potato. The older leaves are
more fibrous, unpleasant to eat and curiously laxative once the
plant has flowered. If every gardener who grumbled about Ground
Elder gave up their weed poisons and started harvesting the young
growth instead, it would help to keep it under control and become
a valuable friend rather than an enemy. It appears in March and is
happy to grow in flower beds or cover expanses of open, damp ground.

Common Hogweed
~ edible ~

Wild Angelica
~ edible ~

Cow Parsley
~ edible ~

Hemlock
Water Dropwort
~ deadly ~

Pignut ✳

Conopodium majus

A fine, small, ferny plant that likes well-drained slopes on woodland and field margins. You can eat the leaves and seeds which have a very delicate, mild-carrot flavour but the prize is underground. (Remember to get the landowner's permission to dig any roots.) Unlike other Apiaceae, Pignuts don't have a taproot like a Carrot but wriggle away underground via a fine white root thread that ends in a hazelnut-sized tuber – although foraging legend is that you can find them as big as golf balls! Pignuts can be maddening to dig up as the plants hide the 'nut' under rocks and roots, while the thread often breaks before you score. Unless you find a particularly fine tilth to dig in, it can take an hour to find a dozen. Harvest them in the autumn or early spring before the new shoots get going in earnest. Once spring has sprung they are smaller. The tubers taste like a cross between a Sweet Chestnut and a Parsnip and are delicious raw or lightly boiled. If you can resist crunching them up raw, you can make a fine flour, good for savoury dishes, which is easy to process by drying and milling the 'nuts'. Watch out though: according to the seventeenth-century herbalist Nicholas Culpeper, Pignuts *'maketh men lusty'*.

In Shakespeare's play The Tempest (Act 2 Scene 2), Caliban says 'I prithee, let me bring thee where crabs† grow. And I with my long nails will dig thee pignuts.' († *crabapple trees*) It's a curious sentence and, as is often the case with Shakespeare, has a double meaning. On one hand, Caliban is trying to prove his usefulness as a native of the land who can provide sustenance. On the other, Shakespearean audiences would have known about the aphrodisiac quality of pignuts, and crabs… well, I'll leave that to your imagination.

Sweet Cicely ❋ *Myrrhis odorata*

I adore Sweet Cicely. It is easily distinguished by its velvet-soft foliage, the strong smell and taste of aniseed, and its white markings on the lower opposite pairs of green, ferny basal leaves, unique to Sweet Cicely, which at first glance resemble bird droppings. She loves damp water meadows and stream sides, and all parts are edible. Chop the leaves finely and use instead of Fennel or Dill or add to salads. Boil the stems and leaves in milk to make a green custard. Use equal parts of chopped Sweet Cicely stems with Rhubarb instead of adding sugar (anethole, a key compound, is sweeter than sucrose). Cooking Sweet Cicely with windy greens like Brussels Sprouts and Cabbage also reduces the flatulent effect. Boil the green seeds in sugar to make breath-freshening aniseed sweeties. The shoots are best picked from April when they are juicy. Gather the seeds when small and green in midsummer as they quickly get too fibrous. The dried seed loses its aromatic oils quickly.

Alexanders (Alisander) ❋ *Smyrnium olusatrum*

Alexanders was originally brought to the UK by the Romans as a pot-herb and later widely cultivated in monastery gardens. With its Mediterranean heritage, it particularly loves the warmer, sandy soils of the coast. It is one of the Apiaceae with yellow flowers so do not confuse it with Hemlock Water-dropwort or Wild Parsnip. The leaves are more commonly eaten due to restrictions on digging the roots which are tender, substantial and have a strong aromatic flavour. The first-year roots are very tasty if parboiled first (which reduces the bitterness) then roasted with a little honey and olive oil drizzled on them. Dried, powdered roots make a slightly spicy addition to other wild flours – the flavour is too strong to use alone. The seed makes an excellent spice not dissimilar to Black Cumin *Nigella sativa*. The leaves have a pungent, fragrant flavour so a little goes a long way. Finely chopped, it can be added as a flavouring herb like Lovage, or steamed with a blander vegetable such as Sea Beet. The stems, leaf buds and encapsulated flower buds all work extremely well as a pickle.

Wild Angelica ✳ *Angelica sylvestris*

The leaf has a serrated edge reminiscent of rose leaf and a domed white flower head that help to distinguish it. It likes damp grassy meadows and ditches. Common Angelica's spicy-bitter root has traditionally been used to make gin, while candied Angelica stems were used to decorate cupcakes in the 1960s and '70s. All parts of Wild Angelica are edible. I harvest leaves from April, seed in the summer and roots in the autumn.

Wild Carrot ✳ *Daucus carota*

This is the wild ancestor of the domesticated Carrot. It has luxurious ferny foliage (that is bipinnate and tripinnate), a hairy stem and feathery forked leaf bract under the flower heads – a helpful identifying characteristic. Each inflorescence is made up of many white flowers with an additional single dark red-purple flower in the centre to attract insects. As the seeds ripen the umbel stems curve upwards, reminiscent of a basket. All parts are edible and can be harvested from April to autumn. The leaves are used as a herb. The taproots – while often disappointingly tough and wiry – can be eaten if you find a luscious one growing in a looser, sandier soil than my local cold clay. Although I seldom find them tender enough to boil, nevertheless they can be ground and dried to make a pleasant flour that has a carroty hint. You should pick them in the autumn of their first year when they are less woody. Wild Carrot seeds were once chewed as a contraceptive but no tests have been done to prove their reliability.

Caution

You must be absolutely sure of identification with plants in this family as mistakes can be fatal. Remember that Celery allergy is common and be aware, if you are allergic, that there might be cross-sensitisation. Handle all of them with care, as many have phototoxic sap.

Most of the dangerous plants that you may be tempted by are in this family. Apiaceae species that you should learn to identify to avoid confusion with their tastier relatives include:

Fool's Parsley ✳ *Aethusa cynapium*, also known as Lesser Hemlock, which contains a poisonous alkaloid called cynapine. The leaves have a glossy shine on both sides but please consult a good field guide for identification with all of these. All parts of it are poisonous and symptoms come on within an hour of eating it. Poisoning can lead to seizures and even death. Treatment includes anticonvulsants, airway management and protection against rhabdomyolysis, electrolyte abnormalities and renal insufficiency. It is found all over the UK but rarely in the Scottish Borders or Highlands. Although the leaves are finer, it can be confused with Flat-leaf Parsley.

Giant Hogweed ✳ *Heracleum mantegazzianum* – while the plant itself is not poisonous, it can cause serious burns that require hospital treatment if the sap gets on your skin and is activated by sunlight (known as a severe phototoxic reaction). It can be confused with its smaller relative, Common Hogweed, but it is larger, has white crystal spikes on the stem rather than white 'stubble', and the stem is marked by angry-looking purple splotches. If you do get sap on you, wash it off and immediately protect the area from sunlight. If a burn has started and you don't have access to medical help, use dock gel (the gel from around the basal shoots of dock *Rumex* sp.) on the burn area until you can seek treatment – it acts like aloe vera.

Poison Hemlock ✳ *Conium maculatum* can cause death through paralysis of the respiratory system. It can be confused with Cow Parsley (page 48). My friend Mark Williams teaches the rhyme 'more hairy, less scary', to help people remember to avoid the hairless Hemlock stems. I think of the O-shaped profile of their hollow leaf stalks, so different from the U-shaped gutter of Cow Parsley basal leaves, and it's 'O for Oh no!' Symptoms of poisoning are: nervous system stimulation followed by paralysis of motor nerve endings; central nervous system (CNS) stimulation and later depression; vomiting, trembling, problems in movement, low and weak pulse, rapid respiration, salivation, urination, nausea, convulsions, coma and death.[7] It is found all over the UK but rarely in the mountainous regions of Wales, Cumbria and the Scottish Highlands. It is extremely common at the coast, particularly the eastern seaboard. Ironically, I once saw it growing at the entrance to Addenbrooke's Hospital in Cambridge.

Hemlock Water-dropwort ✳ *Oenanthe crocata* is probably the deadliest plant in the UK and can cause severe sickness and death through its compound oenanthotoxin, which poisons the central nervous system. Even a small amount can cause convulsions, seizures, nausea, diarrhoea and a fast heartbeat. It is easily confused with Wild Celery (see opposite) and likes to grow in damp ditches, riverbanks and water meadows. The vibrant-green, shiny leaves are tripinnate to tetrapinnate with toothed, wedge-shaped lobes that make them look a little like flat-leaf parsley. The stem is hairless, hollow, grooved and has a yellowish sap when cut. The flowers are white with yellow seeds, so sometimes look cream. Hemlock Water-dropwort has attractive tubers that range from cream like a Parsnip to purple like a Sweet Potato. They are often exposed when snowmelt or flooding erodes soil from riverbanks. One tuber is enough to kill a cow. For some reason it prefers the west coast of Britain and is common throughout Ireland (except in the Midland region). Do be aware that there are other water-dropworts and this whole family needs to be approached with extreme caution.

Cowbane ✳ *Cicuta virosa*, also known as Northern Water Hemlock, is an imposing wetland plant that grows in ditches, marshes, bogs and the edges of streams. It can grow up to 2.5 metres tall but is more often 1.5 to 2 metres. Its stems are striped purple, it has toothed leaves and the usual array of white flowers on umbels. If eaten, it causes tremors and seizures. It is rarely found outside Cheshire, the Norfolk Broads and inland Ireland except in isolated patches. Luckily its even more poisonous relative Spotted Cowbane C. *maculata* is only found in the Americas, where it is sometimes called Suicide Root.

There are other unpleasant members of this family so do make sure you know the ones in your area and take special care with this group. However, it is worth getting to know them as there are also some very tasty species.

Cow Parsley
~ edible ~

Wild Carrot
~ edible ~

Wild Celery
~ edible ~

Sweet Cicely
~ edible ~

Don't experiment,
be sure! The book
that I recommend
below is a
'must have' for
this family.

Poison Hemlock
~ toxic ~

Fools Parsley
~ toxic ~

Further reading

Tutin, T. G. (1980), *Umbellifers of the British Isles: BSBI Handbook No 2* (Botanical Society of Britain and Ireland). An authoritative reference guide to seventy-three of Britain's most common Apiaceae plants (previously called Umbellifers). It features keys, descriptions and line drawings to help identify them.

Asparagaceae – the asparagus family

Wild Asparagus ✳ *Asparagus officinalis*
Wild Asparagus is mainly found in the warmer south of the country, especially coastal areas, and prefers sandy, loose soils. Its branched, feathery foliage looks just like commercial asparagus but the plants are often stragglier and the edible spears are not as stout. The delicious spears are picked in the spring and steamed.

Wild Asparagus spears are generally much slimmer than their chubby, cultivated counterparts.

Asteraceae – the daisy family

The Asteraceae, or daisy family, is one of the largest and most diverse plant families, comprising over 32,000 species spread across nearly every habitat on Earth. Many of our most common garden flowers are in this family, and we use many as food plants – from Lettuce to Artichoke and Sunflower – or pick them for their beauty – such as chrysanthemums and dahlias. It's a family with many tribes – *Artemisia, Achillea, Lactuca, Cynara, Helianthus, Taraxacum* – including some excellent plants for foraging, with only a toxic few in Britain, like the ragworts. Many species are used medicinally, like Chamomile. Asteraceae plants play significant roles in many ecosystems, providing nectar and pollen for a variety of pollinators and often thrive in challenging environments.

The centre is made up of multiple tiny flower heads, with or without ray petals around it.

Seeds are often dispersed by the wind on fluffy parachutes.

Many leaves are used either as herbs, like yarrow, or as salad leaves, like Dandelion.

Starchy roots like Burdock are often a useful source of calories.

Key features

The flowers of the Asteraceae family are composite. This means they look like an apparently single, symmetrical flower head but look closely and you'll see they are composed of multiple, tiny flower heads (sometimes microscopic). Each tiny flower within the centre is a disc floret made up of many petals, sepals, stamens and pistils all jammed together. The crowded centre is often surrounded by large or colourful ray petals. Another common pattern is multiple rows of bracts that hold the back of the flower together. Many of the fruits are single-seeded achenes with a fluffy parachute like the seeds of Dandelion and the many thistles.

MAIN FORAGING SPECIES

Yarrow ✳ *Achillea millefolium*

Yarrow is a common verge plant used to treat cuts, as well as a pot-herb. It especially likes the grasses adjacent to woodlands but doesn't like shade. Leaves and flowers are edible and can often be picked all year round, even when the flowers have dried on the stems. I often use it where others would use Rosemary. If you're fishing, gut the fish, pack the belly with Yarrow and roast it whole on hot stones. The first of its binomial name comes from Achilles, the Greek warrior who used Yarrow in battle to stop wounds bleeding, while *millefolium* literally means 1,000 leaves, referencing the finely divided feathery leaves. Polished Yarrow sticks were used to cast the Chinese oracle, the I-Ching, so it has a very long history. In fact, it was found in the tomb of a shaman some 8,000 years ago.

Yarrow's close cousin Sneezewort *Achillea ptarmica* is popular with children due to the temporary numbing sensation in your mouth when you chew it, leaving a fizzy 'fresh-mint' aftertaste.

Pineappleweed ✳ *Matricaria discoidea*

With a yellow disc that smells and tastes of pineapple, but no white ray petals to hint at its family connections, Pineappleweed is closely related to Wild Chamomile *Chamaemelum nobile*, which is rare in Britain. The leaves taste like chamomile and I use it in herbal teas in the same way. You can infuse the pineapply heads in vodka to make a lovely wild cocktail ingredient. Pineappleweed loves being trampled at farm gates and on dry off-road tracks. The edible flowers and leaves are harvested in the summer.

Common Daisy ✳ *Bellis perennis*

Found on lawns and roadsides, both the garden species of Common Daisy and the large Ox-eye Daisy *Leucanthemum vulgare* are edible and can be found flowering all year round, with Sea Aster *Aster tripolium* at the coast, and Michaelmas Daisy *Aster amellus* right into the autumn. Hate them if you want a perfect, bowling-green lawn but love them if you like a cheeky face as they always make a lawn look more cheerful. I add the spicy leaves to salads and use whole flower heads to decorate puddings – I leave a bit of the stalk attached and push them into panna cotta, for example. When put in the fridge the flowers close, but when brought back out in the light again they open up, much to the delight of the recipient. This trick, of being the 'days-eye', is how they got their name. Daisy leaves can also be used as a good alternative to Arnica for bumps, bruises and other household emergencies. Soak the leaves in vegetable oil for a few weeks and then add 30 per cent melted beeswax to make a simple first-aid salve. Harvest in the spring and summer.

Mugwort ✳ *Artemisia vulgaris*

Mugwort is mainly used as a herb for flavouring and in herbal teas. In bedtime teas it has the reputation of encouraging lucid dreaming, while the smoke from a mugwort smudge stick can accompany shamanic rites. It is called 'moxa' in Chinese acupuncture. Other Artemisias found in Britain include Sea Wormwood *Artemisia maritima*, which makes an excellent herb salt and is great in gravadlax marinades. Wormwood *Artemisia absinthium* is mainly used as a medicine as it is very strong. It was traditionally used to make the drink absinthe. However, it contains a toxic compound α-thujone, which had the reputation of causing blindness, seizures and hallucinations – although this is muddled by the use of cheap alcohol.

Burdock ❋ *Arctium lappa* and *Arctium minor*
A member of the thistle sub-family, the leaf stems, young flower stem and first-year roots are all edible. The roots are dug up in the autumn of its first year – the year when it has only produced a basal rosette – but you will need a very long, strong spade and a lot of patience. Burdock has a very long root which can seem to go down for ever. Julienned or grated roots can be marinated in soy sauce and spices, then fried to make Japanese gobo, a most delicious dish. Alternatively, bake them with a little honey. You can dry the root and powder it into a starch. It makes a flavoursome gnocchi flour. In the UK it was traditional to make a dandelion and burdock beer (a non-alcoholic root drink) to cleanse the liver. In the second year it produces its flowering stem and, by this point, the roots are very woody. In late spring, you can gather leaf stalks and the tender stem. They're bitter, but blanching them, then throwing away the first change of water, helps to make them palatable.

Burdock produces seed head clusters. Each seed has a tiny hook on it and gets tangled on clothes and fur. Bur hooks were the inventor George de Mestral's inspiration for Velcro when he examined their mechanism closely while de-burring his dog. In South Queensferry, not far from where I live, there is a festival every year where a local man, the Burryman, is covered head to toe in thousands of Burdock burs and spends nine hours walking through the town to bring good luck while drinking a lot of whisky! The origins of this festival are obscured by the mists of time.

Spear or Bull Thistle ❋ *Cirsium vulgare*

All parts of *Carduus*, *Cirsium* and *Silybum* thistles are edible. The developing stems are particularly tasty in the late spring, before flowering when they toughen up. Use a knife or potato peeler to make sure all prickles have gone. With Milk Thistle *Silybum marianum* just cut the prickles off the leaf edge with a pair of scissors as the leaves make an excellent vegetable. Some thistle stems are sweet and can be eaten raw, while others are bitter and benefit from pre-soaking or a change of water while cooking. I'm also fond of the young white thistle roots that colonise the vegetable patch in early spring. Washed, steamed and eaten with butter, salt and pepper, they make a day's weeding very rewarding. If you like Globe Artichoke you'll love thistles. I use a strong solution of unripe thistle seed as a vegetable rennet when making cheese.

Dandelion ❋ *Taraxacum officinale*

A multipurpose food crop, the Dandelion offers all of its parts except the stem and calyx as food. Cookery books up until 1900 invariably included a recipe for dandelion salad and wilted dandelion greens. There are about 290 varieties of dandelions in the UK, each adapted to a different habitat, so you can find them almost everywhere. The leaves are bitter and can be used like rocket mixed into a salad of milder greens. You can often find them even in the depths of winter. To blanch a Dandelion, put a flowerpot over the young plant in the spring. This will prevent the emerging leaves from getting light, making them less bitter. Pick the fibrous yellow flowers – removing the bitter green calyx – for wine, vinegars and jams in the spring and summer.

First-year Dandelion roots are tender and you can boil and eat them like carrots. A change of water during the cooking helps if they're very bitter. I prefer to roast them with parsnips julienned to a similar size. Drizzle over a little olive oil, a trickle of birch or maple syrup, grated Parmesan and some black pepper before roasting and you have one of my favourite dishes. Older roots can be roasted until they are dark brown and snap between your fingers, then ground and boiled to make a great (decaf) alternative to coffee. If you roast the roots before grinding them into a flour, it will give biscuits a slightly coffee-like flavour. I like it to mix it with sweet chestnut flour when baking a 'wild cake'.

Sow Thistle ❋ *Sonchus arvensis*

Older Sow Thistle makes very bitter greens unless found growing in long, shaded grass. However, they are highly nutritious and lovely in a gremolata. Leaves and young stems can be eaten raw or cooked after harvesting in spring and summer. Avoid older stems with their milky white latex-like sap, although some indigenous peoples have used it as chewing gum.

Nipplewort ❋ *Lapsana communis*

This is a milder green than its relatives Sow Thistle and Dandelion. The leaves are a useful vegetable as it is very common, found throughout Britain and Ireland, and is eaten mainly in spring and summer.

Caution

Avoid toxic Ragworts and the invasive species Wolfsbane *Doronicum* sp. in this family.

Berberidaceae – the berberis family

The berberis family contains two important genera of wild foods, *Berberis* and *Mahonia* (as well as some interesting medicinal plants like Blue Cohosh *Caulophyllum* sp. and Horny Goatweed *Epimedium* sp.). They are mainly found as ornamental hedging plants when urban foraging.

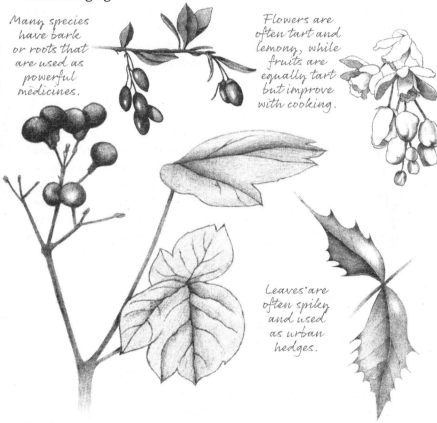

Many species have bark or roots that are used as powerful medicines.

Flowers are often tart and lemony, while fruits are equally tart but improve with cooking.

Leaves are often spiky and used as urban hedges.

Key features

Deciduous shrubs with alternate, simple, often spiky leaves – resembling miniature holly and occasionally divided into leaflets – although most *Mahonia* sp. are evergreen. The stems have spines at the nodes and the plants often have bright yellow inner bark – a sign of berberine concentration (a useful medicine for stomach and bladder infections). The flowers are usually yellow, occasionally red. The fleshy red, blue-black or purple-black berries are generally sour and full of pectin.

MAIN FORAGING SPECIES

Common or European Barberry ※ *Berberis vulgaris*

Common Barberry is found across the temperate and semitropical regions of Europe, Asia, Africa, North America and South America. This is the most common British native in the berberis family – its edible berries were nicknamed 'pipperages' – but sadly there is little left in the wild. It has been destroyed in farming areas as it hosts a fungus, Wheat Rust *Puccinia graminis*, that lowers the yields of cereal crops like wheat and barley. In the past the vitamin C-rich pipperages were collected and used to make jam, jellies and tart pickles but the use has declined over the centuries partly due to the plant being found less often. We know it was eaten as far back as 2600BC as it was found in Grime's Graves, a large Neolithic flint mine in Norfolk, East Anglia, where black flint was mined to make flint spear heads and hand axes.

I mainly use the red berries gathered in the early autumn, and occasionally add the dangling racemes of yellow flowers to salads in the spring. In a recipe for pigeons with rice from *A New Booke of Cookerie* in 1615, we are exhorted to 'Garnish your Dish with preserved Barberyes'[8] and they certainly brighten up a dish just as well as goji berries, or imported pomegranate seeds. Barberries still feature a lot in Persian and Eastern cooking, their vivid red colour adding jewel-like qualities to rice dishes such as 'zereshk polow' and 'zereshk polo ba morgh', where rice is cooked with tangy red barberries, saffron and pistachio nuts to accompany lamb or chicken. It is also used in desserts such as orange, barberry and sumac cheesecake and the tangy tarts described in 'Modern Cookery for Private Families' by Eliza Acton published in 1845. Dried barberries can be rehydrated in apple juice to sweeten them.

In Russia, Georgia, Armenia and Slavic countries the tart, sour barberries were simmered into a popular lemonade-type drink, and a fizzy version is still marketed today. Twenty species of moth rely on the leaves of Common Barberry to feed their larvae, including the endangered Barberry Carpet moth *Pareulype berberata*, which is entirely dependent on it.

Japanese Barberry ✳ *Berberis thunbergia*

Often used as a suburban hedging plant, this barberry has green leaves in the summer that turn to a purple wine-red in the autumn. It has orange-yellow flowers and oval red berries like our native Common Barberry, which are used in the same way. While it is not host to the Wheat Rust fungus, except when it hybridises with the Common Barberry, it is nevertheless a popular shelter for ticks.

Darwin's Barberry ✳ *Berberis darwinii*

Native to South America, this species is planted in many gardens in Britain as an ornamental shrub or a hedge. The leaves look like tiny holly leaves. The yellow-orange flowers are borne in spring in clusters called racemes and taste of lemon sherbet powder. The round dusty-blue berries that ripen in the summer are edible and delicious cooked with a little honey.

Oregon Grape-root ✳ *Mahonia aquifolium*

Planted as a large, dense shrub, Oregon Grape's leaves also look like holly but are three or four times the size of Darwin's Barberry leaves. It fruits prolifically yet is rarely picked as most people assume they are poisonous and those that don't quickly find out how spiky the leaves are, when trying to reach the racemes of tempting fruit! Pick the tart, astringent dusty-blue berries in the summer to make excellent sauces and preserves.

Boraginaceae – the borage family

This is a hairy-leaved family whose general prickliness comes from mineralised bumps (cystoliths) made from silicon dioxide and calcium carbonate that can irritate the skin. It includes Borage, Viper's Bugloss, Alkanet and Comfrey as well as the diminutive Forget-me-not. Few of them are used much due to the off-putting cystoliths and the discovery of their pyrrolizidine alkaloid (PA) content. When taken in excess, this group of plant chemicals can cause liver lesions.

Tuberous Comfrey ❋ *Symphytum tuberosum*

Comfrey was part of the British pharmacopeia for many years and often drunk as a tea. In numerous parts of the world, including Israel and South Africa, comfrey is cultivated as a vegetable, the leaves eaten in dishes such as ratatouille. However, there are now controversies around eating it, as too much could be harmful to your liver. There are not many actual reports of humans experiencing problems with PAs when ingesting normal amounts. Most of the research has been on high doses given to rats. Reported human cases have been when people have taken very high doses, usually as medicinal supplements, or for long periods of time. Each person must make their own judgement about the risks that they take. I've looked into the evidence about comfrey and choose to eat it, but never in excessive amounts or out of season. I avoid the tall Russian Comfrey *Symphytum uplandicum* and any crosses with *S. officinale* as the former contains the highest amount of PAs.

I eat our local Tuberous Comfrey *Symphytum tuberosum*, which has the lowest amount of PAs. The plants are low and spread vigorously to cover the ground, forming dense patches. They have creamy, pale yellow flowers. The leaves, slightly sandpapery to touch when uncooked, can be steamed or fried. For those not on a pure foraged diet, half-closed comfrey leaves dipped into a lemonade tempura batter and deep-fried is a real treat. It is a useful vegetable, especially as it comes up very early, before spring has really arrived.

Tuberous Comfrey has plentiful fat crunchy tubers which taste like Jerusalem artichoke. They are easy to dig up as they run lateral to the soil surface, unlike many deep taproots. Thinning the tubers doesn't cause ecological damage, as even the smallest piece left in the ground will grow again vigorously. Rather, thinning provides more space and less competition for new plants to flourish. Clean the tubers and lightly boil them, serving with oil or butter, salt and pepper. You would be advised to only eat small amounts as, being full of the prebiotic inulin, they cause a lot of wind. I have tried roasting and fermenting them – both taste nice but it doesn't lessen the gastrointestinal side effects. You can dry the tubers and grind them into a flour. Heat is the key to coping with the inulin – using comfrey root flour in a loaf of bread decreases its prebiotic benefits and reduces the windy side effects, making it more edible.

This family is also host to Borage *Borago officinalis* whose blue flowers are used to decorate salads and frozen inside ice cubes for decorating drinks. A crushed Borage leaf imparts a cucumber flavour to a gin and tonic. It is more often used as medicine than as a foraged food as it also contains controversial PAs. The old proverb 'Sow Borage, sow courage' and the saying 'Borage for courage' came about because Roman soldiers drank borage wine before battle, and crusading knights (who had it embroidered on their pennants) imbibed it before jousting tournaments.

Common Comfrey
Symphytum officinale

Brassicaceae – the mustard/cabbage family

This is a large family containing many of our most frequently cultivated vegetables: Cabbage, Broccoli, Cauliflower, radishes, Horseradish, Watercress, Nasturtium, Turnip and the mustards. Some of these can be quite a challenge to tell apart, but luckily none of them will kill or poison you, so many people get by just learning the family characteristics.

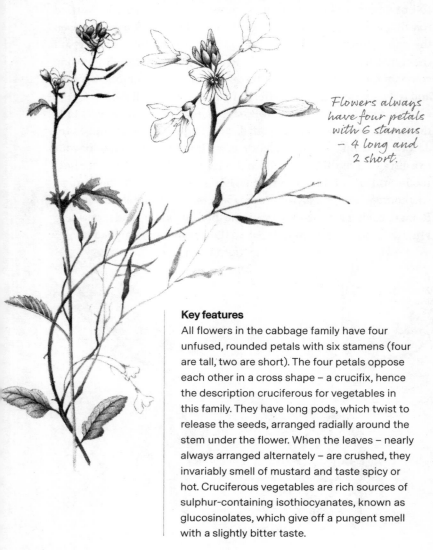

Flowers always have four petals with 6 stamens – 4 long and 2 short.

Key features

All flowers in the cabbage family have four unfused, rounded petals with six stamens (four are tall, two are short). The four petals oppose each other in a cross shape – a crucifix, hence the description cruciferous for vegetables in this family. They have long pods, which twist to release the seeds, arranged radially around the stem under the flower. When the leaves – nearly always arranged alternately – are crushed, they invariably smell of mustard and taste spicy or hot. Cruciferous vegetables are rich sources of sulphur-containing isothiocyanates, known as glucosinolates, which give off a pungent smell with a slightly bitter taste.

Seeds are in pods, often long, arranged in stalks at the top of the stem. Occasionally they are in single capsules on a stalk.

Leaves can vary although lobed and pinnate are common.

The leaves never have bracts unlike Apiaceae. This helps to distinguish Watercress (below) from Fools Watercress.

All form a basal rosette to start with before putting up a flower stem.

MAIN FORAGING SPECIES

Garlic Mustard ✷ Allaria petiolata

Garlic Mustard is also called Hedge Garlic or Jack by the Hedge and, as you might expect, it is commonly found in hedgerows and in front of long walls as it likes a little sheltered warmth. Despite its common names, this mustard is not in the same family as Wild Garlic. Its fresh young leaves, stems and flowers are a gourmand's delight in spring and summer. Large ones can be folded into parcels filled with savoury rice. In India, there is a traditional version of sag paneer that uses half Garlic Mustard greens and half Nettles instead of Spinach. It's delicious. The pods which ripen in late summer and early autumn will give you a large supply of mustard seed to make your own wild mustards and dressings.

Dame's Rocket ✷ Hesperis matronalis

You wouldn't suspect Dame's Rocket of being in the cabbage family, but the four-petal arrangement of its purple or pink flowers gives it away. It is sometimes called Sweet Rocket and often found in great swathes UK-wide, especially along riverbanks as it likes lightly shaded, damp ground. It flowers in May to July but it's worth looking for before then, as the leaves are an excellent vegetable when picked young.

Another related edible plant that looks similar, but with broad leaves and only mildly peppery, is Honesty Lunaria annua. It is best known for its silvery-transparent seed pods that are used in dried flower arrangements. However, its leaves are also used as a cabbage green.

THE CRESSES

Hairy Bittercress ✳ *Cardamine hirsuta*
Hairy Bittercress has an explosive seed
mechanism by which seeds can be shot
out up to 1 metre away. If the wind
catches them they'll go even further.
This means that it gets everywhere.
It likes bare soil beds, gravelly paths and
even city pavements. Bittercresses grow as
a rosette of leaves and the taste resembles
miniature Watercress with a similar hot,
peppery taste. They reproduce really quickly, often several times a
year, putting up a single flowering stem with a spray of tiny white
four-petalled flowers, before their tiny but classic *Brassicaceae* pods
appear. Use the hairy leaves to spice up a salad or blend into a hot
green pesto all year round even in the depths of winter.

The following brassicas taste very like the seedlings of Cress
Lepidium sativum grown for egg-and-cress sandwiches. They just
have varying degrees of heat and small differences in leaf structure
and shape, which help to tell them apart.

Wavy Bittercress ✳ *Cardamine flexuosa*
This tastes like Hairy Bittercress and is just as prevalent. It has hairy,
branched, wavy stems that zigzag but hairless leaves, and loves moist,
shady places like the edges of streams.

Cuckooflower ✳ *Cardamine pratensis*
Also called Lady's Smock. This pretty plant with
pink flowers and hairless stems is especially
fond of water meadows and damp ground near
streams. The leaves are delicious and the
flowers pretty in a salad. Cuckooflower is
host to the Orange-tip butterfly and, as the
name suggests, arrives with the sadly vanishing cuckoo in
late April/May and flowers throughout the summer.

Shepherd's Purse ✳ *Capsella bursa-pastoris*
Found in lawns, flower beds and waste ground in late spring to autumn, Shepherd's Purse grows everywhere except mountain peaks. It's very easy to identify once the heart-shaped pods start to form. If you turn the seed upside down by its stalk you will note the resemblance to a ram's scrotum from which the proverbial shepherd made drawstring pouches. The leaves, flowers and seeds are edible.

Watercress ✳ *Nasturtium officinale*
Watercress grows in slow-flowing streams and ponds. It has a pinnately compound leaf with rounded edges and white flower – look closely to avoid confusion with Fools' Watercress *Apium nodiflorum* and Brooklime *Veronica beccabunga*, which are both edible, and Hemlock Water-dropwort and other dropworts which can be deadly (see pages 53–55). One useful tip is that Brassicaceae do not have leaf bracts whereas Apiaceae do. This small difference is key in separating lookalikes in the two families. Attention to detail saves lives. Take care, when eating all plants that live in the water, to avoid infection from liver flukes carried in streams by water snails if animals, especially sheep, graze upstream. Sterilise the leaves in a solution of 5 per cent acetic acid (white vinegar) or baby bottle sterilising fluid. If in doubt, don't eat them raw but cook them well into soups or as a vegetable as boiling makes them safe to eat.

Wintercress ❋ *Barbarea vulgaris*

Wintercress has much larger leaves than the other cresses, reminiscent of watercress leaves, but this yellow-flowered plant prefers disturbed land and piles of building rubble. It is palatable in the winter – especially the tender heart leaves – but gets very bitter the later in the year it is picked. I prefer it in a mixed salad rather than on its own.

Swine-cress ❋ *Lepidium coronopus*

Swine-cress is exquisitely spicy and hot, similar to other members of this family but more intense and peppery. This bold taste makes it an interesting addition to dishes in small amounts, especially as a seasoning or garnish. The young leaves are the most palatable and can be used raw in salads, added to sandwiches, or blended into pestos for a spicy kick.

It forms a large flattish rosette jostling with lobed leaves. Some just have a single lobe, others three, which look like little toes. It has white flowers a mere 2–3 millimetres long and, sadly for me in Scotland, is mainly found south of the Pennines.

Lesser Swine-cress ❋ *Lepidium didymum*

This is very like Swine-cress but the white flowers are tiny and arranged on side stems somewhat reminiscent of a bottlebrush. The leaves are opposite pinnate (divided into two lobes) with a single terminal one. The plant tends to spread into a dense, low mat across sandy or light soil and is also more common further south.

Field Pennycress ❋ *Thlaspi arvense*

Mainly found in waste ground and cultivated fields along the east coast and in the south. The seeds are in single round pods with a notch at the top. The leaves, flowers and seeds are edible, flowering from May to July.

THE ROCKETS

Early Yellowrocket ✳ *Barbarea verna*
Early Yellowrocket is closely related to Wintercress (page 73) but it doesn't go bitter, staying hot and peppery like watercress although it is named as a rocket. It has a yellow flower and a rounded watercress-like leaf, enjoying the Midlands, west and south coasts.

Perennial Wall-rocket ✳ *Diplotaxis tenuifolia*
Particularly fond of London and Newcastle, Perennial Wall-rocket – which escaped from gardens to become Wild Rocket – has yellow flowers and deeply pinnate leaves. It reliably re-sprouts year after year and once you have found a patch, you can return time and time again for this lovely addition to salads and pesto.

London-rocket ✳ *Sisymbrium irio*
Another 'Wild Rocket', London-rocket (guess where it lives) has a yellow flower and it can be hard to tell it apart from Perennial Wall-rocket. It also looks like Black Mustard *Brassica nigra* (opposite) but the elongated seed pods are waisted (i.e. pinched in) between the seeds. Wild Rocket can also refer to escaped garden rockets *Eruca* spp.

All mustard seeds react with cold water to give mustard its characteristic 'bite'. Using hot water damages the reaction and the resulting condiment will have less 'bite' and more bitterness. Don't forget to pound the seeds in a mortar first and add a little acid – like verjuice or lemon – to set the flavour.

THE RADISHES AND MUSTARDS

Horseradish ✳ *Armoracia rusticana*
Horseradish leaves are mild enough to finely slice and add a mustardy kick to salads. The root is extremely pungent and makes a delicious sauce to go with cold meat or fish. Even the act of chopping it will clear your sinuses. It loves the south but also escapes quickly from areas where it is cultivated.

Wild Radish (White Charlock) ✳ *Raphanus raphanistrum*
Wild Radish has white flowers with green veins and hairy stems and leaves. It flowers from May to September, inhabiting roadsides, field edges and other disturbed ground. All parts of it are edible.

Black Mustard ✳ *Brassica nigra*
Another of the many mustards, Black Mustard likes to live on farm waste, spoil heaps and coastal sites in England and Wales, with most of the Scottish plants colonising Glasgow. The young leaves are tender but very hot and spicy, like Sea Radish which is a personal favourite of mine and can be relied upon to clear the sinuses! It has yellow flowers and its seeds are worth collecting to make mustard sauce.

Other Brassicaceae species you may find include farm escapees such as *Sinapsis arvensis*. It's called Field Mustard or Charlock when it is cultivated and Wild Mustard when it escapes.

AT THE COAST

Scurvy Grass ❋ *Cochlearia anglica*
Previously called *Cochlearia officinalis*, a paste made of the fleshy, round leaves tastes very like Japanese wasabi sauce *Cochlearia wasabi*. Scurvy Grass survives the winter, so was an important source of vitamin C in the darker months when scurvy (vitamin C deficiency) was a risk, before the importation of citrus fruit. You'll find it amongst rough grasses in sand dunes, the scrubland at the edge of the beach, and between rocks on cliffs and the upper shore. One peculiar phenomenon is the spread of closely related, but more adventurous Danish scurvy grass *Cochlearia danica*, which has left the coast to follow the salty, central reservations of the British motorway system. Do not be tempted to leave your car to examine its low mounds of pale pink or white flowers.

Sea Kale ❋ *Crambe maritima*
As the name implies, this one is a Kale/Cabbage-like plant but with a far superior flavour. I find it less bitter than Kale. The young shoots of its heart, tucked under overlapping leaves, are particularly delicious. Remember to go back in the autumn to harvest and spread the seeds to support the population in the relatively few shingle habitats where it is found. A bad storm raking over beach pebbles can wreak havoc on established colonies.

Caution
None of this family is toxic to humans but try small amounts of the strong-tasting ones to start with to avoid stomach upsets.

Sea Radish   *Raphanus maritimus*

Rough, coarse and hairy, Sea Radish looks as formidable as it tastes, apart from the lemon-yellow petals. The young juicy leaf stems are amazing – if you like hot flavours, that is. The young green seed pods look like bulging pea pods with two or three 'peas' in each. If picked swiftly before the shells become fibrous, they are a treat – lightly pickled or crunched raw. The pickles have a short shelf life and need to be eaten quickly or the fire dissipates. It prefers the warmer Atlantic coastline with a only few hardy groups facing the North Sea.

Sea Rocket   *Cakile maritima*

It would be remiss to forget Sea Rocket as it rings the entire coastline of Britain and Ireland. It is a pretty, delicate plant with pink flowers and lobed leaves that are very reminiscent of the Tomato seedlings that spring up for a short time from seeds discarded from beach picnics. However, biting into it will soon dispel the illusion as it is a true firecracker!

It is quite easy to get unsuspecting friends to taste them without suspecting the bitter heat that's about to hit their tastebuds.

Dittander (Dittany or Sea Horseradish)   *Lepidium latifolium*

The flowers are tiny and white if you look closely enough. Metre-high Dittany has alternate oblong leaves that remind me of eucalyptus leaves. It isn't nicknamed Pepperwort or Pepperweed for nothing, as the leaves are extremely hot. Best finely chopped and mixed in towards the end of cooking a wild curry to adjust the heat. The root can be grated and blended with cream and a little vinegar as an alternative to horseradish sauce.

Further reading

Rich, T. C. G. (1991), *Crucifers of Great Britain and Ireland: BSBI Handbook No. 6* (Botanical Society of Britain and Ireland). The go-to reference to identify cruciferous plants in the British Isles covering some 148 species. Includes keys, descriptions and line drawings.

Cannabaceae – the hemp family

The hemp family includes around 170 species. The three best-known genera are: *Cannabis* (hemp), *Humulus* (hops) and *Celtis* (hackberries). Although the genus *Cannabis* was formerly in the same family as Nettle, they are not DNA close relatives after all. This is not a large family and the only plant foraged is Wild Hops.

Wild Hops ✳ *Humulus lupulus*

Wild Hops are often found scrambling through hedges and into shrubs and trees in the warmer central and south England, but still smattered across the north and Scotland. The young shoots, before the leaves open out, can be gathered and steamed. They taste very like slightly bitter French beans and are delicious as a side vegetable. You could pickle them but the taste doesn't really survive the process, so I prefer to lightly blanch and freeze any excess.

The flowers, known as strobiles, can be gathered and dried for teas – especially soothing at bedtime or for nervous stomachs – or to make home-made beer. Once gathered, they should be frozen or dried at a low temperature and kept in a sealed, dark pouch to preserve the volatile oils where the flavour resides.

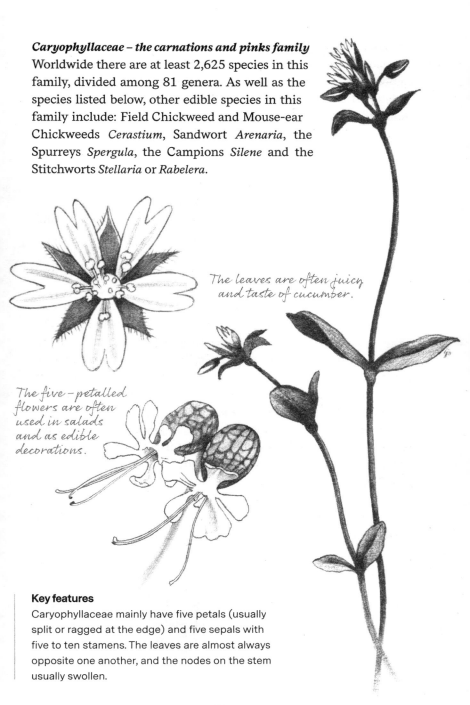

Caryophyllaceae – the carnations and pinks family
Worldwide there are at least 2,625 species in this
family, divided among 81 genera. As well as the
species listed below, other edible species in this
family include: Field Chickweed and Mouse-ear
Chickweeds *Cerastium*, Sandwort *Arenaria*, the
Spurreys *Spergula*, the Campions *Silene* and the
Stitchworts *Stellaria* or *Rabelera*.

The leaves are often juicy
and taste of cucumber.

The five – petalled
flowers are often
used in salads
and as edible
decorations.

Key features
Caryophyllaceae mainly have five petals (usually
split or ragged at the edge) and five sepals with
five to ten stamens. The leaves are almost always
opposite one another, and the nodes on the stem
usually swollen.

MAIN FORAGING SPECIES

Chickweed ✳ *Stellaria media*

Chickweed loves gardeners. It will sprout anywhere the soil has been disturbed, especially if it is also damp, and will inhabit a greenhouse or protected spot all year round. It also grows in light grasses in the shaded edges of copses. It has a lovely cool, light flavour for salads that offsets the more bitter or tart plants that add depth of flavour. I often refer to it as the forager's iceberg lettuce. It makes a wonderful soup, but cut it into bundles of 2–3-centimetre lengths before cooking, or it will wrap itself inextricably around the blades of your stick blender. It is often used in pakora as clumps of it hold a batter well. It is easy to identify because of a line of tiny hairs that grows down one side of the stem.

Mouse-ear Chickweeds *Cerastium* spp. and Stitchworts *Rabelera* spp. are also edible members of this family but not as juicy as Chickweed.

Sea Sandwort ✳ *Honckenya peploides*

Although it is a seaside succulent with juicy leaves, Sea Sandwort is sometimes called Sea Chickweed. The flavour – slightly bitter cucumber – is also cool, like Chickweed. It has pointed leaves closely packed around the stalks in alternating opposing pairs and grows in thick vivid-green mats (from 4–8 centimetres tall) on sand above the high-water mark all round Britain and Ireland. It's best picked in the spring as it gets more bitter as the summer progresses. Sea Sandwort is great gathered young and then lightly pickled, as it keeps its crunchy texture well.

This illustration shows it side on but when foraging you'll spot it from above with the white five-petalled flowers nestled on the four-armed crosses of the leaves.

The Campions, Bladder Campion *Silene vulgaris* and Red Campion *Silene dioca*, also have edible flowers and leaves. White Campion *Silene latifolia* has quite a high amount of saponins as it ages so is only eaten when very young, if at all, although the flowers are mild and pretty in a salad.

Soapwort ✳ Saponaria officinalis

Although Soapwort isn't edible, you can use it to make soap as it contains high amounts of foaming saponins. To make a liquid soap for either your hands or clothes, simply whizz it in a blender with a little water and strain. (See Laundry page 274). Its botanical name of *Saponaria* comes from the Latin *Sapo*, which means soap, hence Saponia. Soapwort roots contain around 20 per cent saponins compared to imported soap nuts at 15 per cent. The soap it makes is gentle and gives lustre and is said to have been used to clean both the Bayeaux Tapestry and the Shroud of Turin.

Although it can cause nausea and stomach upsets in large quantities, it is used in the Middle East as a emulsifier to help bind the oils in tahini and halva. The pink flowers smell sweet and slightly of cloves.

Crassulaceae – the stonecrop family

There are about 1,400 species worldwide and they have their own special way of doing things called Crassulacean acid metabolism or CAM photosynthesis. They photosynthesise during the day but, unlike other plants, don't exchange any gases until the evening, when they take in and store carbon dioxide, and release oxygen. They do this so that they can keep their pores – known as stomata – shut tight during the day to avoid water evaporation. Plants never cease to amaze me.

Members of this family are characteristically succulent, whether growing on old dry stone walls, like navelwort, or ditches, like orpine.

Key features

They have fleshy, succulent leaves often arranged in rosettes or whorls, which don't have stipules. Enjoying symmetry, the flowers have the same number of sepals, petals and carpels.

MAIN FORAGING SPECIES

Navelwort ✳ *Umbilicus rupestris*

In many parts of the country, Navelwort is better known as Wall Pennywort (or Penny Pies). It loves growing in the chinks of tumbledown walls and old granite tors, especially in Wales and the south-west of England and Ireland. Its botanical name *Umbilicus* is a dead giveaway: each round leaf has a bellybutton-style dimple in the middle. It is a tasty succulent and a very welcome winter vegetable, surviving all but the harshest frosts. It can often be picked all year round, but the tenderest, juiciest leaves are found in the spring and early summer.

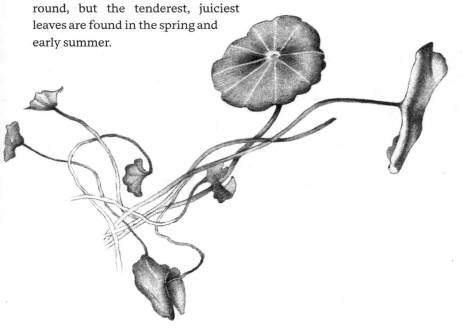

More widespread but in damp ground, you can also find Marsh Pennywort *Hydrocotyle vulgaris*, whose leaves are used in the same way, and is especially delicious eaten in salads with a tangy dressing.

Orpine ✳ *Hylotelephium telephium* (syn. *Sedum telephium*)

This evergreen is often grown in gardens and then makes a break for the countryside, where it will naturalise along shady hedge and ditch edges. It is a 60-centimetre-tall succulent with red flowers. Its young leaves, eaten raw, are crisp and juicy with a pea/asparagus/cucumber flavour. However, the leaves and roots are normally cooked before eating.

Orpine is tolerant to about -20 degrees C so can often be found in the winter but, like most leaves, tastes better in the spring. Do not confuse Orpine with yellow-flowered Biting Stonecrop *Sedum acre* (also known as Goldmoss or Mossy Stonecrop), whose toxins will irritate your stomach if you eat more than a little. It's a good idea to avoid all yellow-flowered *Sedum* spp. White Stonecrop *Sedum album* is slightly hot to taste but can be eaten when young, preferably cooked.

Roseroot ✳ *Rhodiola rosea*

Roseroot can be eaten in the spring in the same way as asparagus. However, outside western Scotland there is not a huge amount of it in the UK, so it is better just admired. It is grown and harvested in Scandinavia and Russia as an energy-giving adaptogen medicine, which has put pressure on wild populations. Think about growing your own if you have a garden.

Elaeagnaceae – the oleaster family

Sadly, in the UK only one of this family is really used – the Sea Buckthorn. Non-resident relatives of this family include the Northern American Silver Buffaloberry *Shepherdia argentea* and the Russet Buffaloberry *Shepherdia canadensis*, which the Inuit peoples gather, dry and smoke to preserve as food. In Japan, the Cherry Silverberry (natsugumi) shrub *Elaeagnus multiflora* bears berries used to make alcohol.

Sea Buckthorn   *Hippophae rhamnoides*

From October to January these hardy coastal bushes, their silver-grey foliage barricading the sand dunes and scrub, are laden with bright orange Sea Buckthorn berries. They are very high in vitamin C and have an antioxidant profile just below acai berry – with no need to fly them in from the Amazon. The berries are full of a bright orange juice – the perfect substitute for lemon juice. Until diluted it's akin to battery acid, but once diluted into a syrup with sugar its citrussy orange flavour develops.

The fun starts when you try to pick them: they are so full of juice (with just one black seed inside full of nutritional oils) that they explode as soon as you put any pressure on them. So the first challenge is getting them off the bush. Rather than picking the berries, cut some berry-laden twigs from the bush itself. You might find a pair of gloves handy, and nothing beats using a pair of secateurs. If you take the small twigs from further down the stem you won't spoil the visual impact for other people. Don't forget to leave plenty for the birds, and remember that the bush fruits on the previous year's wood, so don't over-prune them – leave plenty there for the bush to thrive next year. If this is a hot resource in your area, get together with other foragers and make a community harvesting plan.

Once you're home with your bounty, you'll still need to pick the berries from the twigs. An easy way to handle this is to put them in the freezer. The hard, frozen berries are much easier to pick off the twigs as they don't explode in your hands. This is suitable if you are going to simmer the berries to extract the juice and then strain it in a muslin bag.

If you don't have room in your freezer, as I never seem to, squeeze the juice off the twigs without picking the berries. First, wash your hands and get a large saucepan. (It's best to sit outside, if you can, as until you get the hang of it the juice can go everywhere.) Take a twig in your hand and, with your fingers pointing down into the saucepan, gently squeeze. If your fingers are pointing down, this directs the juice into the pan and not up the walls and into your eye. Turn the twig round by a quarter and apply more pressure, then turn again. If you've ever milked a cow, you will quickly notice the resemblance to milking. Milking the berries is a fast way of processing them without the painstaking task of picking them off one by one. (If you want to save a few for decoration, use a fork to spring them off.) Although the empty berry skin stays attached to the twigs, you hardly waste any juice. Once they are all squeezed, you are left with cold-pressed Sea Buckthorn juice, and a few leaves and twig bits. First mash with a potato masher to get any berries that have detached fully pulped. Then, strain through a sieve and then through a muslin bag to remove any debris.

I recommend pasteurising Sea Buckthorn juice at a gentle heat to preserve it. Alternatively, and to make it more palatable, heat it with sugar to make a syrup, but only after you've used some fresh to make marinades, sauces, sorbet, coulis and a whole host of tasty dishes. It is wonderful for possets, curds, cheesecakes and mixing with Prosecco to make what forager John Wright calls a 'Sea Bucks Fizz'.

The ancient Greeks noticed that when horses were fed on Sea Buckthorn leaves, their coats turned glossy and shiny. This is where the botanical name of Hippophae comes from. Hippo- means horse and -phaos means to shine.

Ericaceae – the heath or heather family

While heather flowers are lovely and heather honey one of the nicest honeys (it makes great mead, too), the Ericaceae family is most interesting to the forager for its many berry-bearing plants. It embraces the subfamily Vaccinioideae, whose members include Cranberry, Bilberry, Lingonberry and the American Blueberry and Huckleberry. These wild berries are pumped full of antioxidants and are extremely good for our health. For more about berries see Chapter 5.

These are small diminutive shrubby plants that can be told apart by closely examining the leaves or, easily, by the colour of the berries when fruiting.

Key features

Plants in the Ericaceae family like growing on acidic and poor soils. Many are evergreen or have glossy deciduous simple leaves. Most are small bushes and bear single berries not in bunches. Surprisingly, rhododendrons, hydrangeas and azaleas are also in this family and also enjoy acidic soil, which enhances the blue colour in their flowers.

MAIN FORAGING SPECIES – RED BERRIES

Cranberry ☀ *Vaccinium oxycoccos*
Sometimes called the Marshberry for its propensity to grow in boggy places, the bright red berries of the Wild Cranberry are considerably smaller than the cultivated varieties. But what it lacks in stature it makes up for in taste, albeit sour. The plant with its sparse glossy leaves is often quite prostrate. In the Scottish Highlands we also find the (very) small Bog Cranberry *Vaccinium microcarpum*. Flowers are reddish-pink and the petals curl back, borne on long thin stems on which the red berries are later held, ripening from September onwards – in time to make cranberry sauce for Thanksgiving or Christmas as it is popular with turkey.

Lingonberry ☀ *Vaccinium vitis-idaea*
The Lingonberry or Cowberry also has red berries but on short stems. Its shiny evergreen foliage is denser and more upright than the cranberry. The berries are also sour. Bell-shaped flowers are white or pale pink. The berries are usually ripe for picking from September to October but can sometimes fruit twice a year with a late-summer crop in July. They are mainly found in Scotland, down the Pennines, and in North Wales with a smattering in Northern Ireland.

Bearberry ☀ *Arctostaphylos uva-ursi*
Bearberry is predominantly found in the Scottish Highlands and better known in the south for its leaves, which are a popular herbal medicine for cystitis. Its glossy foliage is very similar to that of the Lingonberry and it also bears its edible red berries on short stems in late autumn. Its bell-shaped flowers are greenish-white to pink.

BLUE AND BLACK BERRIES

Bilberry ✳ *Vaccinium myrtillus*
This tiny wild relative of the modern blueberry is also called the Blaeberry (Scots), Whortleberry (Northern England) and Whinberry (Southern England). The leaves are similar to Lingonberry but lack the glossy surface. They can be used in teas and help to balance your blood sugar. The lantern-shaped flowers are pale green tinged with pink. Bilberry grows in thick bushes in acidic soils along the edges of roads, paths and clearings. The dusky dark blue berries are full of vitamins and antioxidants (reputed to improve eyesight), and packed full of flavour if you can pick them before the rabbits, deer, mice and other creatures get there, in the summer and early autumn.

Crowberry ✳ *Empetrum nigrum*
The black berries of Crowberry don't have a huge flavour but are welcome when found by a hungry forager in autumn and winter. The leaves are stiff and a little spiky, very like heather. The barely visible, tiny pink or purple flowers grow between the leaves and the stems. It grows to the north of the line made by joining Bristol to Hull but is rarely found south of it. In Ireland it is predominantly found in Donegal and Northern Ireland.

Fabaceae – the pea or legume family

This family contains the Soy bean, garden Pea, Alfalfa, Chickpea, Fenugreek and Liquorice as well as wild peas, vetches, Broom and Gorse. Worldwide, it supplies humans with a range of food, medicines, dyes and timbers. Many of these species need to be treated with some caution. Some people have a hereditary allergy (G6PD deficiency) to the Broad Bean (Fava Bean) *Vicia faba* and *Vicia sativa*. This condition is called favism. For these people, eating these beans, or even walking through a field of flowering beans, can cause the blood to lose iron (haemolytic anaemia). This could be problematic for some people harvesting Common Vetch. Many vetches contain canavanine in their seeds and first roots and shoots to deter insects from eating them. Canavanine can cause a disease called lathyrism, the disease thought to have killed the American adventurer Christopher McCandless; he may have eaten too many Alpine Sweet-vetch *Hedysarum alpinum* seeds, which contain L-canavanine, while weakened from malnutrition.

Key features

All the flowers will remind you of Sweet Pea flowers. The petals are fused to make a standing 'hood', a lower lobe and wings on either side. Seeds are usually round or oval discs, arranged in long, flat pods that swell as they ripen and fatten, eventually splitting to release the seeds. Many are twining vines with trifoliate leaves. The shrub forms often have nasty, curved spines.

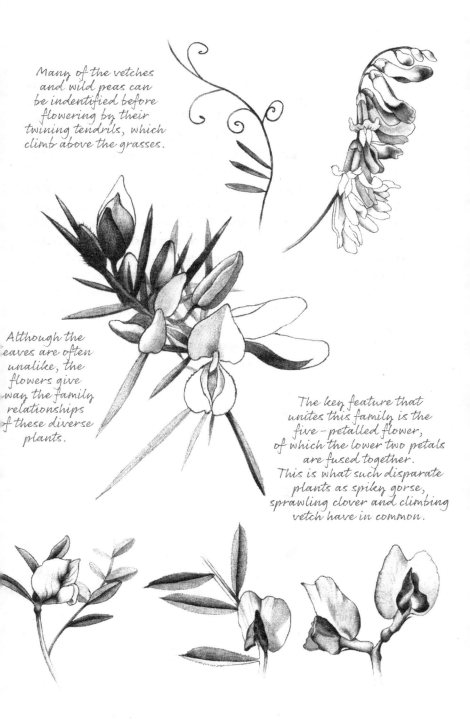

Many of the vetches and wild peas can be indentified before flowering by their twining tendrils, which climb above the grasses.

Although the leaves are often unalike, the flowers give way the family relationships of these diverse plants.

The key feature that unites this family is the five – petalled flower, of which the lower two petals are fused together. This is what such disparate plants as spiky gorse, sprawling clover and climbing vetch have in common.

MAIN FORAGING SPECIES

Common Vetch ✳ *Vicia sativa*

Common Vetch shoots look and taste delicious, just like the delicate, cultivated pea shoots and tendrils decorating a fancy salad. They are edible in small quantities as a garnish and there is evidence that our ancestors cultivated them. But because of canavanine, don't eat the dried seeds in any significant quantity unless they've been properly soaked, drained and then cooked thoroughly in fresh water. Very young vetch shoots contain only small amounts of canavanine and this continues to lessen as they grow. The leaves and flowers are edible and gathered in the late spring and summer. The pink flowers are arranged on individual stalks but grouped in pairs and look just like Sweet Pea flowers. The pods are brown when mature.

Bush Vetch ✳ *Vicia sepium*

The flowers and young shoots of Bush Vetch are tasty in spring and summer dishes. They can be distinguished from Common Vetch by having smaller lilac-blue flowers clustered in groups of four or five and black seed pods. The seed pods are singles not clusters and have around six seeds although usually only three or four mature. The seeds are tiny, however.

Tufted Vetch ✳ *Vicia cracca*

Also called Bird or Cow Vetch, Tufted Vetch is cultivated as a fodder crop for cattle, but humans can enjoy it too. The raceme of blue flowers is arranged in a tall stack and the pods are brown and arranged in clusters. As the pods dry they twist to release five to six seeds per pod each 2–3mm across. Unlike the similar Hairy Vetch *Vicia villosa*, it has a smooth stem. It is eaten like Bush Vetch.

Bitter Vetchling ✳ *Lathyrus linifolius*
(formerly *L. montanus*)

Bitter Vetch or Vetchling has tubers attached to its roots that were eaten in the past before potatoes became popular. Records from the Scottish Highlands show that this was an important food up until the 1800s, the roots being simply boiled and eaten. It suppresses the appetite, reducing thirst and hunger pangs so was used by marching soldiers to keep hunger at bay. The mistresses of King Charles II also apparently used it to keep their figures trim.

There are many vetches but my favourite is the Large-flowered Vetch *Vicia grandiflora* that grows in Poland. Its large lentil-like seeds make you believe you could make a reasonably sized meal out of them.

Red Clover ✳ *Trifolium pratense*
Both Red and White Clover *Trifolium repens*
are edible. I find the leaves fairly tasteless, but
the flowers are sweet and I harvest a lot
of them in the summer to use in tea
blends. Christine Krauss taught me
to add flour to damp clover flowers
(50:50 by weight), press them into a lined baking tray,
and bake them into a delicious crispbread.

Gorse ✳ *Ulex europaeus*
When warmed by the sun, the essential oils
of Gorse flowers – the only edible part of this
plant – smell heavenly of coconut or
old-fashioned suntan lotion. On a
sunny day you can actually tell
whether you're facing north or
south by the taste. The flowers on
the southern sunny side of the bush
taste coconutty while those on the cooler
north side taste of garden peas. It flowers
most of the year except for short spells at
the height of summer and in winter. The
cheery yellow flowers keep their colour even
when mixed into bread dough and baked to make gorse rolls. Don't
eat the 'pea pods' as the quinolizidine alkaloids they contain are not
good for your heart or your health.

Common Broom ✳ *Cystisus scoparius*

Common Broom has edible flowers in the summer that are used like Gorse. Don't eat the leaves or confuse it with Spanish Broom *Spartium junceum*, which contains high levels of cytisine, a toxic alkaloid. The seeds of Common Broom are reputed to have low toxicity and can be roasted as a coffee substitute. The young green pods may have low to zero toxicity. The dried seeds are not eaten, although in a famine situation pre-soaking and a long boiling time might render them edible.

Wild Lupins ✳ *Lupinus perennis*

Lupins are divided into wild (bitter) or cultivated (sweet) lupin varieties. Wild Lupins *Lupinus perennis* come in many colours. The ancient Egyptians and Romans grew them for food; however, Wild Lupins contain a toxic alkaloid called lupanine. You must soak the seeds for five days before cooking for an hour to reduce the alkaloids. I recommend changing the soaking water daily. The cultivated varieties, developed in the 1920s, are low-alkaloid. *Lupinus albus* is a 'sweet' white and *L. angustifolius* is a 'sweet' blue. Sweet Lupins are cultivated as a high-protein food alternative to soya in lower-temperature countries. Soak the seeds overnight and boil them for one hour, and the prepared seeds work well as flour, hummus or a mince substitute. However, wild and cultivated varieties can hybridise, so always assume they need a five-day soak. Pick the seeds in August.

Caution

Many peas, beans and seeds in this family contain lectins and other anti-nutrient factors to protect themselves between the summer and the following spring. Avoid eating the pods, particularly of the larger species, unless you are absolutely sure of their edibility.

Grossulariaceae – the currant family

Many garden fruit plants hop the fence and go feral. I often find wild European Gooseberries *Ribes uva-crispa* (which seem particularly fond of the Scottish right to roam), the White- and Redcurrant – both *Ribes rubrum* – and Blackcurrants *Ribes nigrum*.

Another charming escapee is the Flowering Currant *Ribes sanguineum*. It has flowers that taste as if Lavender, Rose, Rosemary and Thyme all got mixed up together. The leaves are lovely in a tea or used to scent and flavour a delicate carragheen jelly, and I am partial to the flowers in a gin and tonic.

Juncaceae – the rush family

Rushes, with their very thin, tall leaves and tiny brown flowers look somewhat like sedges and grasses but are their own family. They are slow-growing and form thick mats of rhizomes. Many of the Juncus and Luzula species in this family have edible seeds. I have tried the seed of the Soft Rush *Juncus effusus* and it's nutty and rather nice.

Great Woodrush ❋ *Luzula sylvatica*

Great Woodrush can be invasive in many woods, forming a thick impenetrable mat. Knowing that it wasn't poisonous, I tried it, determined to find some virtue to it. You can easily grasp it at the base, just between the two outer leaves, and pull. The white stalk that comes out is mildly nutty and crisp. The taste reminds me of Chinese Water Chestnuts *Eleocharis dulcis*. The seeds are also edible.

Common Club Rush ❋ *Schoenoplectus lacustris*

Also known as the Lakeshore Bulrush, Common Club Rush grows on the edges of lakes and ponds around Britain and Ireland, especially in the Central Midlands of both countries. The seeds can be processed into a flour or porridge, though they are small and take significant effort to collect and prepare. It has edible rhizomes that can be harvested, cooked, or ground into flour.

Juncaginaceae – the arrowgrasses

Sea Arrowgrass ❋ *Triglochin maritima*

It's lovely to have a grass growing on the merse that tastes of coriander. But I'm often asked if it's safe to eat, as Sea Arrowgrass contains the cyanogenic glycosides taxiphyllin and triglochinin, which can turn into dangerous hydrogen cyanide gas under certain circumstances. These glycosides are often at their highest levels in a late dry summer, especially on a non-salty site, and in new growth of leaves and spikes in spring. Cattle grazing on Sea Arrowgrass's relative Marsh Arrowgrass *Triglochin palustris* have died. Note *cattle*, not humans.

Triglochin is hydrolysed in a cow's *rumen* by gut microorganisms to produce hydrogen cyanide. Horses are rarely (if ever) affected by plants containing cyanogenic glycosides as their digestive system does not include a rumen and so cannot easily convert glycosides to free cyanide. Humans do not have a rumen either. We digest our foods with acids, rather than fermenting them as a cow does. This makes a big difference. Even if we did have a rumen, with fresh plant material a fatal intake would be less than 0.5 per cent of a cow's body weight. On that basis, a 70-kilogram person might be in trouble at 350 grams if we digested it like cows. That's about three and a half full 100-gram supermarket salad bags in one sitting – if we were cows.

Bamboo shoots also contain taxiphyllin. Cyanide gas poisoning has occurred from Chinese villagers fermenting Bamboo shoots in large amounts in a 27-metres[3] well. The gas was released when it was fermenting but that doesn't mean that eating Bamboo shoots is dangerous. So go ahead and enjoy adding Sea Arrowgrass's coriander-flavoured spikes and green seeds to your wild salads and meals, but don't try grazing a field of it or fermenting huge quantities in an enclosed space.

Laminaceae – the mint family

Many of the most aromatic wild herbs are in the mint family: wild mints, sages and thymes. This is a large family that also includes Lavender, Oregano, Rosemary, Hyssop, Bugle, the dead-nettles, the woundworts and horehounds. With the exception of Pennyroyal *Mentha pulegium*, Bugle *Ajuga reptans* and Wood Sage *Teucrium scorodonia*, all of them can be eaten safely – although that doesn't mean you'll like all the flavours.

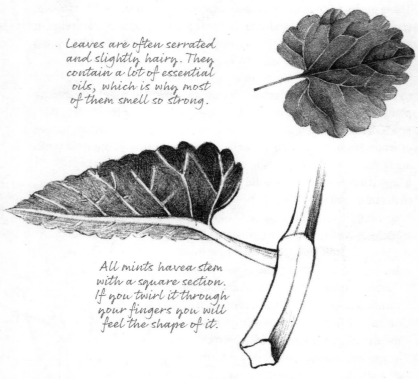

Leaves are often serrated and slightly hairy. They contain a lot of essential oils, which is why most of them smell so strong.

All mints have a stem with a square section. If you twirl it through your fingers you will feel the shape of it.

Key features

Mints are easily identified by their distinctive aroma, the classic square stems and alternating opposing leaves. Each opposite pair of leaves rotates 90 degrees from the pair below it. Most of the plants are high in essential oils and fragrant, especially when crushed, although some have a musky odour. Historically, this family was called Labiateae, which means lipped. It referred to the appearance of the flower, which has five fused petals. Often, two will make the 'top lip' and three make the 'bottom lip'.

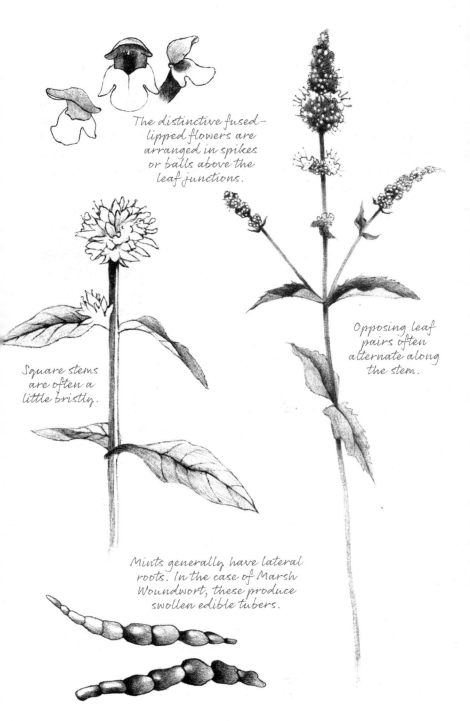

The distinctive fused-lipped flowers are arranged in spikes or balls above the leaf junctions.

Opposing leaf pairs often alternate along the stem.

Square stems are often a little bristly.

Mints generally have lateral roots. In the case of Marsh Woundwort, these produce swollen edible tubers.

MAIN FORAGING SPECIES

Water Mint ❋ Mentha aquatica

Found in many streams in spring and summer. Both the leaves and flowers are fragrant and edible but should be rinsed in a vinegar solution or sterilising fluid to avoid liver fluke carried by grazing animals in infected areas. The leaf veins are often brownish-purple highlighted against the green. The lilac flowers are on the upper leaf axils (junctions) with some held above on the stem tips like pompoms. Although Water Mint has square stems like other mints, the main stem can sometimes be round in profile. Water Mint sorbet is a real summer treat. I dry a lot of it for use year-round in herbal teas.

Spearmint ❋ Mentha spicata

Spearmint is often a leggy plant with few branches. The leaves are deeply incised along the veins and the flowering spikes are long with multiple whorls of lilac flowers. It smells strongly of Spearmint toothpaste. A lot of the mints interbreed to produce an astonishing variety of flavours. For example, the cross between Spearmint and our native Applemint became *Mentha spicata x suaveolens* – now known as mojito mint *Mentha x villosa*. Peppermint, a cross between Watermint and Spearmint, becomes *Mentha x piperita*. Bushy mint, a cross between Corn Mint and Spearmint, becomes *Mentha x gracilis*, with further variations on this known as ginger mint and basil mint.

Horse Mint ✳ *Mentha longifolia*

With a peppermint scent, Horse Mint can be
easily recognised as it produces its lilac flowers
in tapering pyramidal spikes held above the
leaves. I often find it on barren ground such as the
waste ground left by former building works. You
can use it in digestive herbal teas, mint juleps or
make it into a refreshing sorbet. It can grow up
to 1 metre high in the right conditions.

Corn Mint ✳ *Mentha arvensis*

Corn Mint is often found in arable fields and meadows and
both the stems and leaves are very hairy. Its smell and taste are
not as strong as the other mints but it is welcome when there is nothing
else. It produces its lilac flowers in the axils (junctions) of the leaves.

White Dead-nettle ✳ *Lamium album*

White Dead-nettle has soft edible leaves that don't sting and produces
sweet-tasting flowers, but it hides in nettle patches hoping no one
will notice it. A trained eye can easily spot the difference though. It's
a great plant to cook and add into a Georgian pkhali mix of minced
boiled leaves and walnuts pressed into snack-sized balls. It's in
season from late spring and into the summer. I eat a lot of it in salads.
There is also the Red Dead-nettle *Lamium purpureum* and the Yellow
Archangel *Lamium galeobdolon* but I personally prefer the taste of
the White Dead-nettle.

Ground Ivy ✳ *Glechoma hederacea*

Ground Ivy has both a geranium and minty taste.
Once used to flavour beer, it was known as
ale-hoof. The leaves and pretty blue flowers
are edible. Add them to salads, infuse it in
vinegar for a remarkable dressing, or make
a green syrup frozen into a sorbet. I love
making a syrup with it, cooling it (to avoid
its coagulating effect) and churning it with a
creamy custard to create our house favourite
– ground ivy ice cream. You'll find it growing in
a mat and creeping vigorously across the ground
in woods or flower beds. Harvest it from spring to autumn.

Marsh Woundwort ✳ *Stachys palustris*

Marsh Woundwort has long, thin, white, sprout-
like tubers that are tasty and crunchy, reminiscent
of slightly sweet bean sprouts with a hint of
bitterness. They can be eaten raw, lightly steamed
or pickled – just like fancy Chinese Artichoke
(crosne) *Stachys affinis* in Michelin-star
restaurants. The slender ones are best steamed
and mashed for gnocchi or dumplings. The tubers
of Marsh Woundwort were crossed with the non-
tuberous Hedge Woundwort *Stachys sylvatica*
becoming *Stachys×ambigua* in one of the first examples of
deliberate Neolithic plant hybridising. Marsh Woundwort tubers
are one of my favourites as they are relatively easy to dig up, don't
require a lot of processing and taste great. They are also easily dried
and powdered as a flour. I harvest them from October to February.
Although the leaves have a fairly strong, mousy smell, don't be put off
as Marsh Woundwort makes a delicious tea. It is very similar to the
taste of Nettle – in fact its relative Hedge Woundwort is sometimes
called Hedge Nettle. The tea is the best natural antihistamine that
I've come across and has saved the day with many a horsefly bite.

Wild Thyme ✳ *Thymus polytrichus*
Wild thymes of different kinds grace our hillsides and coastal dune meadows, covering the land with a carpet of beautiful pale purple-pink flowers between May and September. Wild-creeping or Elfin Thyme *Thymus serpyllum* is another of these tiny plants. Pick both when young and before the soft stems become woody, as it is fiddly to remove the stems. Use as a culinary herb.

Other useful aromatic mints include Wild Marjoram *Origanum vulgare* and Lesser Calamint *Calamintha nepeta*, also known as *Clinopodium nepeta*. Many more are used medicinally such as Self Heal *Prunella vulgaris* for wounds; White Horehound *Marrubium vulgare* for coughs; Hyssop *Hyssop agastache* spp. for digestion; Common Skullcap *Scutellaria galericulata* for anxiety; Gypsywort *Lycopus europaeus* used as a sedative and to reduce hyperthyroid activity.

Caution
Wood Sage ✳ *Teucrium scorodonia*
Wood Sage contains a derivative of humulene, also found in hops and hemp, so has been popular in traditional beers and vermouths as a bittering ingredient. However, it also contains a compound called teucrin A that can affect the liver. Under EU law, the maximum permissible amount of teucrin A per 1 kilogram of finished product must not be greater than 2 milligrams (5 milligrams if you're in Italy) to prevent liver poisoning. Wall Germander *Teucrium chamaedrys* has a concentration of 0.13 per cent teucrin A and there may not be more than that in Wood Sage.[9] By all means use a few leaves at a time but be wary of using large quantities.

Further reading
Lawton, B. P. (2002), *Mints: a family of herbs and ornamentals* (Timber Press, Oregon).

Malvaceae – the mallow family

This family contains Common Mallow, Tree Mallow and Marshmallow, all of which have edible leaves and roots. It also contains the Linden (European Lime) trees (see page 156), Hibiscus and popular garden plants like the Hollyhock.

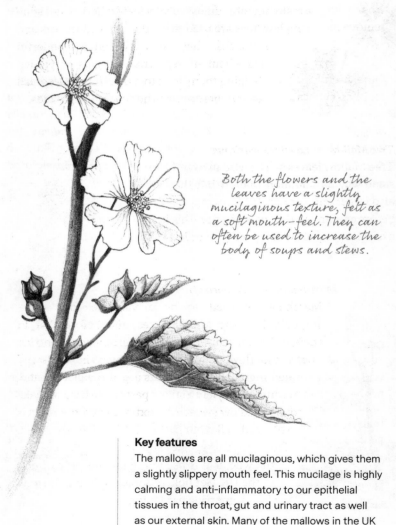

Both the flowers and the leaves have a slightly mucilaginous texture, felt as a soft mouth-feel. They can often be used to increase the body of soups and stews.

Key features

The mallows are all mucilaginous, which gives them a slightly slippery mouth feel. This mucilage is highly calming and anti-inflammatory to our epithelial tissues in the throat, gut and urinary tract as well as our external skin. Many of the mallows in the UK have broad, palmate leaves with five pronounced veins that separate the leaves into lobes.

MAIN FORAGING SPECIES

Common Mallow ✳ *Malva sylvestris*
I like to use Common Mallow leaves the way that *Malva* sp. leaves are
used in Syria, Palestine, Israel, Lebanon and Egypt – to make a
soup called *molokhia* or *khobiza*. The leaves thicken the
soup as they are mucilaginous. When you touch it, it has
a really smooth, almost velvety feel. In herbal medicine
mallow teas are used to soothe irritated throats and
stomachs. They are tasty and a wonderful
ingredient in vegetarian burgers or patties,
helping them stick together. It is widespread
everywhere except the Scottish Highlands.

Tree Mallow ✳ *Lavatera maritima*
Tree Mallow leaves can be used in exactly the
same way as Common Mallow but they are
also larger and very useful for wrapping food
before cooking in the coals of a fire. This is very much
a coastal plant although poorly recorded.

Marshmallow ✳ *Althaea officinalis*
Marshmallow used to be a valuable food
ingredient in the Middle Ages, and before that in
ancient Egypt, China and Mediterranean countries.
Both the flowers and young leaves make lovely
salad ingredients. The roots are also collected and,
traditionally, yield a sticky paste once used to make
marshmallow sweets. An extract from the roots is
still used to flavour *halva*, a Middle Eastern sweet.
However, this species should not be taken from
the wild as it is becoming increasingly rare in
the UK. Get hold of some seeds and do some
guerrilla gardening.

Montiaceae – the miner's lettuce family

Montiaceae is a small family of flowering plants known for their adaptability and preference for cooler climates. This family includes around 14 genera and 230 species, many of which thrive in nutrient-poor or rocky soils. Plants in this family are typically low-growing and succulent-like, storing water in their leaves and stems to endure dry conditions. Other notable members include species of *Lewisia*, often cultivated for their attractive, colourful flowers.

Pink Purslane ✳ *Claytonia sibirica*

This pink-petalled plant with its slightly fleshy heart-shaped leaves has often been my only green vegetable in the winter months. It appears as the weather cools and the buttercups and grasses have died back and is a November treat for which I am truly grateful. The leaves are lovely raw in a salad, or steamed like spinach. In Scotland the Stewarton flower is a white-petalled subspecies.

Spring Beauty ✳ *Claytonia perfoliata*

Spring Beauty tastes just like Pink Purslane, with mild, slightly sweet, and crisp leaves. It has similar basal leaves but differs in that it develops a single 'feature leaf', through which the flower stalk emerges from the middle. It has white flowers but comes up in the spring much later than its cousin. Both like the shade of woodland or hedges, disliking open, sunny ground. In North America it is called miner's lettuce, named for its historical use by miners during the California Gold Rush, who ate it to prevent scurvy in the spring when there were few other plants out that contained vitamin C.

Onagraceae – the evening primrose family

The evening primrose family of around 650 species of herbs, shrubs and trees ranges from willowherbs *Epilobium* spp. to fuchsias *Fuchsia* spp. as well as its namesake Evening Primrose.

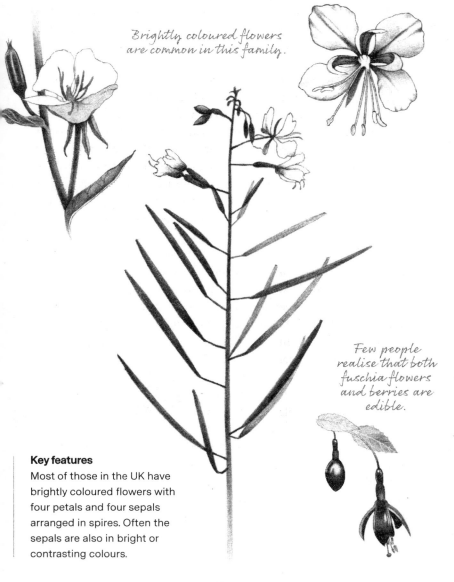

Brightly coloured flowers are common in this family.

Few people realise that both fuschia flowers and berries are edible.

Key features
Most of those in the UK have brightly coloured flowers with four petals and four sepals arranged in spires. Often the sepals are also in bright or contrasting colours.

MAIN FORAGING SPECIES

Rosebay Willowherb (Fireweed) ✳ *Chamaenerion angustifolium*
Young, red-green Rosebay Willowherb shoots start to appear in late spring. They are delicious nibbled raw or gently steamed/boiled with some melted butter, salt and pepper – much like you'd prepare asparagus shoots. I strip the leaves off first as these are a little bitter. I pick lots of mature leaves off the 2-metre-high stems, just before they flower at the end of June, and dry them to make a green tea. It's also easy to make a traditional Russian tea, Ivan chai, by fermenting the leaves (see page 256). The pink flowers are useful as decorations or as a food colouring for jellies. The nickname Fireweed comes from its ability to regenerate after fires and much admired after the London Blitz.

Evening Primrose ✳ *Oenothera biennis*
Evening Primrose is also a tall plant and
you can see the relationship to Rosebay
Willowherb. It has large, floppy, yellow
edible flowers and oil-rich seeds. The flower
buds are lovely in salads. Both the leaves and
the roots have a mild taste and can be
eaten raw or cooked – the former like
spinach, the latter like potatoes. The raw
roots are pretty spicy, so not everyone
likes them, but once cooked, the spiciness
diminishes. As the plant is a biennial, the
root is best harvested at the end of its first year.

Hedge Fuchsia ✳ *Fuchsia magellanica*
Many people don't realise that many fuchsias have edible berries.
When fully ripe, they taste like a delicious cross between a fig and
a grape. Counter-intuitively, they are often purple when
unripe and go green when ripe. Hardy fuchsias
such as the Hedge Fuchsia often go wild in
the UK and seem to survive the winters well,
even in the north-west of Scotland. A couple
of large bushes can yield several kilos of
delicious fruit in August.

Oxalidaceae – the sorrel family
This family features the exotic Carambola or Starfruit in the genus *Averrhoa* as well as over 800 of the *Oxalis* sourgrasses: wood sorrels, pink sorrels and yellow sorrels. However, there is only one species commonly foraged in the UK.

Wood Sorrel ❋ *Oxalis acetosella*
Wood Sorrel is very cute. It's a tiny, diminutive plant with three heart-shaped leaves joined to a delicate stem by their point, which is why this genus are sometimes called false shamrocks. Wood Sorrel tastes of green apple peel or lemon and can be eaten most of the year. Unfortunately, it doesn't have a large tasty underground tuber, unlike its relative the Peruvian Oca *Oxalis tuberosa*.

Wood Sorrel is another species subject to misunderstanding. I see medical warnings about the dangers of consuming it posted on the internet because it contains oxalic acid. Oxalic acid binds with calcium in the urine and causes little oxalate crystals that irritate the kidneys (a condition called hyperoxaluria) – around 75 per cent of kidney stones contain oxalates. In vast quantities, it can even be fatal. Oxalic acid's unique claim to fame is that it was the first compound to be synthesised by humans – the German chemist Friedrich Wöhler, in 1824. Commercially, it's used to clean rust off iron and as a bleach in tooth-whitening products.

Yes, Wood Sorrel contains oxalic acid but let's do some maths: the lethal dose of oxalic acid is around 600 milligrams of oxalic acid per kilogram of body weight. On average, humans consume 50 to 200 milligrams of oxalates per day but 30 to 70 per cent of dietary oxalic acid is excreted daily. The oxalic acid content of wood sorrel has ranged from 0.31 to 1.25 grams per 100 grams of fresh leaves when tested. Using the higher value, if you weighed 70 kilograms you would need to eat 3.36 kilograms of wood sorrel in one meal to kill yourself. This is slightly higher than the lethal dose of 4.2 to 5 kilograms of rhubarb leaves. That is about thirty-three salad bags (100-gram size) of wood sorrel. You'd need to give up your day job to gather that much Wood Sorrel.

---

* Lethal dose at 70kg is:
42g divided by [grams per 100g] = x times 100 = divided by 1,000 = y kg.

Plantaginaceae – the plantain family

Plantago is the largest genus in this family and there are four commonly used by foragers. With the exception of Buck's-horn Plantain, they have long leaves with tough leaf fibres, small flowers and fibrous seed husks. Plantaginaceae also contains the genus *Veronica* within which French foragers used *la Veronique mâle* (Speedwell) as an adulterant for tea, earning it the epithet *le Thé d'Europe*. The poisonous Foxglove (from the fairy folk's-gloves) of the genus *Digitalis* is also in the broader family.

Ribwort Plantain ❋ *Plantago lanceolata*

Both Ribwort and Broadleaf Plantain *Plantago major* have edible leaves when young, before fibrous 'strings' start to form, running parallel to each other through the backs of the leaves. Ribwort Plantain has long narrow leaves and black flower buds that look hardly different before or after its tiny show of flowers. The buds taste of mushrooms and are lovely pickled and served with a cheese salad. Harvest them in the spring when they are tender from virtually anywhere in the UK.

Sea Plantain ❋ *Plantago maritima*

This has long but succulent leaves like Ribwort Plantain, but the seed head is more like Greater Plantain. This is a lovely mild, slightly salty coastal vegetable that I pick from the merse mud flats in summer. It keeps well and is not stringy like its roadside relatives.

Broadleaf Plantain ✳ *Plantago major*
The edible leaves of Broadleaf Plantain are much
wider and almost spoon-shaped. Mature, large ones are
a good source of fibre, which can be stripped out and twined
to make impromptu string. It's a plant that's hugely variable
in size: in frequently cut lawns it becomes
miniaturised, but in a grassy hedgerow the
leaves can reach 10 centimetres or so. After
flowering, the seed chaff can be collected. It is
not as abundant as its relative *Plantago ovata*, which
is the source of psyllium husk sold in health food shops
to increase dietary fibre. One level teaspoon of
psyllium husk contains the same amount of fibre
as a whole bowlful of porridge.

Buck's-horn Plantain ✳ *Plantago coronopus*
Another lovely salad vegetable when the leaves are young, with
a slightly nutty flavour and not too stringy. The leaves have side
lobes that are reminiscent of a young deer's antlers.

Portulaceae – the purslane family
The only UK plant encountered in this family is nutritious
Common Purslane *Portulaca oleracea*, which has lobed green-gold
leaves on fleshy red stems. It is only found sporadically in the
south of England. The Claytonia purslanes in the distantly related
Montiaceae family (page 106) are far more widespread.

Primulaceae - the primrose and cowslip family
This spring-flowering family contains primroses, cowslips and
oxslips. The often wrinkly leaves are arranged in rosettes with round
umbels of tubular flowers on stout stems. Both our native Primrose
Primula vulgaris and Cowslip *Primula veris* have edible flowers and
the leaves are welcome in spring salads.

Polygonaceae – the buckwheat family

This plant family contains the buckwheats, docks, knotweeds and knotgrasses. Cultivated rhubarb *Rheum×hybridum* is probably one of the best known. Many plants in this family – especially the docks and knotweeds – have leaves that are high in sour-tasting oxalic acid. Take care eating excessively large amounts, as this can lead to problems with oxalates. See page 111.

Many traditional recipes call for docks, sorrels, rhubarb and spinach to be served with cream or sour cream. Cream is high in calcium which chelates oxalic acid so it can no longer be absorbed by the blood. This is why rhubarb cooked with cream can sometimes taste a little gritty. Once in the gut, a probiotic bacterium called *Oxalobacter formigenes* – a Gram-negative anaerobic bacterium – degrades oxalate, making high-oxalate foods safer to eat.[10] During the period from winter to spring 2021, whilst I was eating only wild foods, my oxalic acid intake increased dramatically. So the *Oxalobacter* in my gut (analysed by stool samples) increased by over 1,100 per cent to compensate for the extra amount I was eating. It's interesting how our bodies and their inhabitants react to protect us while eating a range of different foods.

The genus *Fagopyrum* provides the pseudo-cereal grain known as buckwheat, mainly found in Asia and China. Although it's not native to the UK, Common Buckwheat *Fagopyrum esculentum* has escaped from farms and bird feeders into the wild. Similar native species like Broad-leaved Dock also have an edible seed.

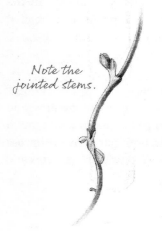

Note the jointed stems.

Key features

Poly – as in Polygonaceae – means many in Greek and gony means knees or joints. One key identification feature for this family is the many swollen nodes that make jointed 'knees' or 'elbows' – the knots – along the plants' stems. They also have many seeds.

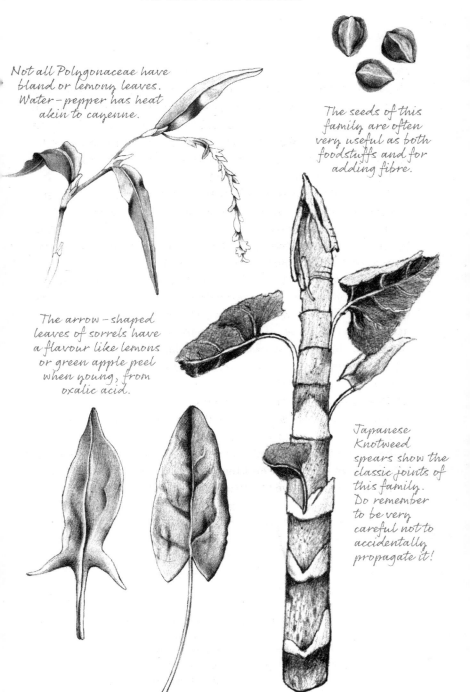

Not all Polygonaceae have bland or lemony leaves. Water-pepper has heat akin to cayenne.

The seeds of this family are often very useful as both foodstuffs and for adding fibre.

The arrow-shaped leaves of sorrels have a flavour like lemons or green apple peel when young, from oxalic acid.

Japanese Knotweed spears show the classic joints of this family. Do remember to be very careful not to accidentally propagate it!

MAIN FORAGING SPECIES

Common Sorrel ❋ *Rumex acetosa*
Sorrel is a common herb of any grassland and tolerates mowing and grazing. The distinctive leaves are arrow-shaped with backward-pointing spurs. Sorrel is rich in acetic acid, giving the whole plant a refreshing lemony zing. It can be nibbled on raw, added to salads or used as a garnish. Wilted over stock with some fried onions and blitzed together it makes an excellent sorrel sauce to have with fish, or any oily or fatty dish. The green apple-skin/lemon-flavoured leaves can be eaten most of the year. A 100-gram (supermarket salad-size) bag of Sorrel will provide 50 per cent of your daily Vitamin C needs, 130 per cent of your vitamin A, 25 per cent of your magnesium RDA and 15 per cent of your iron. It's also high in antioxidants like kaempferol, myricetin and quercetin, which help to protect your cells from the ageing effect of oxygen. To be on the safe side, do not eat more than 50 grams in one sitting, due to the oxalate content.

A big point in Sorrel's favour is that it's often available right through the winter. It is particularly fond of hiding in large tussocks of grass that are home to Broad-leaved Dock too.

Sheep's Sorrel ❋ *Rumex acetosella*
I'm guessing from the name Sheep's Sorrel that the leaf of this smaller dock is supposed to look like a sheep's face; however, I think the leaf has bunny-shaped ears. Perhaps it was just a favourite snack for sheep to nibble on as, although it is small, it is very tasty and sometimes called Field Sorrel.

Caution
Don't mistake Common Sorrel leaves for Arum Lily *Arum maculatum*, also known as Cuckoo Pint, in the Araceae family. The high levels of oxalates and saponins in Arum Lily leaves irritate the skin, mouth, tongue and throat, resulting in swelling, difficulty breathing, burning pain and an upset stomach. It requires special preparation (see page 230).

Japanese Knotweed ✳ *Fallopia japonica*

You might see the old scientific name *Polygonum cuspidatum* used in some references. It's the same plant and a much-feared invasive species, particularly when it comes to home insurance, as the complex and tough root system can undermine building foundations. However, it's a treat for foragers who like rhubarb as it's a perfect replacement: stewed knotweed with cream, candied knotweed, knotweed jam, knotweed wine, knotweed crumble ... In spring, pick the young shoots that look like giant purple-pink asparagus spears. Make sure you clean and prepare the shoots on site, not when you get home; even tiny pieces of it can grow and it's illegal to spread it to new areas. Don't trim the ends off at home and put them into your compost bin as they will grow. If I have any leftover pieces, I boil them before discarding them to be absolutely sure.

Not only is it very tasty – not as sharp as rhubarb – Japanese Knotweed is also very good for you. It contains high amounts of the phenol resveratrol, which is also found in Blueberries, Bilberries, Raspberries, Cranberries, Mulberries, Scots Pine, Peanuts, Grapes and red wine. Plants use resveratrol to protect themselves from infections and ionising radiation. In humans, it acts like an antioxidant that helps to protect cells from ageing and cancer. The majority of commercial resveratrol is extracted from Japanese Knotweed root. Clinical studies have also proved that *in vitro* it will kill the *Borrelia* bacteria that cause Lyme disease, so it is used in the herbal treatment of Lyme arthritis. Even those we perceive as invasive villains can be bearers of gifts.

Broad-leaved Dock ❋ *Rumex obtusifolius*

The leaves of this dock are so bitter that I only eat the very young growth – the unfurled shoots are less bitter and mildly lemony – and the rhubarb-flavoured flower stems. The seed is abundant in the autumn and comes off easily just by running the dry seed heads through your hands. It doesn't have a huge amount of flavour but it is excellent for mixing with tastier nut flours into biscuits and protein bars to make them go further. It also provides a good deal of healthy fibre.

This is the plant that children are taught to use as an antidote to nettle stings. If you've tried it yourself and it hasn't worked, you were probably using the wrong part. Rather than crumpling up a leaf and rubbing it over the skin, the trick is to use the gel found inside the young, furled leaf sheath. Dock leaves work thanks to the presence of phytochemicals called anthraquinones. In aloe vera gel – a well-known, pain-relieving gel – two of the most important anthraquinones are aloin and emodin. Both are painkilling (analgesic) and laxative compounds. Dock root also contains anthraquinones, of which two are emodin and aloe-emodin. In addition to being inherently analgesic, these anthraquinones can generate salicylic acid (nature's aspirin) via enzymes when under attack. Dock is also very high in chrysophanol and physcion, which are both anti-inflammatory. I've found that dock gel soothes nettle stings, eczema and burns.

Alpine Dock ❋ *Rumex alpinus*

Also known as Poor Man's Rhubarb or Monk's Rhubarb, Alpine Dock is recognisable by its enormous leaves – dock on steroids. You can eat the leaves in the spring and autumn (they are bitter in the summer) as an alternative to spinach – they should be cooked and not eaten raw to reduce the bitterness. They have fairly high levels of oxalic acid so should not be eaten in large quantities. The stems can also be used as a rhubarb substitute.

Bistort *Bistorta officinalis*

The old North English country classic Dock Pudding doesn't contain Broad-leaved Dock but Bistort leaves, commonly known as 'Easter-ledges' or 'pudding dock'. Around Easter the young leaves would be finely chopped with Nettles, Dandelion leaves, onions and herbs. These were then mixed with barley or oatmeal and beaten egg, shaped into a ball, tied up in a pudding cloth and boiled in hot water until set. Pre-farming, the earliest containers were probably the stomach membranes of deer or other animals. Hunter-gatherers would have noticed the foods in the crops of birds or stomachs of animals, and boiling such organs could well have resulted in the ideas behind these types of boiled puddings. Gather Bistort leaves in spring before the plant puts up its rosy-pink flowering spires.

Water-pepper *Persicaria hydropiper*

Known by the nickname 'Arse-smart', this is as hot as chillies and will make a fiery sauce if chopped into vinegar. In Japan, the young red shoots known as *benitade* are used as a sushi garnish. A low plant, it loves the centre of a woodland track or the gravelly edge of a stream. It looks like the land-dwelling, non-fiery Red Shank *Persicaria maculosa*, with lance-shaped leaves that are slightly wavy at the base with fine hairs on the edges. Unlike the Red Shank, which is edible but not peppery, Water-pepper is a smooth, mid-green without any dark smudges on the leaves. They can both be eaten from spring through to autumn.

Further reading

Akeroyd, J. R. (2014), *Docks and Knotweeds of Britain and Ireland: BSBI Handbook No. 3* (Botanical Society of Britain and Ireland). An illustrated handbook that helps identify knotgrasses, knotweeds, persicarias, docks, sorrels and other relatives. The book includes descriptions of eighty-three species in eleven genera with sixty-seven illustrations.

Rosaceae – the Rose family

With over 4,800 members, the rose family gives us many of our fragrant flowers and juicy fruits. It contains many genera and has diverse characteristics. The four main fruit types are:

Apple (*Malus*), whose seeds have a protective leathery skin, then fruit flesh and an outer skin. This includes rosehips, hawthorn, quince and rowan berries.

Plum (*Prunus*), whose seeds have a protective shell, then fruit flesh and an outer skin. These 'drupes' include cherries and almonds.

Raspberry (*Rubus*), structured like miniature plums but bundled together into the berry. This includes blackberries, cloudberries, the American Salmonberry and the Japanese Wineberry.

Strawberry (*Fragaria*), whose pips are the actual fruits with flesh around them – technically a 'false berry'.

This family of plants is popular with children as it includes the brambles, wild raspberries and wild strawberries. Other useful members include Wild Cherry, Crab Apple, Damson Plum, Bullace, Sloe, Medlar, Quince, Chokeberry, Rowan and Hawthorn. Non-fruit-bearing members include Meadowsweet, Lady's Mantle, Silverweed and Wood Avens. Some members of this family are discussed in the chapters on trees.

Key features

The leaf groups are arranged alternately along the stems. Once the leaf cluster branches off the stem, the tannin-rich leaves are often in opposite pairs. (The leaves themselves tend to have serrated edges.) There is a lot of variation and they can be simple, trifoliate, palmate or pinnate and some, such as Meadowsweet, are opposite. Many of the fruits feel hairy or bristly from the numerous pistils of the flowers.

The flowers typically contain five petals and five sepals (although this can vary from three to ten), with at least five stamens. If there are more, they are often in multiples of five. The flowers and therefore the fruits are rarely found singly and are usually in corymb bunches.

Many flowers in the Rosaceae family are highly scented and attractive to insects and birds. The scent of almonds, whose seeds contain a cyanide precursor, characterises the Prunoideae sub-family.

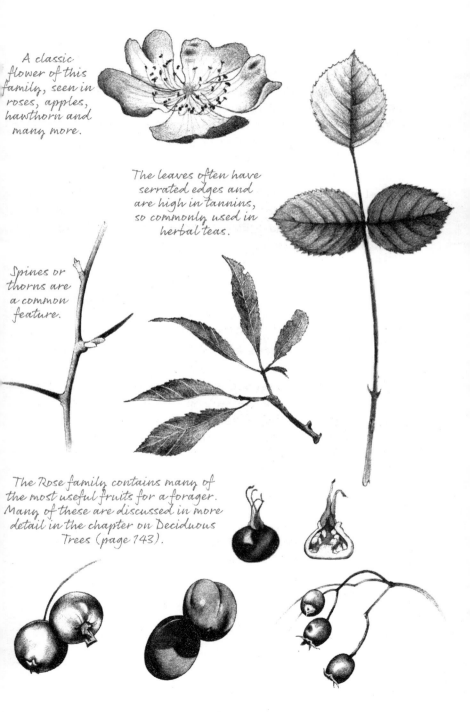

A classic flower of this family, seen in roses, apples, hawthorn and many more.

The leaves often have serrated edges and are high in tannins, so commonly used in herbal teas.

Spines or thorns are a common feature.

The Rose family contains many of the most useful fruits for a forager. Many of these are discussed in more detail in the chapter on Deciduous Trees (page 143).

MAIN FORAGING SPECIES

Dog Rose ❋ *Rosa canina*

Our native wild rose has five pale pink petals and small hips that ripen late in the year. Like all roses, including domesticated garden varieties, the flowers and hips are edible. (It is important with all types of rosehips to remember to remove the irritating hairs from around the seeds, by scraping or straining them out, as they can cause throat, gut or anal irritation.) The Dog Rose is most often used to make vitamin C-rich rosehip jelly, rosehip syrup and a delicious concentrated rosehip juice reduction.

THE ROSE RIDDLE

On a summer's day, in sultry weather,
Five brothers were born together.
Two had beards and two had none,
And the other had but half of one.
Who am I?

Answer: the dog rose flower (look at the sepals behind the petals)

The rose riddle is attributed to Albertus Magnus, 1193–1280.

Japanese Rose ❋ *Rosa rugosa*

Planted on many verges by county councils, this is now considered an invasive species. The flowers are highly fragrant and a rich dark pink and infuse into a delicious rose vodka; they also dry well as an addition to herbal teas. The large hips are easy to process and a savoury-fruity alternative to tomatoes and sweet peppers. They can be roasted, sun-dried and, like Dog Rose, preserved as rosehip purée – a perfect substitute for tomato purée. I process them by cutting around the circumference and scooping out the seeds and hairs with a small coffee spoon, before giving them a quick rinse. When making the purée, I simmer them whole and use a mouli, or food mill, to remove the seeds and fibre after cooking. Once pasteurised, these jars will easily keep for a year.

Bramble ❋ *Rubus fruticosus*

The Bramble – our native wild blackberry – is widely known. There are many subspecies, all edible, which accounts for the dramatic difference in flavour from bush to bush. Pick the berries in late summer into autumn to eat fresh, cook into crumbles, or infuse to make bramble whisky. The leaf is a good tea flavour. Root bark was traditionally stewed as a treatment to stop diarrhoea and dysentery. The young spring buds taste of coconut when they are chewed.

Wild Raspberry ❋ *Rubus idaeus*

Wild Raspberry is easily identified and extremely common in Britain, especially in Scotland. Pick the berries in the summer and eat them fresh. Alternatively, preserve them as raspberry jam and raspberry vinegar, or dehydrate them and add them to home-made muesli. The leaves also make a good tea, traditionally used as a gargle for sore throats, mouth ulcers and infections, loose dentures, and to prepare women for birth due to its tonic action on the uterus.

Cloudberry ✳ *Rubus chamaemorus*

Although mainly thought of as a Scandinavian berry, the Cloudberry grows at high elevations in the highlands of Scotland, where it loves an upland bog. It then makes its way down the Pennines as far as Sheffield. It has white flowers (very like a Bramble's), delicious orange-red berries and a leaf that is shaped like Lady's Mantle but serrated like a rose leaf.

Meadowsweet ✳ *Filipendula ulmaria*

Meadowsweet leaves are very astringent and taste of antiseptic cream or aspirin. They are mainly used in medicinal teas for acid reflux and pain. The edible flowers are honey-scented and used to make cordials and to flavour desserts, especially white chocolate ones. The name probably comes from 'meades swete' referring to its use as a popular mead flavour where it does double duty as a food preservative. You can gather the drifts of white flowers from early July through August, but make sure they are fully open so your cheesecakes taste of honey and not Savlon cream!

Silverweed ✳ *Potentilla anserina*

Silverweed's starchy, secondary roots are best steamed and mashed for gnocchi or dumplings. Larger ones are easiest to work with. Cultivated ones can grow roots that are 10–12 millimetres in diameter, but in the wild they can be as thin as spaghetti, typically 3–7 mm wide. However, their nutrient profile is similar to that of the potato, with higher levels of magnesium and calcium, so they're very nutritious despite their small size. In the Outer Hebrides, Silverweed is known as the 'poor man's potato', a famine food. It was widely cultivated before the actual Potato arrived on our shores, being 31 per cent carbohydrate. The roots can be dried and ground into a gluten-free flour. They have a pleasant, nutty taste and are crunchy.

Wood Aven ✳ *Geum urbanum*

Found alongside most woodland paths, especially in beech leaf litter. The lateral white roots taste of Cloves, albeit milder than tropical clove buds. Both plants contain eugenol, a popular dental ingredient in toothpastes and mouthwashes as it is mildly anaesthetic. The flavour is volatile so needs gentle cooking. Infuse the cleaned roots in a tub of sugar, then melt to make a syrup. Or extract the flavour in a clear spirit (e.g. vodka). Harvest Wood Avens roots in early spring or autumn. When they grow in woodland leaf mould, it is easy to loosen the plant and cut off the tasty side roots without uprooting it completely. Its close cousin Water Avens *Geum rivale* is reputed to replace hot chocolate when the root is boiled, but I am yet to be convinced.

Wild Strawberry ✳ *Fragaria vesca*

We don't often remember that before the Middle Ages, there were few large fruits in Britain other than apples and pears. So our wild fruits were highly valued. Despite its diminutive size, being hardly longer than a centimetre, the woodland Wild Strawberry has more flavour than its modern supermarket cousin. They fruit in June and can be prolific in sunny glades. You can spot them before they fruit as they have three serrated leaves that unite at one end on the stalks, looking exactly like dwarf strawberry plants. They also reproduce by sending out runners so can form dense patches. Despite not having much flavour, the leaves were traditionally a vitamin C-rich addition to herbal teas as, gram for gram, they have five times more vitamin C than an orange.

Further reading

Graham, G. G. and Primavesi, A. L. (1993), *Roses of Great Britain and Ireland: BSBI Handbook no. 7* (Botanical Society of the British Isles, London). A handbook with descriptions of thirteen native and nine introduced taxa of Rosa, with briefer descriptions of seventy-six hybrids. Line drawing illustrations by Margaret Gold.

Rubiaceae – the madder family

This is a very interesting family as it contains both Coffee *Coffea arabica*, which millions of people drink daily, and Madder *Rubia tinctorum*, a significant medieval dye plant. It is characterised by highly aromatic plants.

Members of this family are easily distinguished because the leaves are arranged in whorls around the stem with bare intervals between them.

Key features

Many plants in this family contain coumarins, which smell like newly mown hay when the plant is dried. The leaves are arranged in whorls clustered together on the stem with a clear gap in between whorls.

MAIN FORAGING SPECIES

Cleavers ✳ *Galium aparine*

Twining, climbing and tumbling over your plants when your back is turned, Cleavers is a particularly energetic climber. It has many common names, including Goosegrass and Sticky Willy. It is covered in hooked hairs that help it climb, but also make it stick to animal fur and clothes. The simplest use for Cleavers is a cold infusion: pick a small handful of young shoots and put them into a jug of cold water to infuse overnight. Drink in the morning for a refreshing coconutty-cucumbery-tasting pick-me-up. It acts on the lymphatic system so is a useful detoxifier and diuretic – great if you ever get swollen ankles or fluid retention. In the spring, the young tips are edible raw before their climbing hooks develop – they're good in a salad. Later in the season, I like to juice bundles of Cleavers in my wheatgrass juicer and add a shot to apple juice. Or gather bunches of long stems, chop them, then cook them into soups or stews. As the plant develops, it clings to fur and fabric with tenacity, often leaving little green bobbly seeds behind. These can be toasted or roasted, then ground and boiled on the stove to be drunk as an alternative to coffee (see page 257).

Sweet Woodruff ✳ *Galium odorata*

Sweet Woodruff has little smell until you dry it, when it develops the amazing, sweet scent of vanilla. Each summer I hang a bunch in my car and it makes the best air freshener ever. In the Middle Ages it was used for scenting floors, mixed in with the straw. It also makes a great food flavouring essence (recipe pages 270–71), as it tastes like tonka bean and vanilla. In Germany, the first of May was traditionally celebrated with a delightful sparkling Maiwein drink. This was a bottle of Riesling white wine, infused overnight with three to four sprigs of Sweet Woodruff and then mixed with a bottle of champagne on May Day morning. You wouldn't want to make this too strong as the plant's coumarins can give you one hell of a hangover. Pick it from April to the late summer from the edges of open woodland as it likes a little shade.

Typhaceae – the cattail family

Reedmace ❋ *Typha latifolia*

Known also as a bulrush, or as a cattail in North America, Reedmace is a valuable plant that will provide food all year round. It has an edible rhizome, edible leaf stalks, stamens and pollen. You can pull the leaf stalk out of its socket, which yields a dense core of young white leaves, rather like pulling a leek. Nibble this inner stalk raw, slice it into crisp rounds for salads, pickle it or cook it. It tastes a little like water chestnut with cucumber.

The flowers first produce cobs that are not dissimilar, when boiled, from corn on the cob. Later, the plant is full of nutrient-dense yellow pollen to add to your wild flour mix for pancakes and biscuits. When left unharvested, the mature cobs develop into the characteristic fat brown cigar-shaped tops, waving on top of long stalks.

In the spring, the underwater rhizomes produce root buds. Once broken off, these are delicious lightly boiled or roasted. Also tender and appetising are reedmace hearts – the denser, crispier part of the root, where it meets the leaf stock. The large lateral rhizome sections can be quite fibrous, albeit full of flavour – after boiling, just pull them through your teeth like globe artichoke leaves.

To make a fine gluten-free flour, you need to wash the tasty starch out of the pounded fibres. It is quite a bit of work. To harvest the rhizomes, you need to get into the pond or stream with them. I borrow a set of fishing waders as the water temperature in early spring can be Baltic. There is no other way than to run your hand down the stems and into the mud to loosen the rhizomes. Once located, cut them out with a sickle or homi. After harvesting, I spread them out on the grass and use a pressure washer to clean off the mud. I don't peel them, but just scrape off any hairy rootlets. I only peel off the stiff outer skin if there is engrained dirt.

Chop the rhizomes lengthwise into skinny sections and soak them in clean, warm water. Soaking loosens the starch so it can be washed off the root fibres. It is then easiest to massage the fibres with your hands, to help the starch come away. Let the starch settle on the bottom of the bowl, skimming off any root debris. After settling, siphon off the excess water, add more clean water and stir the starch to rinse it further. Once settled again, siphon off the excess water and ladle the starchy mass onto dehydrator trays (on greaseproof paper liners cut to size) and heat until well dried. Reedmace starch can be stored in brown kraft paper pouches or jars and used like cornflour, or added to seed or nut flours.

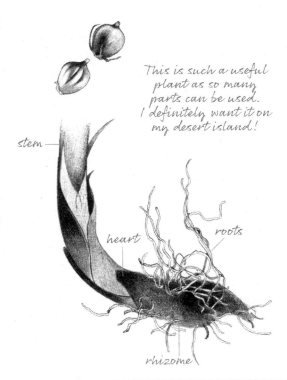

This is such a useful plant as so many parts can be used. I definitely want it on my desert island!

cob

leaf

stem

heart

roots

rhizome

Caution
Do be careful if picking Reedmace stems not to confuse them with irises like Blue Flag *Iris versicolor*. Blue Flag – which is toxic – tends to have an oval section through the stalk base while Reedmace is round.

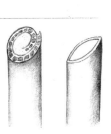

Urticaceae – the nettle family

Stinging Nettle ❋ *Urtica dioica*

The Stinging Nettle is a European superfood. Nettles grow on disturbed soil around houses and farmyards and in parks. They are a rich source of minerals such as magnesium, iron, calcium and silica – which help to keep bone, skin and hair strong – along with potassium and manganese. They are also high in vitamins A (beta carotene), Bs and C, and they are high in protein too.

Pick the young shoot tops to cook as a rich earthy vegetable in spring. You can use it exactly as you'd use spinach – except you can't eat raw nettles unless you enjoy a stung tongue. I like it steamed and eaten as is, or added to a quiche, ravioli parcels or tempura leaves. You are limited only by your imagination. Don't collect them in late summer (unless it is new growth after strimming), as mature plants have more unpleasant acids in their leaves.

Collect the plump seeds in late summer and toast them to bring out their nutty, hempseed-like flavour and add them to bread or oatcakes when you're baking. Or grind the green seeds and soak them in a little vodka for a month. Then use this tincture a *teaspoonful* at a time as a winter blues pick-me-up. Drink nettle tea to avoid hay fever and rinse your hair in it to retain strength and shine.

You can dry Nettle leaves to use in the future as a tea, or to reconstitute them for soup or stews later in the season. One kilogram of dry material is obtained from 5 kilograms of fresh leaves. Nettle is also an important fibre and cordage plant and many fine linen-weight textiles were used in the past.

The cluster of leaves that form the nettle's tip are the most useful as a vegetable. However, the seeds add fibre and boost a low mood while the root is a useful medicine, used predominantly for balancing male hormones.

Violaceae – the violets and pansies

Violaceae is a group of flowering plants that includes about 1,000 species spread across temperate and tropical regions. Known for their delicate, often fragrant flowers, this family includes well-loved species like Wild Violet *Viola odorata* and Heartsease *Viola tricolor*. Violets are appreciated for their beauty but they have also been used since the 14th century to flavour and decorate desserts, candied to make sweets or added to wine.

All the violets have edible, vitamin C-rich leaves and edible flowers. They are tiny, though, and disappearing as their habitat vanishes. It is lovely to transform a short grassland or a woodland by scattering the seed and when you have created a large new colony then foraging some seems a fair trade-off. Although depleted in numbers, you can still find:

Sweet Violet ❋ *Viola odorata*
Common Dog-violet ❋ *Viola riviniana*
Early Dog-violet ❋ *Viola reichenbachiana*
Hairy Violet ❋ *Viola hirta*
Heath Dog-violet ❋ *Viola canina*

With the exception of the Heath Dog-violet, all have heart-shaped leaves with mildly serrated edges, distinguishing them from pansies, which have distinctly scalloped edges on their leaves. The five-petalled flowers are very similar, though pansy flowers seem more substantial and are often two-toned with purple and yellow. Pansies are edible too. The most commonly found are:

Wild Pansy or Heartsease ❋ *Viola tricolor*
Field Pansy ❋ *Viola arvensis*

Violets are generally used as edible flowers and leaves in spring salads. The leaves can also be added to teas as a spring vitamin boost. If you make a syrup with violet flowers it will have a bluish colour. If you then add an acid – like a squeeze of lemon juice – it will turn pink. Many blue petalled flowers are sensitive to pH like this.

Key features

The flowers typically have five petals arranged in a distinctive asymmetrical shape, with a spur at the back that contains nectar. They also have five sepals, five stamens, and one pistil. The leaves can be simple or divided, and are often heart-shaped or toothed.

Sweet Violet

Hairy Violet

Dog Violet

Field Parsley or Heartsease flower

Dog Violet leaf

Heart-shaped leaves are characteristic of both violets and pansies. The flowers can be single-coloured or two tones and often have additional marks on them that children think look like fairy faces.

Poisonous Plants and Trees

It is rare that people poison themselves as most of those who take up foraging are aware of the dangers and take the time to educate themselves. It is useful to familiarise yourself with the few species that can harm you, though. Remember the golden rule: never put anything in your mouth unless you are 100 per cent sure that it has been identified correctly and it is safe to do so.

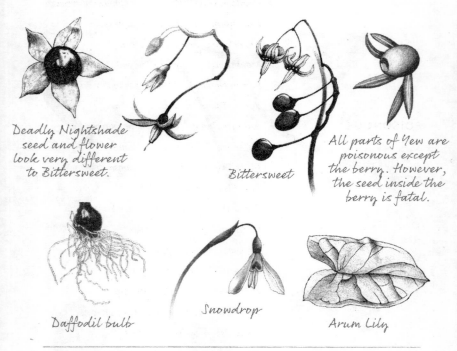

Deadly Nightshade seed and flower look very different to Bittersweet.

Bittersweet

All parts of Yew are poisonous except the berry. However, the seed inside the berry is fatal.

Daffodil bulb

Snowdrop

Arum Lily

Caution

Quite a few plants can be both poisonous and edible, depending on the preparation.

Black Nightshade *Solanum nigrum* – unripe, green berries are very poisonous but fully ripe cooked black berries are edible.

Tulip *Tulipa* spp. – flowers can be eaten but the bulbs are only edible once the toxic centre and outer skin have been removed and they have been well cooked.

Yew *Taxus baccata* – all parts are deadly except the edible red flesh around the seed (the aril), which is sweet and similar in flavour to a lychee. Nevertheless, hidden inside is a poisonous black seed that must be removed before eating. All other parts of the yew contain highly toxic taxines and eating even a few leaves can be fatal (see page 175).

Common most dangerous plants and trees:

HIGHLY POISONOUS	Common/cherry laurel * Prunus laurocerasus
	Cowbane * Circuta virosa
	Deadly Nightshade * Atropa belladonna
	Fool's parsley * Aethusa cynapium
	Foxglove * Digitalis purpurea
	Hemlock Water Dropwort * Oenanthe crocata
	Laburnum * Laburnum anagyroides
	Arum Lily * Arum maculatum
	Monkshood * Aconitum napellus
	Poison Hemlock * Conium maculatum
	Yew * Taxus baccata
POISONOUS	Autumn Crocus * Colchicum autumnale
	Bittersweet * Solanum dulcamara
	Black Bryony * Dioscorea communis
	Blue Flag * Iris versicolor
	Bluebells * Hyacinthoides non scriptus
	Common Ivy * Hedera helix
	Crocuses * Crocus spp.
	Daffodils * Narcissus spp.
	Delphinium * Delphinium spp.
	Dog's Mercury * Mercurialis perennis
	Groundsel * Senecio vulgaris
	Honeysuckle berries * Lonicera spp.
	Hyacinths * Muscari spp.
	Leopard's Bane * Doronicum pardalianches
	Snakeshead Fritillary * Fritillaria meleagris
	Snowdrops * Galanthus spp.
	Ragwort * Senecio jacobaea
	White Bryony * Bryonia dioica
DANGEROUS	Giant Hogweed * Heracleum mantegazzianum
	Wild Parsnip * Pastinaca sativa

CHAPTER 5

A Note on Berries

A lot of children are told that *all* berries are poisonous, but this is not the case and it only helps to foster a fearful approach to nature. When shown, children learn the differences between species faster than adults do. While some berries are toxic, there are also many more plants (including poisonous plants) that have edible berries. Being 'safe to consume' encourages animals to eat them and spread seed to locations much further away than the plant could reach by itself. Fruits do often contain a laxative, though – to encourage the animal to expel the seeds into a nice pile of fertile manure.

As with all wild foods, it's important to learn to identify every species correctly, as each has its own special qualities.

Here is a table of twenty edible wild berries and when they should be harvested:

Edible wild berries:

Barberry, Common	*Berberis vulgaris*	Autumn	edible when cooked
Bilberry	*Vaccinium myrtillus*	July–September	eat raw or cooked
Bramble	*Rubus fruticosus*	August–October	eat raw or cooked
Cloudberry	*Rubus chamaemorus*	August–October	eat raw or cooked
Cowberry	*Vaccinium vitis-idaea*	August–October	edible when cooked
Cranberry, Wild	*Vaccinium oxycoccus*	August–October	edible when cooked
Crowberry	*Empetrum nigrum*	August–December	eat raw or cooked
Dewberry	*Rubus caesius*	August–October	eat raw or cooked
Elderberry	*Sambucus nigra*	Summer–Autumn	edible but must be cooked
Gooseberry, Wild	*Ribes uva-crispa*	Summer	eat raw or cooked
Hawthorn	*Crataegus monogyna*	Autumn–Winter	edible when cooked
Lingonberry	*Vaccinium vitis-idaea*	Summer or late Autumn	eat raw or cooked
Raspberry, Wild	*Rubus idaeus*	Summer and Autumn	eat raw or cooked
Rowan	*Sorbus aucuparia*	August–November	edible when cooked
Sea Buckthorn	*Hippophae rhamnoides*	Winter	edible when sweetened
Service Tree, Wild	*Sorbus torminalis*	Autumn	edible when cooked
Strawberry, Wild	*Fragaria vesca*	Summer	eat raw or cooked

Tasty urban berries

For foragers living in towns and cities, many cultivated hedging and garden plants also have edible berries that often go unnoticed and are never picked. I recall gathering several kilos of feral *Fuchsia* berries while on holiday in Applecross and several holidaymakers approached me concerned I was about to poison myself. I had these delicious berries – that, when fully ripe, taste like a cross between a fig and a grape – all to myself. My favourites, picked from quieter streets and parks with low pollution from car fumes, are:

Darwin's Barberry	*Berberis darwinii*	Harvest in late Summer	best cooked
Fuchsia	*Fuchsia* spp.	Late Summer	all have edible berries (the taste varies) when fully ripe
Himalayan Honeysuckle	*Leycesteria formosa*	Late Summer and Autumn	bitter if unripe but when fully ripe taste like caramel
Mulberry	*Morus alba* and *M. rubra*	Fruits in Summer	eat raw or cooked
Oregon Grape	*Mahonia aquifolium*	Harvest in Summer	tart, so cook with a little honey or sugar

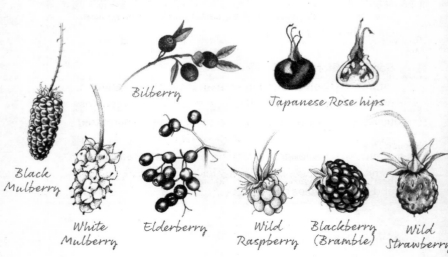

Bilberry

Japanese Rose hips

Black Mulberry

White Mulberry

Elderberry

Wild Raspberry

Blackberry (Bramble)

Wild Strawberry

BERRY NUTRITION

Berries are exceptionally good for us, being packed full of vitamins, minerals, nutrients and antioxidants that reduce the risk of many age-related illnesses. Although sweet-tasting, they improve blood glucose control and help lower inflammation. Here are some examples of the goodness contained in them:

Bilberry

Vitamins C, A, D, and some vitamins from the B group plus rutin, pectins, tannins, carotenoids, flavonoids, anthocyanins, organic acids, iron mineral salts, manganese, potassium, lithium and molybdenum.

Dog Rose hips

Vitamin C (mainly in fresh fruits), vitamins A, B1, B2, minerals, pectin, organic acids, sugar, carotenoids, tannins, fatty oil, proteins and vitamin E. The seeds (achenes) have high non-saturated fatty acid content, vitamins A and E.

Elderberry

Vitamins C, A, B3, B6, colourants (anthocyanic glycosides), organic acids (malic, citric), sugars (sambubiose), flavonoids (rutin, isokvercitrin, sambucin), tannins, bitter substances and pectins.

Sea Buckthorn

Vitamin C (twelve times higher than the vitamin C content of oranges), A, B1, B2, B6, B12, E, amino acids, carotenoids (lycopene, lutein, zeaxanthin, α-carotene, β-carotene, γ-carotene), tocopherols, phytosterols, flavonoids (e.g. quercetin), polyphenols, organic acids, polyunsaturated fatty acids (especially omega-7 palmitoleic acid, linoleic and linolenic acids).

Berries that should not be eaten:

Alder Buckthorn	*Frangula alnus*	Summer and Autumn	**Medicinal.** Berries are a bowel purgative.
Arum Lily	*Arum maculatum*	Summer and Autumn	**Toxic.** Red berries clustered on an upright spike. Also called Cuckoo Pint and Lords-and-Ladies.
Bittersweet	*Solanum dulcamara*	Summer and Autumn	**Toxic.** Egg-shaped red berries follow purple flowers on a shrub. Also called woody nightshade.
Black Bryony	*Tamus communis*	Summer and Autumn	**Toxic.** Round red berries follow small green flowers on a climbing vine.
Buckthorn	*Rhamnus catharticus*	Summer and Autumn	**Medicinal.** Berries are a bowel purgative.
Butcher's Broom	*Ruscus aculeatus*	Summer and Autumn	**Toxic.** Red berries follow purple flowers on a prickly bush.
Deadly Nightshade	*Solanum nigrum*	Summer and Autumn	**Toxic.** Black berries follow white flowers on a shrub.
Dogwood Berries	*Cornus sanguinea*	Autumn	**Mildly toxic.** The berries aren't fatal, but eating them will make you feel very unwell. Use them for making ink instead.

Holly	*Ilex aquifolium*	Autumn and Winter	**Mildly toxic.** Holly berries may not kill you, but eating more than a few can cause nausea, vomiting, diarrhoea, dehydration and drowsiness.
Mistletoe	*Viscum album*	Autumn and Winter	**Toxic.** Popular with the druids and used in some cancer treatments, mistletoe can be deadly. Eating berries can cause blurred vision, stomach cramps and diarrhoea at best, and death at worst.
Snowberry	*Symphoricarpos albus*	Autumn	**Mildly toxic.** The white berries of this shrub are poisonous. Not native but has often become naturalised.
Spindle tree	*Euonymous europaeus*	Autumn	**Toxic.** Bright orange fruit in a pink capsule.

There are also many cultivated and garden plants with berries that are not edible. I have only listed those often found in habitats that you may be foraging in.

CHAPTER 6

Deciduous Trees

In Spring I look gay,
Decked in comely array,
In Summer more clothing I wear;
When colder it grows,
I fling off my clothes,
And in Winter quite naked appear.
Who am I?

A LIMERICK TREE RIDDLE FROM 1813

Trees are a fantastic source of bounty for the forager, as many produce nuts and seeds that are full of calories, healthy fats and other nutrients. Others produce berries, rich in vitamins and antioxidants, that add flavour to a meal. Some produce drinkable sap.

Deciduous trees are those that lose their leaves in the autumn and are bare through the winter, unlike evergreen trees such as conifers. Their leaves often change colour as they are dying, giving us the beautiful copper, orange and red tones of autumn. The 'fall' is triggered by changes in the amount of sunlight and temperature. During the winter the trees are dormant, conserving water and energy. New leaves grow back in the spring as the soil warms and they awake once more. Deciduous trees play an important role in many ecosystems. They provide shelter and food for a wide range of wildlife, from birds and squirrels to other mammals and insects. They also help to regulate the local climate by providing shade and absorbing carbon dioxide from the air.

Many deciduous trees have tasty, edible leaves that are especially delicious in salads or added to sandwiches instead of lettuce. However, you need to keep your eyes open for when they come out – a process known as 'greening' – as they are only tender and tasty for a few weeks in early spring. They quickly become fibrous, drier and less palatable as the tannin content increases, though older leaves are still good for herbal teas.

There are several ways to approach identifying a deciduous tree:

Growth habit
The overall growth habit of the tree provides clues, especially when you're looking at a tree from a distance. Some, like the weeping willow, have drooping branches, while others, like the beech tree, have a more upright growth habit.

Leaf shape
The shape of the leaves can be a useful identifier for many deciduous trees. For example, oak trees have leaves with lobes, while field maple trees have leaves with distinct points.

Leaf arrangement
The arrangement of the leaves on the stem can also be helpful. Some trees have opposite leaves, where two leaves are directly across from each other on the stem, while others have alternate leaves, where each leaf grows on a separate part of the stem.

Bark texture
The texture and colour of the bark can also be a useful identifier. For example, birch trees have distinctive silver or white, papery bark, while oak trees have rough, deeply furrowed bark.

Birch bark

Oak bark

Tree growth patterns:

Columnar

Upright

Pyramidal

Spreading

Oval

Rounded

Vase shaped

Weeping

Deciduous tree twig shapes:

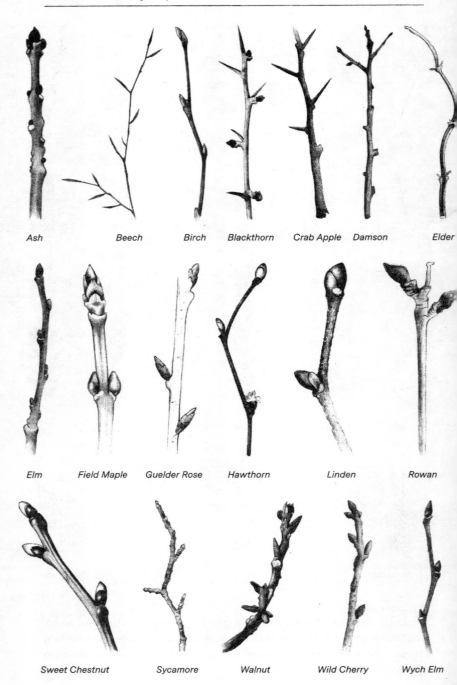

Ash   Beech   Birch   Blackthorn   Crab Apple   Damson   Elder

Elm   Field Maple   Guelder Rose   Hawthorn   Linden   Rowan

Sweet Chestnut   Sycamore   Walnut   Wild Cherry   Wych Elm

Deciduous tree leaf shapes:

Ash   Beech   Birch   Blackthorn   Crab Apple   Damson

Elder   Elm   Field Maple   Guelder Rose   Hawthorn

Hazel   Linden   Oak   Rowan   Sweet Chestnut   Sessile Oak

Sycamore   Walnut   Wild Cherry   Wych Elm

Further reading

Poland, John (2020), *The Field Key to Winter Twigs* (published by John Poland, available from Summerfield Books). This book illustrates and identifies the twig shapes of over 400 trees, shrubs and woody climbers found wild or planted in the British Isles.

Deciduous tree bud shapes:

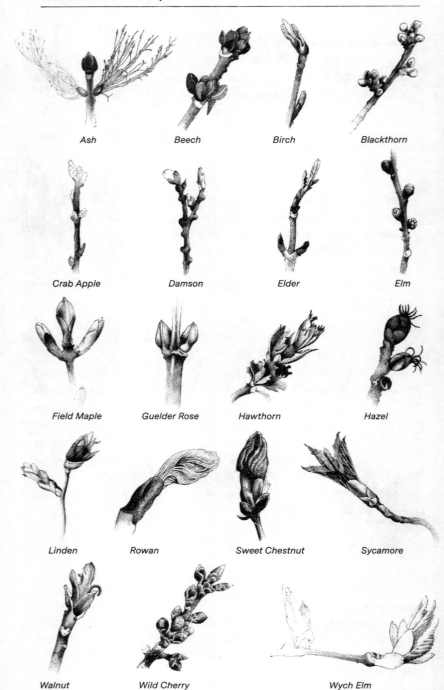

Ash

Beech

Birch

Blackthorn

Crab Apple

Damson

Elder

Elm

Field Maple

Guelder Rose

Hawthorn

Hazel

Linden

Rowan

Sweet Chestnut

Sycamore

Walnut

Wild Cherry

Wych Elm

Common deciduous trees

Here are some deciduous trees commonly found in Britain and Ireland that are useful for the forager and crafter. I will leave it to you to look up all the identifying features but explain why I find them so useful.

Ash ✳ Fraxinus excelsior

The large bundles of winged ash seeds that hang from the trees in the late spring are called keys. These can be pickled as a condiment when immature, if spotted when they've just emerged. However, they quickly become too tough and fibrous. If a pin or fine skewer can pass through them without being forced, you have got them at the right time.

Frenette is a mildly alcoholic drink made from fermented Ash leaves (see pages 266–67 for the recipe). It is an ancient drink, possibly made in Gaul around the time of the Romans, that originated in the north of France and Belgium. Variations on the name include *freinette*, *fresnée* or *frênée*. This 'Forest Champagne' was still widely made in French villages in the 1950s and 1960s, but is not found as often these days. The famous French writer Colette was reputed to love making frenette. Ash is also a very reliable firewood.

Beech ✳ *Fagus sylvatica*

Beech leaves taste slightly of lemon. They are soft and silky in the first two weeks of May but too fibrous to eat later in the month. They are perfect in salads or for making noyau – a liqueur made by infusing the young leaves in vodka with a little white sugar. Dried brown Beech leaves, which stay on the hedges right through winter, make a lovely cold-weather tea. Beech nuts – known as 'mast' – were once ground for flour but they are fiddly and hard to process. If you can get them before the squirrels do, enjoy them peeled and toasted, or just nibbled raw. Beech tree sap makes a tasty syrup but is hard to extract (see page 170).

There are some very old records of extracting an oil (by pressing it) from beech nuts. British herbalist John Evelyn in 1664 says, 'We must not omit to praise the *Mast*, which fats our *Swine* and *Deer*, and hath in some Families even supported men with bread: *Chios* endured a memorable Siege by the benefit of this *Mast*; and in some parts of *France* they now grind the *Buck* in *Mills*: It affords a sweet *Oyl*, which the poor People eat most willingly.' The kernels are 50 per cent fat and you need 5 kilograms to make just 1 litre of oil. It is expensive to produce and needs ageing over five years (in a cool place under 15 degrees C) for the flavour to fully develop. However, it's worth it as the oil is absolutely delicious. In the first two or three weeks of October, in the Carpathian beech forests, the Székely people still get together and put bed sheets under the trees. They climb into the trees and shake down the nuts, which are then cold-pressed in their shells. The oil is shared out equally between the foragers. Sometimes the nuts are sold – their price being twenty-five times the price of acorns – but the oil is kept like a precious golden treasure and drunk as health shots.

Birch ❋ *Betula pendula* and *Betula* spp.

Birch leaves have a very strong taste of wintergreen that is not enjoyed raw by most people, but are great for teas that relieve muscle or joint pain as they contain salicylic acid – a compound similar to mild aspirin. This also has natural preservative properties. A Finnish fisherman told me that before refrigeration on fishing vessels, they would put to sea with plenty of birch brash (the young twigs) which, sandwiched between the layers of fish, would help keep them fresh until they got back to port. In bushcraft, the bark is often used to make containers and, historically, everything from baskets and canoes to coffins, while the inner bark was sometimes dried and ground as meal, to extend flour in times of famine. Importantly for the forager, the Birch is associated with mycorrhizal mushrooms like chanterelles, boletes and other delicacies and the saprophytic medicinal mushrooms like Chaga, the Birch Polypore and the Tinder Hoof.

There are many types of birch trees and they can all be tapped in the spring, as a health drink or evaporated sap that makes a luxury syrup. Silver Birch *Betula pendula* is the species most commonly found and tapped in the UK. In my experience, 20 litres of sap yields around 200 millilitres (180 grams) of syrup, generally a third to a quarter of the yield of Paper Birch *Betula papyrifera* whose sugar content is 0.9 per cent but has the sweetest-tasting syrup. Traditionally, the sap of Black Birch *Betula lenta*, sometimes called Sweet Birch or Cherry Birch, was fermented into a tasty vinegar. All edible tree saps can be fermented and made into wine or vinegar. The Downy Birch *Betula pubescens* and the White Birch *Betula alba* are also common throughout the UK. Find out more about birch sap and tree tapping in Chapter 7.

Blackthorn ✳ *Prunus spinosa*

The Blackthorn fruit (technically a drupe) is the 'sloe' used to make traditional sloe gin by pricking the ripe drupes, then soaking them in gin with a little sugar for a few months. The cooked fruits are edible but mildly laxative. Slightly underripe sloes can be lacto-fermented as a substitute for olives. You can also infuse the leaves in red wine and brandy to make a boozy almond-flavoured fortified drink called épine. This leafy liqueur saves the day in years when strong spring winds damage the Blackthorn blossom, preventing the sloes from forming.

Crab Apple ✳ *Malus sylvestris*

Our native wild apple tree produces tiny, hard apples that are best cooked or pressed to make verjuice or crab apple wine. They last on the tree and the ground throughout the winter, and are often still edible in the following spring. Many have cross-bred with the domestic apple and there is a huge range of wild 'feral' apples about. If you are using sugar you can line a frying pan with them and simmer them in a melted sugar syrup to make miniature toffee apples. They are a delicious treat. Alternatively, dry slices of them in a dehydrator which improves their sweetness, or cook and purée them either to make fruit leathers, or to freeze as apple sauce. They also help to add pectin to wild berry hedgerow jams.

Damson ✳ *Prunus insititia*

Pick these tart wild plums in the summer. Stew them like plums, make sumptuous damson jam, a fruity damson wine or boozy damson gin. I also like to salt damsons in a large ceramic crock, alternating layers of salt and damsons. This is the same way that Japanese *umeboshi* plums are prepared, to make a sweet-and-sour preserved fruit, and a tangy, thick *umezu* liquid as the salt draws the juices out of the damsons. The smaller Bullace and Mirabelle (also *Prunus domestica subsp. insititia*) are other varieties of wild plum similar to the damson and used in the same way.

Elder ✳ *Sambucus nigra*

The elder is a native tree that has been highly valued for centuries and is part of our mythopoetic heritage. The name comes from the Danish *Hyldemoer* – the 'elder' or 'earth mother'. A faerie tree, it was considered very unlucky to bring branches into the house or to cut it down. It is a common deciduous hardy perennial tree or large bush that can grow up to 4 metres high. The leaves are compound, bright green and sharply toothed. From June, the fragrant sweet, creamy-yellow elderflowers which smell of honey are used for teas, cordials, mead, wine and desserts. Infused, they help to reduce itchy, swollen eyes and sinuses in hay fever sufferers. The elderberries are picked around late July to September (it's highly variable across the country) when they are purple-black and the clusters have turned to hang down. They are made into ketchups, syrups, cordials and wines, and can also be pickled as a condiment. Elderberries must be cooked to be edible. Don't make the mistake of blitzing them into a smoothie without cooking them first as they will cause severe stomach cramps. The elder tree is also host to the edible Wood Ear (Jelly Ear) Fungus so popular in Chinese cuisine.

Elm ✳ *Ulmus laevis / U. minor*
and *Wych Elm* ✳ *Ulmus glabra*
Although the inner bark of Elm has been
used as a famine flour boiled into a gruel, the
tree is so rare now, due to Dutch elm disease,
that it should not have bark taken from it.

Both Elm and Wych Elm have tender spring
leaves that taste slightly nutty. The young winged seeds,
known as 'samaras', are the best part though. They are
slightly mucilaginous with a soft mouth feel, taste a
little like garden peas, and can be eaten raw in salads
or cheese sandwiches, or steamed. Be sure to pick the
samaras when green and tender, before they turn
papery and brown. Wych Elm is very common in
Scotland and I pickle the samaras every year but they
should be eaten immediately when still crisp as they go
slimy with storage.

Guelder Rose ✳ *Viburnum opulus*
The shiny bright red berries are not poisonous.
However, most people find them mouth-
puckering, sour and astringent. I might eat one
or two raw berries, but the rest I cook into a jelly
or a caramel sauce to go with ice
cream. I find the best use for
them is to make red herbal
bitters as a wild alternative
to Angostura bitters. The light
yellow-green inner bark, nicknamed 'cramp
bark', when boiled into a tea is excellent for
relieving the soft-muscle spasms associated
with period pain, as well as stomach tension.

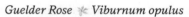

Hawthorn ❋ *Crataegus monogyna*
Hawthorn is one of the earliest trees to produce tender leaves in the spring when the bright green, slightly nutty leaves and buds can be eaten raw, added into salads or sandwiches. These were often called 'bread and cheese' although the reason why is lost to history. The fruits are called haws and collected after the first frosts in the early winter. Haws are used to make jelly, fruit leathers, liqueurs like haw gin, and to make haw ketchup or, with spices, haw-sin sauce. Haws help the body to digest meat and fats better. The leaves and flowers make a tasty circulatory tea that can be drunk daily to modulate high blood pressure.

Hazel ❋ *Corylus avellana*
Early Scots and Britons could not have survived winter without hazelnuts gathered in the autumn from these small trees. Widespread in woodlands and hedges, it has been a staple nut since Palaeolithic times. Hazelnuts, also known as cobnuts or filberts, can be gathered from any tree in the genus *Corylus*. Our native British species is *Corylus avellana*. The nuts keep for months if harvested at the right time and dried properly. Don't pick them too early while they are still very green, as it takes time for the nut to fully swell inside the casing. Young hazelnuts can be blended with a little water, soaked and then pressed to make hazelnut 'milk' from which a very nice hazelnut 'cheese' can be fermented. Mature hazelnuts can be shelled and eaten raw or roasted, or ground into a delicious flour (see page 235). You can also press hazelnuts in an oil press to yield a delicious hazelnut oil with a strong flavour. Oil press attachments can be bought for some juice extractors.

Linden (European Lime) ✳ *Tilia cordata/europaea*
Linden covers two trees: the Small-leaved Lime
tree and the Large-leaved Lime tree. I use the
term Linden to prevent people getting confused with
the tropical citrus lime. Linden leaves have slight
hints of citrus with a soft mouth feel. Both the
Small-leaved and Large-leaved Lime species
have tender, edible young leaves and flowers
in the spring to eat fresh from the trees.
They have a much longer picking season than
Beech, because the young leaves that skirt the tree trunks are
protected from the elements. Collect the flowers to make a delicious
herbal tea that helps to release tension. However, don't store the
flowers for over a year as they can become narcotic as they age.
You can roast mature seeds to make a substitute for cocoa
powder (see page 243) but gather them on the young
side for the best flavour. They smell a little like
chocolate but taste more like a mocha with hints of
coffee. Unfortunately, linden 'chocolate spread' does
not have a great shelf-life and is best made fresh and
just kept for a day or two. I think it's delicious.

Oak ✳ *Quercus* spp.
The acorns from oak trees provided early humans with an important
food (see pages 231–232). There are two native species of oak in the
UK. The sessile oak *Quercus petraea* sometimes called the Irish or
Cornish oak, and the pedunculate oak *Quercus robur* often called the
English oak. The botanical word 'sessile' means that the acorn cups
have no stalk (but the leaf has a long stalk). The opposite is true of
'pedunculate' meaning that the acorn cups have a long stalk (their
leaf has a short stalk). The easiest way to remember which is which,
is that the word pedunculate – like the acorn stalk – is longer and the
word sessile is shorter. You might also find other non-native species
of oak and can use all their acorns from mid-September onwards.

Maples ✳ **Acer** spp.

Sycamore ✳ *Acer pseudoplatanus*
Sycamore is in the maple family with its classic
five-pointed leaf. According to the food historian
Sturtevant in 1919, 'In England, children suck
the wings of the growing keys for the sake of obtaining the sweet
exudation that is upon them.' I find the leaves too bitter to eat but
tap the trees occasionally for their sap (see page 168 from January
to March. Sycamore sap – with vanilla and caramel notes – can be
boiled down into sugar crystals to make a real treat.

Field Maple ✳ *Acer campestre*, native to the UK, can be tapped
from January to March – as long as the nights are cold but
the days crisp and sunny. In 1919, historian Sturtevant
recorded, 'In the western Highlands and some parts of the
Continent, the sap is fermented into wine, the trees being first
tapped when just coming into leaf. From the sap, sugar may be
made but not in remunerative quantities.'

Sugar Maple ✳ *Acer saccharum*, of all maples, gives you the best
yield although it is not commonly planted in Europe. Around
20 litres of sap will boil down to 500 millilitres of syrup. It is
widespread in North America and the First Nation peoples
poured syrup out on the snow to harden into candy. That must
have been some ice cream topping. You can usually tap around 2
kilograms per tree with high yielders around 15 kilograms.

Silver Maple ✳ *Acer saccharinum* (Previously *A. dasycarpum*)
has roughly half the sugar sap content of the sugar maple
but is more common in Europe. The yield ratio is around
80:1 and it is a lighter syrup. Just three trees can give you
as much as 680 litres each season yielding 18 litres of syrup.[11]

Norway Maple ✳ *Acer platanoides* sap makes syrup with a more
butterscotch-like flavour.

Mulberry ✳ *Morus* spp.

Although not native to the UK, the Black Mulberry *Morus nigra* is fairly common, with fruits that look like slightly elongated blackberries. Known for their longevity, the oldest mulberry tree in Britain is suspected to be more than 470 years old. White Mulberry *Morus alba* – the type that silkworms like to eat – is less common but can sometimes be found. Mulberries are usually late to leaf up – around a month later than beech – waiting until it is properly warm to venture out. Its fabulous berries are ready in August and September but the tree can take from five to ten years to produce fruit. The young leaves of Mulberry taste mild – slightly sweet and slightly grassy.

Rowan ✳ *Sorbus aucuparia*

The Rowan's tart bright orange berries need to be simmered with a little sugar to be palatable for most people, although I love the sharp flavour when nibbling them. They are high in antioxidants such as vitamin C. Pick them in late summer to make a delicious rowan jelly or rowan toffee. The spring leaf buds taste of marzipan. You can infuse them in clear spirit or glycerine to make rowan bud 'almond' essence (see page 270). Harvest leaf buds in March to April and the berries in August to October.

Another *Sorbus* is the Wild Service Tree *Sorbus torminalis* whose berries are edible when cooked. Their date-like flavour develops when bletted. Bletting is a term used to describe the process by which some fruits are left on the bush or tree to become overripe and develop a soft, jelly-like consistency. The fruit's starches are broken down into simple sugars, resulting in a sweeter, less astringent flavour. During bletting, the fruit's flesh may also darken in colour or become translucent.

Sweet Chestnut ✳ *Castanea sativa*

Sweet Chestnut trees are widespread except in mountainous areas. Ready from late September into October over two to four weeks, the fruit ripens on the tree and puts on a lot of bulk in its final two weeks, before falling to the ground – so don't pick the spiky fruits off the trees too early. It's best to go out each morning (before the squirrels are up) and pick those that have dropped to the ground overnight. Remove the plump, shiny-brown nuts from the spiky casings, make a cross on the end with a knife (to stop them exploding when heated) and cook them before peeling. This is easier than trying to peel them raw. The inner pith can be quite bitter if not removed. Roast them for a delicious snack, or dry and grind them into a very versatile sweet flour (see page 235). Sweet Chestnut trees are also often host to the edible Beefsteak Fungus.

Horse Chestnuts have one (occasionally two) nuts per case and are not generally edible.

Sweet Chestnuts usually have two to three nuts per case and are edible.

Caution

Sweet Chestnut *Castanea sativa* with its serrated-edge single leaves is very different from the five-leaved Horse Chestnut *Aesculus hippocastanum*. It bears useful, tasty nuts in spiky pods – smaller and spikier than the conkers of the Horse Chestnut. The larger conker nuts from the Horse Chestnut tree are not edible without a lot of processing as they contain high amounts of irritating saponins, but they can be used to make soap (see page 274).

Walnut 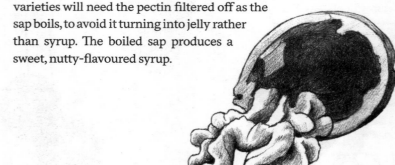 *Juglans regia*

Walnut trees grow throughout Britain. They produce nuts in the south of England but bear poorly in the north. However, the hotter summers may well change this. Walnuts are delicious and high in calories and oils. They're excellent for diabetics as they have a glycaemic index of zero. Shell them and eat them raw; they are best eaten as nuts, or whizzed into nut butter, rather than made into flour as they contain a lot of oil (see page 236).

As the oil content is high, they work well in a blended flour with acorn. Pressed walnut oil is also excellent for salad dressings. The leaves and husks can be used to make a temporary brown hair dye (see page 279) that also helps calm down dandruff.

For tapping, the English Walnut *Juglans regia* likes a freezing cold winter and spring, but some walnut varieties can be tapped from the autumn right through until spring. Most walnut varieties will need the pectin filtered off as the sap boils, to avoid it turning into jelly rather than syrup. The boiled sap produces a sweet, nutty-flavoured syrup.

Caution

Don't confuse walnut fruits in the husk with conkers. Walnut husks have a smooth outer skin and are edible, while conkers husks are bumpy with an occasional small spike.

Wild Cherry ❋ *Prunus avium*

The red 'gean' fruit of the Wild Cherry is small but sweet and palatable. Also look out for the astringent black Bird Cherry *Prunus padus* and the delicious Cherry Plum *Prunus cerasifera* which has often escaped from gardens. The Cherry Plum flowers early in February and the fruits are ready from late July to early September, while Wild Cherry can be a little later. Old Wild Cherry trees often host the edible Chicken-of-the-Woods Fungus.

Bird Cherry

Wild Cherry

CHAPTER 7

Tapping Trees

In the spring, tree sap from deciduous trees can be a welcome source of minerals, especially copper, zinc and magnesium, correcting mineral depletion after the scarcity of vegetables in the foraging diet at the end of the winter. As well as minerals, sap contains nutrients, enzymes, antioxidants, sugars, salts, amino acids and even some proteins. My favourite, Birch sap, with a subtle, earthy hint that reminds you it's not water, contains all of the former plus natural carbohydrates, organic acids, fruit acids, potassium, calcium, phosphorus, manganese, sodium, iron, B vitamins and vitamin C.

I mainly tap Birch trees, but you can tap and drink sap from at least twenty species of tree in Europe. There is a short period of two to three weeks between mid-March and mid-April, when sap flows in Birch trees (see page 167). Birches are the easiest to tap in this country and yield a healthy spring drink or a sweet smoky syrup – one of the few sources of sugar on a foraged diet. Once the ground has thawed, the pressure on the roots, and air within the wood fibres, changes – allowing the sap to rise up the trunks, preparing for the new greening. The effect is most marked in the mornings, but a steady flow will continue overnight as long as it doesn't freeze. A White Birch tree will give you, on average, around 4.4 litres of sap in a 24-hour period. Slightly less in a young tree, slightly more in older trees, with variance according to when in the season you are collecting.[12]

Colourless with a neutral flavour, birch sap is a pleasant, refreshing drink – a living water renowned for its restorative and detoxifying properties. It is to the higher latitudes what coconut water is to the tropics. It is drunk as a tonic and a traditional beverage in northern China, Belarus, Ukraine, Russia, the Baltic states and Scandinavia. In northern Europe, a century ago, people would drink 8 to 10 litres of birch sap every spring as a fortifying detox tonic – waking up a sluggish liver and flushing the kidneys. Ethnobotanical records show that birch sap wine was commonly made in Derbyshire, and, 'in 1814, the Russian soldiers near Hamburg intoxicated themselves with this fermented sap'.[13]

I've noticed that climate change is affecting birch sap production. The tapping period is getting earlier as winters are warmer. Twenty years ago, it was rare for me to tap before April in Scotland. In the last five years, I have always tapped Birch in March and now it tastes sweeter. American tappers have noticed that maple sap yields in the southern states are dropping and their season is starting earlier too, often in December, and is shorter. Higher temperatures associated with climate change produce more phenolic compounds in the bark that make the syrup darker and change its flavour.

Sap-to-sugar ratios

In the table below, I've included a broader range of trees that you can tap than just those native to the British Isles. The popularity of collecting and planting specimen trees in parklands since Victorian times has led to a wide variety of non-native trees being available. I have put in a range of values that covers both my own experience and information from published research papers. You will see that there is a range of yield ratios. This can be due to the age of the trees, time of collection, spring temperature and geography, and how runny the resulting syrup is. However, you will get an idea of which trees are really worth tapping and what yield to expect.

Trees with edible sap and their sap-to-sugar ratios:

Common Name	Botanical Name	Sugar %	Sap:Sugar Ratio
MAPLES AND SYCAMORES			
Amur Maple	*Acer ginnala*	1.5–3.9%	50:1–60:1
Bigleaf Maple	*Acer macrophyllum*	1.5–3%	30:1–50:1
Bigtooth Maple	*Acer grandidentatum*	2%	40:1–60:1
Black Maple	*Acer nigrum*	1.5–3%	40:1
Box Elder	*Acer negundo*	2.9–3.5%	60:1
Field Maple	*Acer campestre*	2.8%	36:1
Gorosoe (Korean) Maple	*Acer mono*	1.5–2%	60:1–80:1
Norway Maple	*Acer platanoides*	3.2%	30:1–60:1
Red Maple	*Acer rubrum*	1.5–4.0%	40:1–50:1
Rocky Mountain Maple	*Acer glabrum*	0.5–1%	100:1–150:1
Silver Maple	*Acer saccharinum*	1.7–4% (av. 2%)	60:1
Sugar Maple	*Acer saccharum*	2–6% (av. 4.5%)	20:1–40:1
Sycamore	*Acer pseudoplatanus*	1–3.2%	60:1–100:1

Common Name	Botanical Name	Sugar %	Sap:Sugar Ratio
BIRCHES			
Downy Birch	*Betula pubescens*	1–2.6%	100:1
Paper Birch	*Betula papyrifera*	0.5–2%	100:1
Silver Birch	*Betula pendula*	1–2.5%	100:1
White Birch	*Betula alba*	≤1%	100:1–110:1
Yellow Birch	*Betula alleghaniensis*	0.5%	180:1
WALNUTS			
Black Walnut	*Juglans nigra*	2–3.5% (< 6.2%)	30:1
Buartnut	*Juglans x bixbyi*	1.5–3%	35:1
Butternut	*Juglans cinerea*	1–3%	Not found
English Walnut	*Juglans regia*	1–5%	Not found
Heartnut	*Juglans ailantifolia*	1.5–2.5%	40:1
Sitka Alder	*Alnus sinuata*	1–1.5%	90:1–100:1
OTHER SPECIES			
Beech (under vacuum)	*Fagus sylvatica*	1% sugar	85–145:1
Elm	*Ulnus* spp.	≤1%	Not found
Hornbean (European)	*Carpinus betulus*	0.9%	Not found
Hickory*	*Carya* spp.	1.7–3%	40:1–60:1
Ironwood	*Ostrya virginiana*	≤1%	120:1
Linden (European Lime)	*Tilia* spp.	≤1%	Not found
Linden / Basswood (American)	*Tilia americana*	≤1%	Not found
Wild Cherry	*Prunus avium*	≤1%	Not found

Common Name	Botanical Name	Sugar %	Sap:Sugar Ratio
TROPICAL SPECIES			
Coconut Palm (bud stem)	*Cocos nucifera*	5–18% (av. 14%)	8:1–10:1
Date Palm (Asian)	*Phoenix sylvestris*	2–10% (av. 4%)	15:1–40:1
Date Palm (Mediterranean)	*Phoenix dactylifera*	2–10% (av. 4%)	10:1–15:1
Fishtail Palm	*Caryota urens*	15–20%	20:1–30:1
Gomuti Palm	*Arenga pinnata*	12–16%	10:1–15:1
Nipa Palm	*Nipa fruticans*	12–18%	20:1–25:1
Palmyra Palm	*Borassus flabellifer*	12–16%	60:1–70:1
Sago Palm	*Metroxylon sagu*	10–15%	25:1–30:1
Talipot Palm	*Corypha umbraculifera*	15–20%	30:1–35:1

* Hickory is seldom tapped because hickory bark, toasted in the oven, can be boiled to give a similar-tasting syrup. This is also how spruce syrup or larch syrup are made – by boiling the needles. In both cases, the flavours are infused by boiling bark or needles in water to make a strong tea. After the plant material has been strained off, an equal volume of brown sugar is added and the solution simmered until a lovely honey-like consistency is reached.

How to tap a Birch tree

Each tree that yields sap can have a slightly different method of tapping and, commercially, vacuum pumps are often used to speed up the process. I have focused on the Birch as this is the one that most people can find and experiment with, in the UK.

I tap birches in the early spring – usually late March or early April in central Scotland. To find out if a Birch tree is ready for tapping, snap a small twig (the width of a drinking straw). If a drop of sap forms at the break, the sap is flowing and the tree is ready. Only tap the trunks of mature trees that are at least 25 centimetres in diameter at chest height. A tree this size can produce about 2 to 5 litres of sap a day from a single tap. Choose the tallest tree in a group as these produce the strongest flow.

You will need: a tree tap with a mallet (or a short length of flexible, food-safe, plastic tubing), a portable drill with an 8-millimetre wood bit, and a container to collect the sap.

1 First drill a small hole into the trunk, at a slight upward angle, about 4 centimetres deep. When you remove the drill you should see sap starting to drip.

2 Hammer the tree tap into the hole with the mallet, following the angle, so the sap flows down to a bucket either hung from the tap or secured to the trunk. If you use the tubing method the drill bit must be the same diameter as the tubing to ensure a snug fit and stop sap leaking around the sides. A diameter of 8 to 10 millimetres is ample as the sap comes out drop by drop. Push the tube into the hole. Put the free end of the tube into an appropriate glass, stoneware or stainless-steel container (plastic can taint the sap). Only use one tap/tube per tree.

3 Once the tap is set up and the sap is flowing into your container, leave it to collect for 24 hours. You'll need to swap containers when you return to continue collection. The sap can run for one or two weeks and you may collect 30 to 60 litres – a small fraction of the thousands of litres a tree produces. The flow will stop when the leaf buds open. You'll notice a change in the sap, from crystal clear to milky, as bud burst approaches. The taste also changes, becoming slightly cheesy, the signal to stop and remove the tap.

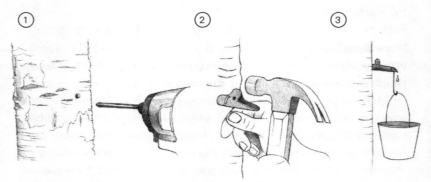

These illustrate the process described on the previous page.

There are various opinions on sealing the hole. I advocate plugging it with a sterilised 8-millimetre dowel, with care not to trap dirt and moulds in the trunk that could cause infection. An alternative is to plug the hole with moss, which is antiseptic. But there's also the option to do nothing: sap will flow into an unplugged hole, washing out any pathogenic microbes, then thicken and harden to form a natural plug.

To avoid making holes in the tree altogether, an alternative tapping method is to cut the end off a small 5-centimetre-diameter branch. Tie or tape a bottle over the cut end and wait for the sap to fill it. This will not collect as much sap as a trunk tap but is less damaging to the tree.

Don't tap the same tree every year, as it can affect its lifespan. Birch trees have a relatively short lifespan – about 90 years on average (but can reach up to 150 years).

The process is similar for maples except the hole depth is different. With Birch and Sycamore trees, the ideal depth is between 3.8 and 4.5 centimetres as the bark is thinner. With Sugar Maple you will need to drill deeper. A study in Vermont found that 'the average yield with the 2.25 inch [5.7 cm] deep hole was 70% greater than that from the 1.25 inch [2.5 centimetre] hole'.[14] Commercially, people also often insert tubing and link trees together.

Raw Birch sap

You can drink birch sap as soon as you have collected it. Just strain it to remove any leaf debris or flies and keep what you don't drink straight away cool in the fridge for up to five days or freeze it. You can also lightly pasteurise it if you want to keep it for longer and free up some fridge space. If you leave it out, unpasteurised, it will start to ferment. This is not necessarily harmful, but it will alter the taste. The herbalist William Thomas Fernie wrote in 1901, 'A fermented liquor may be made from the sap of the birch tree in the springtime, this being collected throughout the mountains and wooded districts of Germany, and Scandinavia. It is possessed of diuretic properties, and is antiscorbutic, being especially commended for modifying the symptoms of diabetes mellitus. As well as being drunk fresh, there is also a tradition of fermenting tree saps into wines and spirits.' Some people go on to make a wine from the sap but for this you do need to add extra sugar, yeast and yeast nutrient. Birch sap can also be used as a mixer but the taste is changed by other flavours.

Birch sap syrup

Birch sap syrup is produced by boiling the sap at a slow, steady simmer to evaporate off the water. I do this outdoors in my old wood-fired Soyer stove with its large cauldron to prevent creating a lot of water vapour in the house. Once most has boiled off, and it has reduced by two-thirds, I transfer it to an induction hob to finish on a low heat, so as not to scorch the syrup as it thickens. Scorched syrup can taste very bitter.

The process takes several hours as the water-to-sugar ratio is 100:1, which means 10 litres of sap only yield 100 millilitres of precious syrup. Use it like maple syrup on pancakes, fresh fruit or in savoury dishes and enjoy its mysterious, smoky, earthy flavour. Unlike maple syrup, which is primarily sucrose (regular sugar), birch is primarily fructose and glucose. These are monosaccharides not disaccharides, so it is hard to boil it into candies and sweets.

Beech sap syrup

Beech sap syrup is a lot like maple syrup. However, beech sap does not flow with the proliferation of birch and maple saps so has to be extracted with the extra pressure provided by hooking the tube up to a vacuum pump. (Small vacuum pumps are not very expensive as they are used to pump oil out of cars during an oil change.) The season starts later than the maples, after the snow melt, once the soil has thawed in slightly warmer late-winter weather before the spring equinox. It carries on until the birch sap starts to flow and the buds to open. The sap is sweet but still has the low sugar content that birches do. The yield varies according to the weather and the efficiency of your vacuum pump, but can vary from 7.5 litres across smaller saplings to 20 litres for mature trees. Of the flavour, American tree-tapper Adam Wild says, 'Beech syrup is somewhat close to the taste of maple syrup yet has its own unique flavour reminiscent of dried plums, pears, and raisins with a slight nutty finish.'[15] A problem when boiling beech sap down to make syrup is that it encourages pectin to form, which creates a thick jelly. So keep a careful eye on it and lower the temperature to stop this from happening.

Further reading

Visser, M., and Salatin, J. (2019), *Sweet Maple: Backyard Sugarmaking from Tap to Table* (Lyons Press).

CHAPTER 8

Coniferous Trees

Identifying conifers

Conifers is the name given to the group of trees that bear cones. Many are called evergreens, with the exception of larch, because they have needles rather than leaves and do not lose them in the winter. The conifer group includes Pinaceae (cedars, firs, hemlocks, larches, pines and spruces), Cupressaceae (cypresses, junipers, redwoods and thujas) and Taxaceae (yews). While there are only three native conifers in the British Isles and Ireland – Scots Pine, Juniper and Yew – there are many foreign conifers that have been planted in parks, gardens and forestry plantations.

To the forager, conifers are mainly a source of flavour, a winter vitamin C boost, and occasionally, in times of hunger, flour is made from the inner bark of some pines. Care needs to be taken with identification though as some contain some very toxic substances. A slip in telling a fir from a yew, when gathering needles for a herbal tea, could result in poisoning and even death.

Looking at how a conifer's needles are arranged helps us identify the tree. This mnemonic is a good introduction to the classification process:

Pines are in pairs
Larches in lumps
Spruces are spiky
Firs flex and are flat
While Juniper's jaggy and smells of jin (gin)

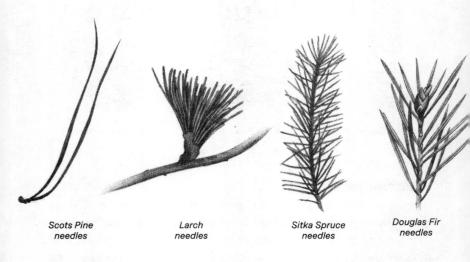

Scots Pine
needles

Larch
needles

Sitka Spruce
needles

Douglas Fir
needles

Spruces also sometimes have a square profile when rolled through the fingers. Firs can't roll, they just turn over. So you can also remember that: spruces are stiff and sharp. Firs are flexible and friendly.

Conifer ID – cones, needles and flowers:

Douglas Fir cone

Larch cone

Monkey Puzzle cone

Norway Spruce cone

Scots Pine cone

Sitka Spruce cone

Monkey Puzzle needles

Norway Spruce needles

Scots Pine flower

Sitka Spruce flower

Douglas Fir flower

Larch flower

Common conifers

Larch ✳ *Larix decidua*

The Larch is the only evergreen that isn't forever green: it sheds its needles in the autumn. There's always got to be someone who breaks the rules. The species name *decidua* is a reminder that it's deciduous. Like Birch, it is a pioneer species and can survive on poor soils. Boil the needles to make a vitamin-rich tea. The young red flower cones can be pickled or crystallised as a treat.

Monkey Puzzle ✳ *Araucaria araucana*

A non-native sometimes called the Chilean pine, the Monkey Puzzle tree was introduced to formal parks and gardens during the Victorian era. Female trees can produce vast quantities of large pine nuts as long as there is a male tree in the vicinity. The 3- to 4-centimetre-long nuts have three layers to peel off which can be a little time-consuming. Boiling them for no more than 10 minutes makes peeling them much easier and, this way, the nuts taste like sweet chestnuts. They can then be ground and dried into a useful nut flour.

Scots Pine ✳ *Pinus sylvestris*

With any method that generalises identification, you will need to learn one or two exceptions. The 'pine needles in pairs' rule applies to our Scots Pine *Pinus sylvestris*. However, some foreign pines have sets of three needles and five needles. The basic rule of thumb is that red pines have two, yellow pines have three, and white pines have five. Spruces and firs have single needles. Scots Pine vitamin C-rich needles can be boiled into a tea. They can be used as a bed for cooking food on outdoors and for smoking food. The Sami people roast the inner bark to neutralise the terpenes in it and grind it into pine bark flour. The young green cones can be cooked into a jam. Collect the pollen to add nutrition to your nut flours. The pollen is also reputed to help men maintain testosterone levels, especially during the 'andropause' in their midlife years.

Sitka Spruce ✳ *Picea sitchensis* and *Norway Spruce Picea abies*
Pick and boil the fresh, bright-green, citrus-pine shoots in the late spring to make a wonderful syrup. I call it spruce honey. Boil the needles to make a vitamin-rich tea.

Most pines can be used in teas and for 'bread' flour and some firs, like the Douglas Fir *Pseudotsuga menziesii*, have particularly aromatic needles and a great-flavoured sap that can be added to drinking water or infused in vodka. I am personally wary of the hemlocks, cypresses, cedars and thujas though, as they can contain some very strong chemicals.

Caution
Yew ✳ *Taxus baccata*
Technically the English Yew tree is not a conifer. The word for the order Coniferales means cone-bearing and they are in the order Taxales (*yew-like*) while *baccata* means berry-bearing. However, like all conifers, Yew trees have flat needle-like leaves. Unlike conifers, Yew trees are poisonous, so it's important not to mistake one for the other. Yew berries, needles or bark contain poisonous taxine alkaloids. Eating just 50 grams of Yew needles can lead to heart failure in an adult and just one or two of the seeds can kill a small child.[16] Technically, the drupes (called *arils*) that look like red berries are edible raw and cooked. A raw paste of them makes a tasty albeit sticky diabetic jam. However, the seed inside the drupe is toxic and must be removed to be safe. See also page 134.

PART THREE

THE
SEAWEEDS

CHAPTER 9

The World of Seaweed

"Hundreds of hands waving in the current.
They wave to the coast and to themselves day in, day out,
on long slender wrists; underwater rounds of applause."
MIEK ZWAMBORN,
THE SEAWEED COLLECTOR'S HANDBOOK

The coast of the British Isles is excellent for foraging seaweed. The water is cool enough for many delicious species to thrive and, luckily for us, there are no poisonous varieties. Well, you might keep an eye out for the featherweeds – four species of *Desmarestia* that grow mainly in deep water and have mastered the knack of producing a little sulphuric acid to put off predators. But foraging for seaweed is far less complicated than trying to identify edible fungi. Learn what a featherweed looks like, and then you can gaily wander an unpolluted shore nibbling and tasting living seaweeds. Do so and you'll soon learn that just because seaweeds aren't poisonous does not mean that they're all choice edibles. Some taste like fish food or have the texture of hair or leather. But there are many that taste exquisite, and you'll be surprised at the variety of flavours.

As well as being a source of culinary delight, seaweeds are nature's multivitamins. They contain a huge variety of vitamins (including B9 and B12), minerals, trace elements like iodine and tyrosine – so crucial to thyroid function – and amino acids. They are superb prebiotics and supercharge the growth of many different beneficial gut microbiota. Iodine is critical to the healthy functioning of our bodies. Our thyroid uses it to make hormones that control the speed of all the chemical reactions in our cells, including the mitochondria, our cell's 'batteries'.

Seaweeds reside in the Kingdom Protista, which is often defined by what's *not* included in it. For example, all organisms that are not animals, plants or fungi. Seaweed scientists (phycologists) disagree as to exactly what should be in this kingdom as the boundaries are fuzzy between protists (microscopic single-celled organisms) and protoctists (multi-celled organisms with a cell membrane that encloses a nucleus and various organelles). The latter includes slime moulds as well as red algae and kelp seaweeds. Here, I'm using the Kingdom Protista for seaweeds as they are a type of alga, although not all algae are seaweeds.

There are three colours that divide the seaweed families:

Brown	Phaeophyta	1,800 worldwide, 186 in Britain
Red	Rhodophyta	6,500 worldwide, 348 in Britain
Green	Chlorophyta	1,500 worldwide, 110 in Britain

In total, around 644 species of seaweed can be found along the British shore,[17] with brown seaweeds (kelp and wracks) being the most abundant. The red seaweeds are the trickiest ones as they can look brown, red, pink or green depending on their age and condition.

I find it mind-blowing that *Laminaria digitata*, the brown alga known as either Oarweed or Tangle, is more closely related to the malaria parasite *Plasmodium falciparum* than it is to plants. (And, astonishingly, fungi-inhibiting compounds made by a Fijian red seaweed *Callophycus serratus* have potential in synergising drugs that fight malaria.[18]) In the tree of life, green seaweeds like Sea Lettuce *Ulva lactuca* are in the clade (ancestral group) Viridiplantae along with plankton and land plants, whereas both Oarweed and the malaria parasite are in the clade Sar (Harosa). While green seaweeds are the ancestors of land plants, red algae branched away from green algae before land plants developed. And both share a common ancestor in the group Archaeplastida.

Fortunately, from a culinary perspective, the complex relationship of the three groups of seaweeds is of minor importance. That they are delicious is far more to the point. I use seaweed in cooking and travel to the coast twice a year just to pick it for my store cupboard. There is nothing I enjoy as much as camping by the sea and eating the seaweed. I tie paracord between the trees and peg up my seaweed to dry in the wind. When fully dry, seaweed stores extremely well and is vital as a quick source of food on busy days when I'm only eating wild food. Dried seaweed and mushrooms quickly make a nourishing dashi soup, while frozen Spaghetti Weed is as quick to make as pot noodles.

Worldwide there are over 12,000 species of seaweed, although scientists believe there could be as many as 1,000,000 – some are microscopic while giant kelps can grow 40 to 60 centimetres a day! Between them, seaweed and algae produce around 70% of the world's oxygen. This brings sharply into focus the dangers of polluting, acidifying and warming the oceans. All life once came from the sea and we are more dependent on it than we can begin to imagine.

Further reading

The best field guide to seaweeds is Bunker, A. R.; Brodie, J. A.; Maggs, C. A.; and Bunker, A. R. (2017). *Seaweeds of Britain and Ireland: Second Edition* (Amsterdam University Press).

For a comprehensive online list of North Atlantic seaweeds visit 'The Seaweed Site: information on marine algae' accessed at **seaweed.ie**

When to harvest seaweed

Many people's view of seaweed has been coloured by their childhood trips to the seaside at the end of July or in August, when temperatures are high and the beaches strewn with washed-up, smelly, slowly rotting seaweed. Summer is not the best time to harvest seaweed.

Higher water temperatures tend to slow down the growth of seaweeds. By high summer they've released their eggs and antherozoids (seaweed spermatozoa) and are settling down to old age. Most seaweed species grow fastest from January to May and are at their tastiest and most productive in the spring – from February through March, April, May and early June. Their growth rate slows down as the water temperatures rise from June to September, the slowest growth rate being in August. Once the sea temperature starts to cool in the autumn, the growth rate begins to pick up again, particularly after November. I do my first picking in February, which is when I find seaweeds taste best. Some green seaweeds are picked in the summer though.

Safety first

Go down to rocks and rock pools when the tide is out so you can harvest from the living plants. This way you are harvesting fresh food and not something washed up that's days or weeks old. Don't be blasé about the tide and the tidal zone. Look up the tide times online, or buy some tide tables. There are lots of websites that provide anywhere from a week to a month of free tide forecast (e.g. **tides.willyweather.co.uk**) and there is also the Meteorological Office (**metoffice.gov.uk/weather/specialist-forecasts/coast-and-sea/beach-forecast-and-tide-times**). Set two alarms on your phone: the first to sound 30 minutes before the tide turns, and the second when the tide turns. This should allow you enough time to get back to the safety of the shore.

Don't go foraging for seaweed alone. Wet, seaweed-covered rocks are easy to slip on. Tell people where you are going and when you will text or phone them to let them know you're back: a simple precaution could be the difference between life and death. Make sure your phone is fully charged and, wherever possible, stick to areas where you have a mobile phone signal.

Some people like to wear lifejackets and carry flares. I always have a first-aid kit in my car and some basics in my pocket. I also recommend a loud whistle. My harvesting knife has a whistle in the handle as I can't whistle for toffee.

Where to harvest

The best places to look for seaweeds are near rocks and rock pools once they are exposed at low tide. Seaweeds need something to hold onto with their holdfasts. The holdfast is made up of lots of finger-like haptera that look like roots – or a bundle of spaghetti. It clings to rocks either by twining around them, or sticking to them with a home-grown chemical adhesive. This gives the seaweed a stable place to grow. So rocks and rock pools are a much better bet than a sandy bay, where you're unlikely to find fresh specimens.

Make sure that you're collecting from an unpolluted source. Avoid beaches near towns, sewage pipes, run-off and industry. Avoid bays where there is a lot of green algae, which is often caused by phosphorous or nitrogen from agricultural fertilisers washed down via rivers. Check specialist websites, such as wild swimming or surfing sites, as bathing water quality is monitored and the results published every year.

I also suggest you learn about the sea creatures you come across. Some, like sea anemones, are clean water indicator species. If they are present, it's a good sign that the water is unpolluted as they cannot survive in dirty water.

Check your beach and water quality
Surfers against Sewage online map **sas.org.uk/map**
The Rivers Trust sewage alerts **theriverstrust.org/key-issues/sewage-in-rivers**
Environment Agency Swimfo: **environment.data.gov.uk/bwq/profiles**
Scotland Environment Protection Agency: **sepa.org.uk/BathingWaters**

Seaweed parts:

1   Blade
2   Stipe
3   Holdfast
4   Hapteras
5   Reproductive parts
6   Air bladders
7   Meristem
8   Midrib

The littoral zone

The littoral or tidal zone is the name of the area that is affected by the action of the waves. Generally, this means the area between the highest high tide and the lowest low tide also known as the foreshore or the intertidal zone. In the UK the foreshore is all technically owned by the Crown. It is administered by the Crown Estate, either directly or through local councils. The littoral zone consists of four distinct areas, each corresponding to different tidal conditions. Like plants on land, seaweeds can be fussy about which part of the shore they call home. When the tidal zone is short – as it often is if the coast is steep – this can be hard to see, as all the seaweeds are jostled up together. When the tidal zone is long, you can more easily see each seaweed's preference.

The four zones are:

Splash zone: Sometimes called the spray zone, this is the highest area on the shore. Here the land is only occasionally soaked by ocean spray and large waves. It remains dry except during extremely high tides, such as spring tides or storms. Channelled Wrack can sometimes be found here. It is the highest up the shore of all the seaweeds. However, loose seaweed are thrown up here by high waves. Don't collect dead seaweed from the splash zone. It's like picking your salad off the floor of a supermarket when everyone else has driven their trolley over it.

High intertidal zone: Submerged during the highest tides, this zone spends long periods exposed to air between tide cycles. It is often thickly carpeted with Bladderwrack and Spiralled Wrack and, if near a river mouth, Horned Wrack.

Mid intertidal zone: This area is usually underwater, only exposed during the lowest tides when the water recedes. Here you will find Serrated Wrack and the carragheens, followed by Pepper Dulse, Spaghetti Weed and Dulse as you near the shelf at the edge of the low intertidal zone.

Low intertidal zone: Also called the sub-tidal zone, this area is briefly exposed at low tide but is underwater most of the time. Here you'll find Oarweed, Sugar Kelp and Dabberlocks as they don't like being out of the water for long!

The littoral or tidal zone:

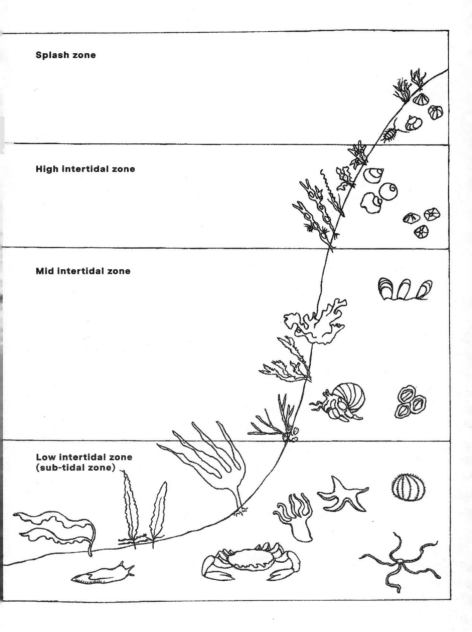

Splash zone

High intertidal zone

Mid intertidal zone

Low intertidal zone
(sub-tidal zone)

Harvesting equipment

You'll need a pair of snips, scissors or a knife. I like the spring-loaded shears used in gardening and dressmaking – they let me work quickly even when my hands get cold. Welly boots with good grip, wool base layers and fingerless gloves are mandatory clothing.

For collecting the seaweed you'll need buckets or bags. My favourite is an old wire shopping basket, which lets the water drain and lightens the load in the process. Water is heavy! I usually take a few small plastic boxes with lids for the more delicate finds. It stops me losing them when everything gets mixed up together but, more recently, I've changed over to the mesh vegetable bags supplied by supermarkets. I can tie them onto my basket so they don't blow out.

How to harvest

Don't yank the stipe off the rocks. You'll not only kill the seaweed and prevent it from growing again next year, but you're also going to end up with sand and flakes of rock in your harvesting basket and on your dinner plate. Picking clean is good for you and good for the seaweed. Cut the blades off above the stipe, leaving enough seaweed behind so that it can reproduce or grow again.

Harvest sparingly over a wide area (rather than intensively in a small one), and don't take more than you can use. Thinning the seaweeds is fine but a scorched-earth, pick-everything approach is not. Take a sustainable approach and you will be able to harvest the same spot for years without damaging the environment.

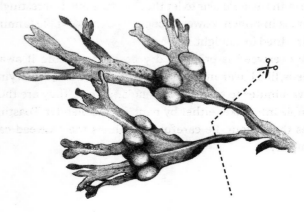

Washing

There's a lot to be said for rinsing the seaweed in the sea as you go along, if you can find a deep rock pool that's free of sand. It saves time once you're home, tired after a day out, if you harvest clean produce. Note that seaweed will taste saltier if you rinse it in seawater rather than fresh water, before drying it. Surprisingly, on its own, seaweed is not particularly salty.

If you take seaweed home, whatever you do, don't put it into a bucket of fresh water and leave it overnight. By the morning you will have a slimy mess. Or, if you had any Dulse in there, a slimy, purple mess. This is caused by the alginates in the seaweed, which are a natural gelling agent extracted for commercial use in everything from toothpaste to puddings. You're best off rinsing the seaweed in a big tub of cold water as soon as you get home and hanging it straight up to dry.

Drying

There are no rules when it comes to drying other than not letting it sit around wet or damp for too long as it will deteriorate. I've dried seaweed on clothes racks, pegged it out on the washing line, stretched clothes lines over the bathtub, and even hung strips from the banisters in a stairwell. When I'm camping by the coast I string a line between two trees. When I'm at home I tend to use the folding wire clothes airer. The very small seaweeds, such as Pepper Dulse, get patted with a towel to remove the excess water and put into a dehydrator. Alternatively, you can put them in the oven at a low temperature with the door ajar to let the moisture out. Interestingly, the polyphenols in brown seaweeds convert to more edible tannins when they are dried in sunlight.

Make sure seaweed is properly dry before you store it away. Some seaweeds, like Laver and Dulse, I will toast in a hot, dry-frying pan for a few minutes to take any last moisture out. They are then easy to crumble into flakes either by hand or in a blender. Toasting also changes the flavour. Be careful, though, as the seaweed can burn very quickly.

Fermenting

People often ask me about fermenting seaweed but it doesn't ferment particularly well on its own. Seaweeds are used to decaying in salty water – basically what brine is – and tend to carry on decomposing rather than fermenting. However, thinly sliced Oarweed or Dulse added to shredded cabbage or kohlrabi works well. I use about 15 grams of seaweed per kilo of greens – coincidentally around the same amount as in Japanese recipes such as 'nukazuke' (rice bran fermented pickles).

Pickling

Like fermenting, pickling seaweed can be a hit or miss affair. Some seaweeds such as *Chorda* or *Dumontia* quickly turn to jelly on contact with vinegar. However, firmer seaweeds like the immature reproductive pods of Eggwrack or very young Bladderwrack tips can be pickled successfully. Ideally eat them within 3 months as inevitably they deteriorate. In Japan, where seaweed consumption is high, they preserve seaweed as 'kombu no tsukudani' by simmering kelp in a vinegar, lemon, mirin, soy and brown sugar syrup. This is the closest I have found to a true seaweed preserve. However, when I'm on a wild food diet, sugar is out! 'Senmaizuke' is another pickle where finely chopped seaweed is tucked between thinly sliced salted turnip, before adding a sweetened rice vinegar.

Storing seaweed

Dried seaweed will keep for years and the flavours often improve with age, as the tasty salts and sugars become more concentrated. The brown seaweeds last the longest. Store them in jars or sealed kraft pouches out of sunlight.

Further reading

To discover more about sea creatures that also inhabit the shore and rock pools:

Bowen, S.; Goodwin, C.; Kipling, D.; and Picton, B. (2018), *Sea Squirts and Sea Sponges of Britain and Ireland* (Vol. 11) (Princeton University Press).

Wood, C. (2013), *Sea Anemones and Corals of Britain and Ireland* (Princeton University Press).

CHAPTER 10

Brown Seaweeds (Phaeophyceae)

The most common species of brown seaweeds found along the British and Irish coasts are the wracks in the order Fucales: Bladderwrack, Spiralled Wrack, Serrated Wrack, Horned (Estuary) Wrack, Channelled Wrack and Eggwrack. Also under Fucales, in the family Sargassaceae, Sea Oak (related to the invasive wireweed *Sargassum muticum*) inhabits the intermediate pools.

On the edge of the tidal zone you will also find the kelps in the order Laminariales: Oarweed, Sugar Kelp, Thongweed and Dabberlocks. When out in a boat on the sea lochs of the west coast of Scotland, you are also bound to find Mermaid's Tresses wrapped around your propellor or tying up your oars sooner or later. Kelps are cool-water species that become stressed by high temperatures. Unfortunately, ocean warming driven by climate change is going to affect the geography, abundance and resilience of kelp beds. They are a home to many marine species, including herbivorous fish, and invertebrates such as the unusual Blue-rayed Limpet *Patella pellucida*. Their decline will have a far-reaching impact on the marine ecosystem.

Following are some of my favourite edible brown seaweeds. As there are many fewer seaweeds than plants to consider, I have not grouped them into families.

Oarweed ⚹ *Laminaria digitata*

Also known as 'Tangle', Oarweed is one of the most common seaweeds around the British coast. It grows at the edge of the subtidal zone and in deep water, so you need a low tide to harvest it fresh. The best times to go are during the especially low neap tides. Although you can harvest it all year round, I prefer the younger growth in the early spring – between the Celtic feasts of Earrach (1 February) and Beltane (1 May). Oarweed grows to between 1 and 2 metres long. Its largest kelp relative is Giant Kelp *Macrocystis pyrifera*, which can reach up to 45 metres in length (as long as a football pitch), growing 30 centimetres a day.

Cut off a few fronds from each plant, leaving the stipe, broad meristem and some other fronds to carry on with life. I harvest only the young fronds, cutting them from the 'palms' as rectangles which I use to make 'lasagne' sheets. I roll up long thin fronds when they are dry but still supple and store them in glass jars. Over time, they become covered in white powder. This isn't mould, it is all the salts and sugars (such as mannitol, a sugar suitable for diabetics) coming to the surface and enhancing the flavour.

I often use Oarweed in the way other people might use bay leaves – just one or two added to a dish. For this, I cut the Oarweed while still wet into strips about 12 centimetres long, and let them dry like that. They keep for several years as long as they're stored away from moisture and humid air.

If you have dried seaweed and dried mushrooms in the house you need never go hungry. A simple dashi soup can be made by rehydrating Oarweed (*kombu* in Japanese) in cold water for 20 minutes, before slicing it finely and simmering for 30 minutes with some rehydrated mushrooms. Season with salt and pepper or a splash of soy sauce. Alternatively, just simmer squares of it and season with butter, pepper and vinegar.

Kelp has been used for sustenance or medicine for centuries. In the eighteenth and nineteenth centuries, families would collect the thick stems (stipes) thrown up on the shore after a storm and roast them slowly at the back of their wood stove. The centre gradually cooks and splitting the stipes open reveals a marrow of thick umami paste that can be spread onto rolls or oatcakes. Records between 1700 and 1800 show that people simmered kelp lightly and drank the infusion with butter to restore the appetite. I wouldn't suggest doing this too frequently, though, as you might end up overdosing on iodine. In traditional medicine, kelp poultices were used to open old wounds that needed cleaning and dilate the cervix to start labour.

Today, kelp is harvested industrially and its alginates extracted to use in food gels, cake mixes, paper coating, medicines and many other things.

Sugar Kelp ✳ *Saccharina latissima*

Also called Sweet Kombu, Sweet Wrack or Seabelt, this brown seaweed only has one blade, so it sneaks into inlets and rocky gullies to protect itself from the storms of the open sea, where the many-bladed Oarweed thrives. The centre of the blade is slightly pockmarked, as if shirred or smocked. The outer edge is thinner and wavy, like the ruffle running down the front of an old-fashioned men's dress shirt.

Sugar Kelp is best harvested during a super-low tide, so that you can get safely down to the sub-tidal level. Cut off the single blade, leaving the stipe, meristem and a reasonable length of the blade to carry on with life. Or harvest *selective* fresh castaways that are in good condition and freshly thrown up after stormy weather. You can harvest it from spring to autumn, but it is best in the spring, when it is around half a metre long. By June it will have reached several metres and won't be as tender.

I use Sugar Kelp in casseroles and stews (like I would Oarweed), or flaked into cakes and biscuits (a great way of enriching food for fussy children). As with Oarweed, a powdery white coating of mannitol develops on the surface of Sugar Kelp when it dries.

Sugar Kelp really comes into its own fried in hot oil as crisps – but this is not for the ill-equipped or faint-hearted. The gel pockets that form across the centre of the blade burst unpredictably, sending hot oil everywhere. You must use a closed fryer ... I speak from experience. Ideally, make friends with a chef who has an industrial chip fryer. In this, pieces of sugar kelp will fry in just a minute or two into the most delicious crisps you have ever tasted. I have seen babies as young as six months old greedy for more.

Young Sugar Kelp is tender and perfect for eating. As it matures, the centre strip becomes pockmarked and the edges distinctly separate and wavy.

Dabberlocks ✳ *Alaria esculenta*

A 2-metre-long brown seaweed, Dabberlocks likes to grow in the same places as Sugar Kelp, and on first glance could be mistaken for it. But Dabberlocks has a hard rib running down the middle of a delicate, wavy blade that has no gel pockets or texture in the centre band. It often tucks itself under rocky ledges in tidal gullies that are seldom fully exposed. It can grow 5 per cent of its length in a single day. Cut it above the reproductive 'wings' at the base of the blade from mid-spring to early summer. Eat it raw or cooked. If the latter, remove the central spine and cook it ahead of the blade, as it takes a little longer. I particularly like it in a quiche with smoked haddock or cobbler. It can also be dried, crumbled and home oak-smoked as a seasoning. It contains vitamins C, K and B, which all peak sequentially from early to late spring.

Sea Spaghetti ✳ *Himanthalia elongata*
Sea Spaghetti, also called Thongweed,
is a brown seaweed that grows from a
button-shaped holdfast disc, putting
out two or three main branched
fronds. It starts growing in the autumn and winter
and can reach up to 2 metres long by the summer, dying back
after it has reproduced. When harvesting, I only take one main
branch. Leaving one frond and the button behind allows the
seaweed to keep on growing and reproducing for around three
years. Each frond grows thick and divides into thongs which do
look remarkably like the straps of rubber flip-flop sandals.

Sea Spaghetti grows on rocks on the lower shore
right next to the sub-tidal zone, exposed at low tides.
It particularly likes gently sloping rock shelves. After a
quick rinse on the day of harvest, Sea Spaghetti keeps in
the fridge for a couple of days. It also pickles well and can be
dried and rehydrated. Eat it fresh, or boil for just a few minutes and
use instead of pasta. Alternatively, freeze it in 100-gram individual
portions. You can cook it directly from frozen by plunging it into a
pan of salted, boiling water for 3–4 minutes, draining it, and serving
it mixed through with rosehip purée, salt and pepper as an instant
meal for two.

It's also very nice raw and doesn't have a fishy taste. It is superb in
sushi rolls and Japanese-style salads, marinated in a little dressing, or
cooked in dim sum parcels.

Dried seaweed flakes can be mixed with seasalt flakes at a 50:50 ratio
to make a range of delicious seasonings. This is especially helpful if
you're following a low salt diet and don't want to compromise flavour.

Mermaid's Tresses ✳ *Chorda filum*

Although *Himanthalia elongata* is commonly called Sea Spaghetti, the epithet should by rights have gone to Mermaid's Tresses *Chorda filum*, which looks the most spaghetti-like of all the algae. *Chorda* also goes by the name of Sea Lace, Bootlace Weed, Dead Man's Rope, Cat's Gut, Sea Twine and Mermaid's Fishing Line ... you can see why I stick to calling it *Chorda*.

Like Sea Spaghetti, *Chorda* also grows from a tiny button, but it is unbranched and grows in a few metres of water, reaching up to 10 metres in length as it swirls around. I typically find *Chorda* on the sheltered, leeward side of the Hebridean Islands, trying to wrap itself round the propellor of the outboard motor. *Chorda*, eaten raw, makes the best sushi salads with a satisfying al dente bite, but don't use too much vinegar as this quickly turns it mushy. Avoid cooking it for the same reason.

The wracks ✳ en famille Fucus

Although the wracks are the most abundant seaweeds on British shores, they are not widely eaten as their flavour is only appealing when very young. They also like to interbreed and can have features (morphology) of more than one species, making identification a challenge. Bladderwrack has the most morphological diversity, changing shape and size – and even whether or not it has bladders – according to salinity and wave action. They are arranged in the mid-tidal zone with Channelled Wrack highest up on the shore and Serrated Wrack nearest the sub-tidal zone.

Egg Wrack ✳ Ascophyllum nodosum

Egg Wrack is easy to identify as it has air bladders along its long fronds, each around the size of a quail's egg in a mature specimen. I don't use a lot of Egg Wrack as it quickly gets tough and its mouth feel is dry. However, the disc-shaped conceptacles (the reproductive parts), which grow from the side of the stem, are delicious when young. Pick them before they mature and fill with gel, and eat them raw – on their own, in salads – or pickle them to eat with cheese. Egg Wrack is also host to a red seaweed, Woolly Siphon Weed *Vertebrata lanosa* (see page 205), a delicious epiphyte. An epiphyte is a seaweed that clings onto another seaweed instead of a rock; *epi-* means 'on top' and *-phyte* means 'plant', so epiphyte means 'growing on top of another plant'.)

Although it is not strictly speaking a kelp, it is sometimes called Norwegian Kelp, Knotted Kelp, Knotted Wrack or Rockweed. Egg Wrack is widely used in the supplements industry for both human and animal health. Its nutrient profile has been studied in depth and it is a great example of how well-balanced seaweed is a natural multivitamin.

EGG WRACK NUTRIENT PROFILE

Vitamins: A (antioxidant), B group (including B12, thiamine, riboflavin, niacin, pantothenic acid, pyridoxin, choline and cobalamin), C (antioxidant), D (colecalciferol), E (antioxidant), H (biotin) and K (menadione).
Minerals: Calcium, Magnesium, Nitrogen, Phosphorus, Potassium, Sodium, Sulphur.
Amino acids: Histidine, Isoleucine, Leucine, Lysine, Methionine, Phenylalanine, Threonine, Tryptophan, Valine, Alanine, Arganine, Aspartic acid, Cysteine, Glutamic acid, Glycine, Proline, Serine, Tyrosine.
Trace elements: Antimony, Boron, Cobalt, Copper, Fluorine, Germanium, Gold, Iodine, Iridium, Iron, Lithium, Manganese, Molybdenum, Platinum, Rubidium, Selenium, Silicon, Silver, Tellurium, Titanium, Vanadium and Zinc.

Egg Wrack is also often used to make garden fertilisers. All along the west coast of Scotland, where it is readily found (preferring the Atlantic to the North Sea), crofters would collect Egg Wrack and Oarweed from the shore after the first winter storms and cover their vegetable beds with a thick seaweed mulch. This leached nutrients as it rotted over the winter, protecting the soil from weeds and erosion. Come spring, it was dug into the soil, enriching it and enhancing moisture retention. You can also soak it in a barrel with comfrey to make a nutrient-dense liquid plant food.

Channelled Wrack ✳ *Pelvetia canaliculata*
Channelled Wrack grows further up the shore than any of the other seaweeds. This is because its stems are curved to make miniature canals in which it can retain water and thus stay out of the sea for a long time. Nutritionally, Channelled Wrack contains essential omega fatty acids three times higher than all other native species tested: Omega 6 and Omega 3 at a 3:1 ratio and Omega 9. It also contains ALA (Alpha-linolenic acid) and EPA (Eicosapentenoic acid) in equal amounts.

When it is very young it can be steamed and eaten. The flavour is mild and it works well added to casseroles or risottos. Alternatively, dry it and blitz it into small pieces to use as a condiment.

It is also delicious pickled in vinegar, keeping its texture well.

CHANNELLED WRACK DETOX DRINK

Simon Ranger of Seagreens® created this delicious antioxidant drink: squeeze a quarter of a lemon into a jug with 25 grams of dried *Pelvetia* pieces, grated ginger root and 4 teaspoons (or teabags) of green tea. Top it up with cold water. Leave for an hour. Strain into a new jug to drink straight away, or keep in the fridge for up to three weeks. Sweeten if desired with pure apple or grape juice.

Bladderwrack ✳ Fucus vesiculosus

The young tips are nice boiled lightly and served with butter, salt and pepper. They're faintly reminiscent of French beans. Young tips can also be pickled in vinegar with spices. Commercially, the bladderwrack extract fucoidan is used in diet pills, and iodine from the algae is used in health supplements. Up to 5 per cent Bladderwrack 'flour' (dried, finely powdered wrack) can be added to bread and pasta flour without causing problems with texture or flavour. This is a good way of adding many of the health properties of seaweed into a modern diet.

Bladderwrack is easy to identify as most have pairs of air bladders on either side of a central rib on the branching fronds. These help to lift the alga towards the sunlight when covered by the tide.

Bladderwrack also goes by the names of Black Tang, Rockweed, Bladder Fucus, Black Tany, Cut Weed, Dyer's Fucus, Red Fucus and Rock Wrack.

Spiralled Wrack ✳ Fucus spiralis
and *Horned (Estuary) Wrack ✳ Fucus ceranoides*
Spiralled Wrack does not have air bladders and twists at the end of the fronds. Horned Wrack, which loves the less saline mouths of rivers, does not have air bladders either, but the edges of its frond tips are often inflated. To make things very confusing, Bladderwrack, Spiralled Wrack and Horned Wrack all interbreed to form hybrids with enthusiasm, leading to some very puzzling specimens. The young tips of both these upper- and mid-shore wracks are tender enough to eat, steamed or lightly pickled.

Serrated Wrack ✳ *Fucus serratus*
Nibble on young Serrated
Wrack – also known as
Toothed Wrack or Saw
Wrack – and you'll find
it tastes like slightly salty
nutty peas. Although
it is cooked into broths
in Japan, I tend to use for
home thalassotherapy, a Victorian spa trend
that involved seaweed baths and body wraps.
It grows from a branched thallus perfect for
hanging over the taps when running a hot bath.
Seaweed baths are very relaxing, easing aches and
pains while lowering the day's stress and aiding a good night's sleep.
They are reputed to be anti-ageing and to improve the suppleness of
your skin, reducing cellulite and wrinkles. Thalassotherapy was also
often used in the past to treat dry or itchy skin conditions. Don't leave
the seaweed sitting in the bath after you've drained it, though, as it
may stain the enamel. Put it straight into the compost.

Sea Oak ✳ *Halidrys siliquosa*
Leaving the wracks on the rocks, Sea
Oak is an olive-brown, zigzag-branched
seaweed that prefers pools that never fully
empty, on the midshore. It has long, thin pod-
shaped air bladders that help to distinguish it.
Like its namesake, the oak, it tastes of tannins
(in this case, phlorotannins) so has a very dry
mouth feel. But I came across Fiona Bird's recipe for
black olive and sea oak tapenade in her *Seaweed in the
Kitchen*,[19] and have picked it ever since purely for this
mouthwatering delicacy.

CHAPTER 11

Red Seaweeds (Rhodophyta)

My favourite edible red seaweeds found along the British and Irish coasts are Dulse, Pepper Dulse, Royal Fernweed, Dumont's Tubular Weed, Woolly Siphon Weed, Carragheen and Laver. There are also exquisite red species that I don't eat but admire for their beauty, such as Sea Beech *Delesseria sanguinea* and Eyelash Weed *Calliblepharis ciliata*. They are seen most clearly when floating in the water, as they collapse as soon as you pull them out. The best way of preserving them for posterity is to gently float them in a bowl and slide a piece of stiff watercolour paper underneath them. Carefully raise the paper so that the seaweed lands on it. With a small paintbrush or tweezers, stretch out the fronds so that, as the water drains away, they look their best. Then sandwich them with sheets of blotting paper pressed between layers of newspaper or paper towel, with a weight on top, until they are dry. Peel away the blotting paper but leave the seaweed mounted on the watercolour paper. The herbarium collection at the Royal Botanic Gardens in Edinburgh has an incredible collection of herbarium seaweeds; I could stand among the stacks and marvel at them for hours.

Dulse ✳ *Palmeria palmata*

Dulse likes hanging off the rocks (preferably east-facing) at the subtidal zone – the edge of the world. It has to be collected during a very low tide. It also hitches an epiphytic ride on the stems of Oarweed (page 190) and Forest Kelp. It's a red seaweed 5 to 30 centimetres long with thin, transparent ends like fingertips. Cut it above the stipe in late spring.

I dry Dulse whole for reconstituting (by soaking it in cold water for 10 minutes) into quiches, tarts and fishcakes. With the latter you don't have to use fish at all – Dulse is a perfect vegan substitute. In quiches and egg tarts I love pairing it with finely chopped Rock or Golden Samphire. Dulse also has a special affinity with potato – Dulse and potato rösti is a dream of a dish. Finely sliced onions, grated parboiled potato and chopped fresh Dulse all mixed together and pressed down hard into a well-oiled frying pan. Cooked slowly on both sides until it is caramelised on the outside and gooey in the middle.

Once dried, I powder a lot of Dulse to make microflakes. Mixed with powdered mushrooms and herbs like yarrow, it makes a wonderful stock seasoning powder. Dried Dulse is often best after a year or few, as the flavour just keeps on improving. I also love putting some smoke through it, especially the lighter maple or applewoods. The smokiness transforms it into a vegan bacon.

Charles Dickens records that as a boy, on holiday in Edinburgh, he'd spend his penny on dried Dulse to chew on, rather than on sweets, preferring its smoky, almost bacon-like taste. It also yields a purple dye that was traditionally used in Harris tweed but is seldom used nowadays.

Pepper Dulse ❋ *Osmundea pinnatifida*

Pepper Dulse looks like miniature Christmas trees, about 2 to 4 centimetres long. While it can go pale brown and even green in the sun, the best Pepper Dulse is so dark it is almost black. Thanks to its intense flavour, it's been dubbed 'the truffle of the sea'. The tastiest is picked from the north and east faces of lower-zone rocks that don't spend too long out of water, as sunlight and heat quickly alter the taste.

While you can dry and powder Pepper Dulse, using it as an alternative to black pepper, I prefer to preserve it in fat. Doing so seals in the flavour, which otherwise deteriorates incredibly quickly, changing just 12 hours after picking. Once I am home from a harvest, I rinse it briefly in cold water and pat it dry. (I learnt the hard way not to use hot water as this makes it release clouds of peppery tear gas. Similarly, setting your dehydrator temperature too high will soon have the house smelling of tear gas at an XR rally). Once patted dry, some goes into the fridge to be used the next morning with eggs. The rest is finely chopped and mixed into either butter at room temperature or soft goat's cheese, then reshaped into blocks and frozen. It is perfectly delicious melted over scallops, fish or a steak, or into mashed potatoes or burdock roots. You can also crush fresh Pepper Dulse, blot up any moisture on kitchen paper, and soak it in olive oil to make 'sea truffle oil'. Adding a little miso wins it a Michelin star.

It is not worth trying to freeze it any other way. It doesn't survive the defrosting process, and quickly becomes sludgy. It's such a tiny, back-breaking species to collect that it is sold as a gourmet product at £13.00 for 10 grams (£1,300 per kilo). I neither envy the pickers nor begrudge them the price.

Royal Fernweed ❋ *Osmundea osmunda*

Royal Fernweed is a close cousin of Pepper Dulse and tastes very similar, if slightly less peppery. Its main advantage is that it grows in large clumps of around 4 to 6 centimetres long so is less backbreaking to pick. It prefers to live in shallow pools and rivulets left by the outgoing tide, while Pepper Dulse is happier to stay out of the water for longer. Treat it and use it in the same way as Pepper Dulse.

Dumont's Tubular Weed ❋ *Dumontia contorta*

Dumont's Tubular Weed is prolific in my favourite harvesting spot, but when I first came across it, no one else – not even my forager colleagues – appeared to know about its edibility. I was determined to identify it as it has such an amazing flavour – umami with a hint of iron – and a lovely bite. In the summer months, when most people visit the beach, it has died back, which might explain why it is still relatively unknown. It starts growing again in November and by February/March is producing its central, curly, pre-Raphaelite tresses where the flavour is concentrated. It also likes to inhabit shallow pools and bared rock in shallow channels that the running tidewater never leaves.

Cut off the central twisted fronds in late winter to early spring and eat fresh within 24 hours. I eat it raw, as it turns to mush when cooked, unless I'm turning it into delicious, delicate lacy fried cakes. To achieve this, pat the alga dry then sift a little mushroom powder or seasoned flour over it. Pull out clusters and drop them into hot oil – safely. It fries in minutes. I also use it to garnish soups, as a raw seaweed 'fettuccine'. It is tasty dried, but the process is laborious for the amount you get from it.

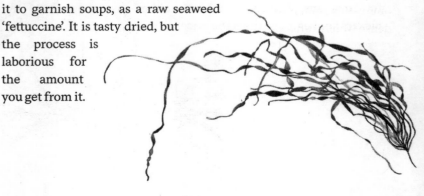

Woolly Siphon Weed ✳ *Polysiphonia lanata*

Occasionally classified as *Vertebrata lanata*, Woolly Siphon Weed is an epiphyte on Egg Wrack. In other words, it piggybacks on it but as a passenger not a parasite. It is easy to spot, clinging to the long, green stipes of Egg Wrack (see 196) in 4–7 cm long red-brown bunches, like pom-poms, miniature wigs or thick armpit hair. Very occasionally you find it growing on Serrated Wrack or Bladderwrack. Although in Britain we call Pepper Dulse the 'sea truffle', in Norway it is Woolly Siphon Weed that claims the title. Norwegians export it to restaurants in France, Iceland and other Scandi countries. As its nickname suggests, it smells and tastes very truffle-like. This is because it contains dimethyl sulphide, the compound that gives earth truffles their distinctive aroma. However, the flavour does vary from season to season and with changes in the weather or different locations. It has an excellent flavour, although the texture can be a little thread-like. I wash it well, dehydrate it and then lightly toast it before pulverising it into a powder. This makes a delicious seasoning to sprinkle over seafood.

A word of advice when gathering it. Pick it off Eggwrack stipes that are draped over rocks or in mounds high above sand. If the Egg Wrack has trailed on sand, you will have a Herculean task to get the grains out of this siphon weed's dense woolly tufts.

Egg Wrack

Woolly Siphon Weed

Carragheen 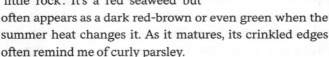 *Chondrus crispus*

This curly seaweed that inhabits the mid-tidal zone was traditionally called Irish Moss. The word 'carragheen' started to be used in the nineteenth century and may come from Carrigan Head in County Donegal, north-western Ireland, where it was commonly gathered, or from the Irish Gaelic word meaning 'little rock'. It's a red seaweed but often appears as a dark red-brown or even green when the summer heat changes it. As it matures, its crinkled edges often remind me of curly parsley.

Carragheen is not eaten as a sea vegetable, but is still useful in the kitchen and your home medicine kit. It contains compounds called carrageenans, which have an affinity with proteins. Boiled in milk, Carragheen makes a vegetarian alternative to gelatine. Powdered Carragheen, known as carragheen finings, is used in home brewing to clear excess proteins in beer and reduce cloudiness. And saline nose sprays with the addition of iota- or beta-carrageenan have been found to lower the transmission rate of Coronavirus proteins found in cold and COVID-19 viruses.[20] It is also antiviral against the herpes viruses that cause cold sores and shingles, and human papillomavirus (HPV).[21]

To make a delicious seaweed dessert, boil a handful of dried Carragheen in around 600 millilitres of water for 20–30 minutes until the water turns into a light jelly. Then squeeze it through a muslin bag – wearing builder-grade rubber gloves as it is hot. The gel will ooze out. You want to combine the gel with 600 millilitres of warm, creamy milk. I infuse the milk first with elderflowers or gorse flowers and often make it up as 300 millilitres of milk and 300 of cream to make it extra thick. When the gel combines with the warm milk, it will start to set. Pour the thickening mix into dessert glasses, or kraft paper cups, and allow it to cool down. Then store it in the fridge while it sets fully. I've tried boiling Carragheen in vegan milk substitutes and while there are not enough proteins in them to set firmly, you will get the consistency of a thick custard.

To make a sumptuous hand or body lotion, boil Carragheen in water to make a gel (as above). Take off 2 tablespoons (30 millilitres) of gel and slowly whisk in double the amount (60 millilitres) of a light oil, such as sweet almond or sunflower. Add ½ teaspoon (2.5 millilitres) of essential oil to scent it and a little preservative (e.g. phenoxyethanol, benzyl alcohol, potassium sorbate or dehydroacetic acid) according to the manufacturer's instructions if you don't want to keep it in the fridge.

When picking Carragheen wait until the early summer, when it's grown to its full size. Rinse it well, as it is host to tiny shrimp- and earwig-like creatures, then dry it. Traditionally it was dried on bed sheets in the sunshine (which will bleach it white), but you can also use a dehydrator. Whether it is bleached or not makes little difference to the efficacy. Before using it, reconstitute it by soaking it in cold water for 20 minutes then draining it.

Grape Pip Weed ❋ *Mastocarpus stellatus*
Grape Pip Weed, aka False Carragheen, colonising the mid and lower-intertidal zone, looks very like true Carragheen *Chondrus crispus* and is used in exactly the same ways. The sides of Grape Pip Weed are slightly thickened forming a channelled centre that true Carragheen doesn't have. Another difference is that when it's mature, its reproductive structures are raised on tiny, sturdy filaments (papillae) up to 1mm away from the frond's surface. In warmer waters, *Chondrus crispus* crowds it out but in colder waters it thrives, as it is better able to tolerate freezing temperatures.

Laver ✻ *Porphyra umbilicalis*

Even though it appears brown, and boils down to a green-black paste, Laver is classified as a red alga. You'll find it draped over midshore rocks. When it dries in the sun and wind, it stretches to look just like thin dark-brown cling film. I look for rocks where it hangs into rock pools, which makes it easier to trim off, without lots of sand and rock flakes added in. Leave plenty on each rock as it will carry on growing. You can harvest it from January to April. It is not dissimilar to the Japanese nori *Pyropia yezoensis*, which is used to make the seaweed paper to wrap sushi rolls, as they are both in the family Bangiaceae.

A native culinary tradition, especially in Wales, Scotland and Ireland (where Laver is called *sleabhac*), is laverbread. Laverbread isn't a bread at all. It's a thick seaweed paste that can be spread on toast, used as a condiment, eaten with cheese and biscuits, eaten hot with pepper, vinegar and butter, cooked with leeks and onions, or eaten cold with oil and lemon juice. To make your own laverbread, wash ten to twelve large handfuls of Laver well in several changes of water, then hand squeeze it to remove excess water but keep it moist. Then stew it for several hours, with half a cupful of apple cider vinegar, until quite tender. This is best done overnight in a slow cooker (or a cast-iron casserole dish in a very low oven or on top of a log burner). Don't try to speed up the process as the best laverbread flavours take time. It will naturally reduce into a thick, glossy paste. Keep what you don't use straight away in the freezer.

My favourite dish is mixing equal amounts of laverbread and oatmeal into small balls and frying them in bacon fat or coconut oil. Even better, roll them in sesame seeds and deep-fry. I also use teaspoons of the paste to add flavour to gravies and other dishes that need an umami kick. In my kitchen, Laver seaweed that isn't turned into laverbread paste is lightly toasted and crumbled, then stored in jars. This is sprinkled into lots of meals.

CHAPTER 12

Green Seaweeds (Chlorophyta)

Green algae are the most diverse of the algal groups, with at least 7,000 species existing on all continents on Earth. Most live in fresh or salty water but many are found in other habitats – even soils, tree bark and snow. Some form symbiotic relationships with fungi to create lichens. The earliest ones, found in fossils, are calculated to be a billion years old. Of these, in the group (taxon) Chlorophyta there are around 1,500 species of green seaweeds in the oceans. The word Chlorophyta comes from the Ancient Greek *khlōrós*, meaning 'green' and *-phyta*, meaning 'plant'. Some can be used as foods but modern technology has harnessed Sea Lettuce into cultivation experiments to produce bioethanol as, like land plants, their photosynthesis produces sugar which converts to ethanol. The green algae produce more ethanol (and fewer gelling agents) than the brown seaweeds but there are still challenges scaling up these experiments. Following are some of my favourite of the 110 green seaweeds found along the British and Irish coasts.

Sea Lettuce ✳ *Ulva lactuca*

Sea Lettuce has vibrant green sheets with wavy edges, and is easy to spot thanks to its resemblance to a 'land' lettuce growing in the upper intertidal zone. By late summer it can grow as big as 12 centimetres wide and high. (Double Ribbon Weed *Ulva linza* is similar in flavour but only reaches 4 to 5 centimetres across.) Sea Lettuce doesn't have much of a stipe and holdfast, but you should still cut it in a way that leaves enough to continue growing. In areas high in fertiliser run-off, for example near river estuaries, it can become so abundant that it's considered invasive, a 'green tide'. Large piles of it rotting on the shore are liable to give off hydrogen sulphide gas as it decomposes. This has caused fatalities in both humans and animals who had the misfortune to breathe in too much of it.

That aside, it is a pretty and versatile seaweed. While not very tender when raw, it can be marinated to tenderise it for Japanese-style seaweed salads and sushi, or lightly steamed as a vegetable, or even fried into delicious, delicate crisps. Handfuls of well-washed Sea Lettuce can be boiled down to a paste like Laver, although the flavour is not as intense.

When dried and flaked, Sea Lettuce keeps its jewel-like emerald colour. The bright green flecks in scrambled eggs or mashed potato are both pretty and nutritious.

Gutweed ✳ *Ulva intestinalis*

Gutweed is made up of very long, thin green tubes found on rocks and boulders on the upper shore. It inflates itself with oblong bubbles of a flotation gas that makes it look like strings of sausages… or intestines. It grows from late spring through summer when it reaches a harvestable size. I tend to pick it from boulders that it is draped over when the tide is out, rather than from rock pools. As each frond is a tube, sand that gets in through any nicks is trapped, and can never be washed out again. However, it makes the best crispy seaweed around in my opinion. Rinse the fronds well, then pat them dry (to prevent spitting) and deep-fry them for a mere minute. Then sprinkle with a pinch of salt, a little brown sugar and some toasted sesame seeds. Gutweed is also tasty as a lightly steamed vegetable, but if served in a salad needs to be marinated a little in the dressing to tenderise it before serving.

When Gutweed is young it is easy to confuse with other *Ulvas*, although this isn't a problem as they are also edible. You're most likely to come across the sea grasses *Ulva compressa* and *Ulva flexuosa*. One of the curious characteristics of the *Ulva* family is that some species can flatten two layers of cells together to form the lettuce and ribbon sheets, while others leave space between the two layers to form tubes. However, which form they choose to use can be entirely dependent on the environmental conditions around them. This can confuse us mere mortals when trying to tell the difference between one and the other!

Velvet Horn ✳ *Codium tomentosum*

Velvet Horn (also known as Spongeweed) is a branched green seaweed with cylindrical spongy stems. It is not abundant where I forage so I consider it a special treat and am careful to harvest sustainably – taking nothing if the populations are too small. It is our native *Codium* and is being displaced by the more invasive *Codium fragile* subsp. *tomentosoides*, which I am also happy to make a meal of. Both need to be picked young, as once the sponge texture has fully developed it makes for quite weird albeit not unpleasant eating. Like Bladderwrack, Velvet Horn also tastes of French beans, but has fewer tannins than young Bladderwrack fronds. I steam it for a few minutes until tender and eat it with melted Pepper Dulse butter, salt and black pepper.

The related species *Codium fragile* subsp. *tomentosoides* and *Codium fragile* subsp. *atlanticum* have both been found around the Irish and British coasts since the early 1800s, but originated in the Pacific. Their common names change from region to region: Dead Man's Fingers, Green Sea Fingers, Felty Fingers, Forked Felt-Alga, Stag Seaweed, Sponge Seaweed, Green Sponge, Green Fleece and the Oyster Thief. Common names can be confusing because they often work overtime. To me, the Oyster Thief is another recent arrival (1908), a brown seaweed shaped like a beige balloon called *Colpomenia peregrina*, which looks completely different. *Codium* likes rock pools on the lower shore and shellfish beds in the subtidal zone. If it attaches to a shell it can float away with it – hence Oyster Thief.

Occasionally you may find squashed, fuzzy, spongy, green balls on the shore, that are obviously made of seaweed threads of some sort. These are usually the Basque Beret *Codium bursa*, made of interwoven microscopic filaments. They look a little like freshwater algae *Cladophora* balls (marimo), now reclassified as *Aegagropila linnaei*, which are popular in aquariums.

PART FOUR

WILD
PANTRY

CHAPTER 13

Wild Flours

Living on an exclusively wild diet for a year forced me to re-evaluate many ideas about food that I took for granted. I realised that I couldn't survive by sticking to the same recipes and style of eating I was used to, because it's not always possible to find substitutes for farmed or agricultural produce among wild species. Many of the food groups that we depend on heavily today – and staples such as flour, sugar and dairy – just don't feature in a wild food diet. Adapting to my new lifestyle was a steep learning curve, but it encouraged me to be resourceful, and I discovered many new tasty or practical uses for the plants, fungi and algae that I foraged, which helped to keep my cupboards, fridge and freezer well stocked.

Thinking beyond wheat

One of the biggest challenges I faced was what to do about flour. Society has taught us to associate flour with wheat, one of humankind's principal foods – but wheat doesn't grow in the wild in Britain. The term 'wheat' covers several grasses producing large grains in the

Poaceae family. On average, wheat grain contains around 70 per cent carbohydrate and, for years, carbs have been the base of most governments' advisory food pyramids. Today, 50 per cent of the world's daily calorie intake comes from just three species: wheat, corn and rice.

In more recent years, wheat grain has got a bad rap, with various diets encouraging people to cut it out of their diets altogether by pointing to the eating patterns of early man. It's not the case, however, that Palaeolithic people didn't eat grain-based carbs at all – they just didn't eat them *all year round*. Palaeolithic and earlier humans gathered grains from many different species of grasses and cereal crops, many of which they saved for the winter months. But before large farm storage complexes, they would have eaten most by the spring. There would then be a natural six-month or so gluten-free period while the next crop grew, produced and ripened seed. Wheat flour, like everything else, has a season.

Carbohydrates are a primary source of glucose, considered to be the body's main fuel, which our bodies store as glycogen primarily in the skeletal muscles, then the liver, with a little in the brain. But our bodies are like a hybrid car that can switch between food sources depending on what fuel is available at the time. If we run out of glycogen, the body can switch to ketone power (called 'ketosis'). Burning fat to release ketones is a slower form of energy release, which is why many people on a no-carb diet experience fatigue. Nature did not intend our bodies to run permanently on ketones. It is the body's emergency back-up system, not the main engine, there in order to make sure that our energy-intensive brain never runs out of power.

A low-carb diet should focus on complex carbs, and not just wheat, corn and rice. Complex carbohydrates, especially from roots, provide nutrients such as inulin that feed the good bacteria in our gut, as well as providing energy. There are seeds, nuts and roots that can be powdered to make flour-like alternatives, although some ingenuity is needed to help them stick together, as, with the exception of the Pooideae grass subfamily, none of them contain the gluten that makes them bind, stretch and rise. In the next pages, I've described some of the wilder or more unusual alternatives, and how you can produce them from species you have foraged.

Eating the lawn

Calories from carbohydrates are an important part of nutrition. One place they come from in the wild is seeds, which are easy to gather. At the end of July or August, when the grass is ripe, brown and dry with full heads of seed, you can harvest grass grains. On a dry day, pick the whole heads by cutting their stems. With some species you can pull the grain off the stem in the field. In past times, people also used seed beaters and would thrash all seed from a field of mixed grasses into a basket.

Break the husk from the stem and discard stems and any stray leafy material. If you need to store it at this stage, keep it in a paper sack to avoid mildew.

I use a bench-top flour mill, on a large setting, to crack and separate the husk and seed casing from the grain. The technical word for this is kibbling. You may need to experiment with the seed size and the setting to get it to crack the seed on the first pass instead of pulverising it. You don't want to crack the grain, just the outer case. Sieving it then separates much of the chaff, which is smaller than the grain. Follow this by winnowing the grain to release the last of the chaff. A second pass of the grain through the mill, on a fine setting, gives a reasonable flour.

Keeping an eye out for ergot

Ergot, or 'rye ergot fungus' *Claviceps purpurea*, is a poisonous fungus that infects rye and other Poaceae cereal grasses. It's not a mushroom but a sclerotium, a type of food storage organ made of densely-packed hyphae, oil and water. The sclerotium contains mycotoxic ergoline alkaloids, for example ergotamine, which constrict blood vessels. Ergot is the precursor of LSD (this is not something to experiment with) and the drug ergotamine, once used to stop post-partum bleeding.

In the Middle Ages, ergotism was widespread as no one associated eating rye bread – popular as it grows in poor soils – with the madness and illness that follows. It was called St Anthony's Fire, as his ordeals of *ignis sacer* – the holy fire burning inside him – suggest ergot poisoning. When blood vessels constrict, neurological problems develop characterised by tics, twitches and spasms, paranoia and hallucinations. When the circulation stops, fingers and toes swell and go numb, as the tissues die. Gangrene sets in, they go black and often need to be amputated. Mental deranged peasants – the nobility ate white bread – suffering convulsions and the feeling of ants crawling under the skin, were assumed to be possessed by the devil or cursed by witches. Black 'bruises' where tissue was dying off were thought to be 'witch marks'. The Finnmark witch trials in the 17th century record very clear accounts of this medieval medical mystery.

Unfortunately, ergot thrives in conditions that are constantly damp, so it's widespread in the British Isles. I've seen it all the way from East Anglia to Scotland! You can spot ergot by closely examining the grains in the grass seed head. It looks like tiny pointed black fingers sticking out of the seeds but can infect grain even when it can't be seen. A fatal dose can be as low as 2 grams, taking effect from one to several days. The European Commission allow a maximum level of 0.5 g of ergot sclerotia to one kilo of unprocessed grain intended for human consumption. Although the alkaloids probably become inactive after around 18 months of storage, do not take risks by eating infected grain.

Poaceae – the grass family

Poaceae (also Graminaceae) is the family of 12,000
plus members that contains most gluten-yielding
grasses, specifically in the Pooideae subfamily. Many
of these are familiar: Wheat (including Durum,
Einkorn, Emmer), Barley, Rye and Oats. There is a wide
range of grasses with a history of human collection in
this family, including cereals, millets and other grasses.
Rye *Secale cereale* (shown here and not to be confused with
Perennial Ryegrass *Lolium perenne*), was the only bread grain
used by many Europeans for centuries, as it is less affected by
the winter frosts, diseases, drought and lack of nutrients in the
harsh climates of Central and Northern Europe. It was often simply
called 'the grain' with a similar nutritional
profile to oats.

MAIN FORAGING SPECIES

Black Bent ✳ *Agrostis gigantea*
Also known as Redtop or Dew-grass and
common throughout most of England, with less
density in the north and Scotland, the grain was
used in medieval Germany to make pottage and
porridge. It can certainly still be used to make both
and flour.

The medieval herbalist Gerard says:

*"Dew-Grass hath very hard and tough roots long and fibrous: the stalks
are great, of three or four cubits high, very rough and hairy, jointed and
kneed like the common Reed: the leaves are large and broad like unto
corn. The tuft or ear is divided into sundry branches, chaffy, and of a
purple colour; wherein is contained seed like Milium, wherewith the
Germans do make pottage and such like meat, as we in England do with
Oatmeal; and it is sent into Middleborough and other towns of the Low-
countries, in great quantity for the same purpose..."* [22]

Cock's Foot ✳ *Dactylis glomerata*
Pick the whole heads by cutting their stems on a dry day. Then winnow and mill. There is a high ratio of husk to seed which makes it arduous to process, with low return. The seed yield is only about 20 per cent, but it does taste good. The rainy, humid summers in Scotland make this species particularly susceptible to infection by the poisonous fungus Ergot, so make sure to check for it before harvesting.

Common Reed ✳ *Phragmites australis*
As well as using it to thatch your cottage, you can dry the young stalks and roots of the Common Reed and mill them into a sweet flour or starch. The root may contain as much as 5 per cent sugar, and a sugary gum can sometimes be extracted from inside the shoots. There are also records of the shoots and young leaves being eaten – or dried, ground and mixed into flour – in Japan. The small seed is difficult to de-husk but toast it to singe off the fluff, then grind into a meal.

Couchgrass ✳ *Elymus repens*
Couchgrass doesn't have much in the way of harvestable seeds – only about twenty-five seeds per plant. The eighteenth-century British botanist William Withering writes, 'The roots dried and ground to meal have been used to make bread in years of scarcity.' He also advises singing off the hair on the grain before using it. The roots are starchy and make a reasonable flour. The juicy, tender, white lateral roots spread invasively, so it's good to find a use for them. In herbal medicine, Couchgrass is used as a bladder antibiotic and tonic for urinary tract infections. The seeds of Crested Wheatgrass, another Elymus species, were also collected and ground into a mush in North America. As far as I can gather, a 'mush' is a thick porridge made by pouring boiling water over the seeds and leaving them to swell before eating it.

Floating Sweetgrass ❋ *Glyceria fluitans*

This may well be referred to in ancient texts by the name *Manna esculentum*. In Germany, Bohemia and Italy it was cultivated for sale and added to bread or used to make pottage, in the same way that the English used oatmeal. In English it was variously called Manna-grass, Dew-grass or Rice-grass.[23]

There are records of use in Germany, Lithuania, Prussia and Poland. Floating Sweetgrass seeds were cooked into 'Schwaden grütze (groats)' or 'Frankfurter grütze' with milk or butter.[24] In Poland, 'manna grass' was the first edible wild grass documented in the 1380s as an alternative to millet, in 1595.[25] Wild Manna grass was used by villagers to pay tax to local landowners by villagers. Various nuts, honey, farmed grains and Manna were paid as a tithe in November at Martinmas. It was considered superior to cultivated Manna, a millet called *Digitaria sanguinalis*, being sweeter and often used in desserts. Some would gather wild Manna just to pay the tax. For although it's a moderately high-yielding weed it is expensive because of the time it takes to harvest it. Eventually, by the 1800s, as its marshland habitat dwindled and paying tithes went out of fashion, its use declined. It has hardly been recorded since 1914.[26]

It grows throughout the whole of the British Isles and is due a revival in popularity. Harvest it in July. It is best picked early on a dry morning before the seeds fall out.

Great Brome ✳ *Bromus diandrus*

Also known as 'ripgut brome' because of its sharp, pointed fruits which can pierce animals' nostrils, Great Brome was sometimes harvested from the wild and used as a food grain, probably mixed with cultivated grains. You can try all of the bromes.

Lyme Grass (Sand Ryegrass) ✳ *Leymus arenarius*

Lyme Grass grows all around the coasts and is an important grass for stabilising sand dunes. It is about a metre high and a distinctive blue-green-grey colour with seed heads that ripen in July. The seed, while delicious, can be difficult to process. It can either be ground into flour or cooked like rice in both savoury and dessert courses.

Marram Grass ✳ *Ammophila arenaria*

Like Lyme Grass, Marram Grass is found around the coast and is harvested in July. Also like Lyme Grass, it sends out underground rhizomes that help to stabilise dunes and stop erosion. So please don't dig it up. The yield of seed to husk is around 50 per cent.

Perennial Ryegrass ✳ *Lolium perenne*

Perennial Ryegrass is found in the UK both wild and sown in the 'improved grass' mixes used to grow hay and silage for animal fodder. It is one the few wild grasses that contains gluten – so can be made into a risen bread – so it's worth adding to your flour mixes. It contains small but prolific seed in large amounts. However, given that in Europe it represents up to 50 per cent of the grass seed market, one might argue that it is no longer wild. I think of it as the pheasant of the grass family.

Red Fescue ✳ *Festuca rubra*
and *Meadow Fescue* ✳ *Festuca pratensis*
Red Fescue is widespread everywhere in the UK
and Ireland. I have found it to give a 15 per cent
yield grain to chaff. Meadow Fescue has relatively
large seeds and has a historic use in Poland, so there
is no reason it couldn't also be used in the UK.

Rice Cutgrass ✳ *Leersia oryzoides*
A rough-leaved grass that likes the
trampled nutrient-rich mud around watering
holes, ponds, ditches, brooks and canals in the south
of Britain, with one instance recorded in Cambridge.
Its range has been decreasing since 1992 as the habitat
changes but it is being reintroduced in some places. As the
name suggests, the grains can be boiled as a wild rice.

Rye Brome ✳ *Bromus secalinus*
A grass with a comparatively large seed head that has a tradition of
food use in Poland.[27] It was boiled into groats – a type of medieval
porridge – or mixed with cultivated grains to make them go further. It
wasn't eaten much on its own as it was thought to have poor nutritional
value. It is mainly found in England as an agricultural weed.

The grain (or seed) is inside a papery husk. Chaff is the word used to
describe the bits you don't want. You release the grain from the chaff
by breaking it (threshing) and separating it (winnowing).

Timothy Grass ✳ Phleum pratense

You can eat the seeds of Timothy Grass, which can be found in abundance throughout the UK. It has long cylindrical heads – about 3.5 centimetres long – and a lot of seed. Not all gluten-free flours will rise with yeast, but Timothy Grass will.

Yorkshire Fog ✳ Holcus lanatus

This is a soft-to-touch grass that grows everywhere. Pick the heads by running the stems through your hand. The seeds detach easily and quickly, filling a sack in no time. Then winnow and mill. The seed is quite small but tasty. The yield from my lawn last summer was around 37.5 per cent grain to chaff collected.

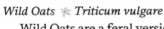

Wild Oats ✳ Triticum vulgare

Wild Oats are a feral version of cultivated oats but with much smaller seed heads. Nevertheless, I am able to get a 60–70 per cent yield ration, and probably with more wholesome bran still attached.

Cyperaceae – the sedge family

Sedges are perennial grass-like plants covering 5,500 species, but they are not classed as grasses. Grasses and rushes have both male and female parts within the same flower. However, sedges are monoecious – meaning they have separated reproductive parts. The male flower spikes are at the top of the stem and the female flower spikes are further down. All sedges are edible although some are much more useful to foragers than others. Many are grown in the UK as ornamental plants, their owners never suspecting their useful value as a food crop. The best known are probably Papyrus *Cyperus papyrus*, the Chinese Water Chestnut *Eleocharis dulcis*, and the Chufa or Tiger Nut *Cyperus esculentus*, which has decent-sized tubers that make a slightly sweet, fine flour.

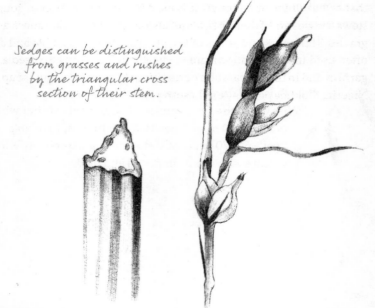

Sedges can be distinguished from grasses and rushes by the triangular cross section of their stem.

Key features

Sedges have triangular stems with no joints, whereas grasses have round stems and jointed nodes. Here is a useful rhyme to distinguish between grasses, sedges and rushes: 'Sedges have edges, rushes are round, and grasses have knees where the leaves are found.' The defining feature of a sedge is a bract (called the utricle) around the female flower that has a long tip (beak) which splits into two at the end.

MAIN FORAGING SPECIES

Pendulous Sedge Seed ✳ *Carex pendula*
This is a native sedge that spreads very thickly in damp areas, in large clumps, often beside low-lying rivers. The arching seed heads are easy to gather and provide abundant seed in July. When I've harvested it, I have got a 90 per cent grain to chaff yield from it after winnowing, the highest of my 'lawn experiments'. Most of the *Carex* species of sedges also have edible roots.

Galingale ✳ *Cyperus longus*
Galingale is the largest *Cyperus* species in the UK. Records show that the tubers were once boiled and eaten by peasants in times of famine. The root is edible and has a nutty flavour that is similar to that of hazelnuts or almonds. It is used in the preparation of soups, stews, curries and other dishes, and also as a thickener in sauces and gravies. The leaves and stems of the plant are likewise edible and are often used in salads and as a green vegetable. They are also used as a garnish and in the preparation of traditional dishes like Egusi soup in Nigeria, Mokhoa oa tsenya in Lesotho and Ugali in Kenya.

Flours from pulses

Like gram flour from chick peas, the peas from vetches like Common Vetch *Vicia sativa* (see page 92), can also be used to make flour. However, it's important to remember that they contain lectins and anti-nutrients. Anti-nutrients prevent your body from using essential amino acids and minerals. In legumes they include: 1) proteins (amylase inhibitors, protease inhibitors and lectins), and 2) other substances (phytates, saponins, tannins, polyphenol compounds, non-protein amino acids and galactomannan gums). You can neutralise many (but not all) of these by soaking pulses in five times the amount of water (overnight or for up to 24 hours), rinsing, then cooking thoroughly and rinsing again. This helps to reduce most of the inhibitory action. Remember that even domestic beans have to be soaked overnight, the water changed and then boiled for at least 20 minutes in order not to be poisonous.

Any pulses you use to make flour substitutes must be cooked then dried again – I use a dehydrator – before milling. Flours made from unsoaked, uncooked pulses will still inhibit your enzymes.

Flour from roots, rhizomes and tubers

Roots, rhizomes and tubers – all types of underground starch storage organs – are often dug up in the late autumn when the plant's energy returns below the ground and fattens them up. They lie dormant during the winter, the future food of a new plant due to come up in the spring. Early spring brings another opportunity to dig them up as the ground thaws, and the first few emerging leaves mark their presence below. Once they are fully in leaf, the new growth has used up the carb store provided by the root and the plant's energy has moved from the root to the leaf. For the best taste and nutritional value, roots should be dug in the late autumn and early spring when there is minimal foliage.

In the UK we don't make as much use of our native wild roots as we could. The law against digging up roots discourages experimentation. Critically – whatever the law – you must harvest sustainably. When I have the landowner's permission, I use the opportunity to do a bit of wild gardening. I make sure that the patch of soil I have dug over is replanted with well-spaced rhizomes or tubers, which allows plants to regenerate. This practice also yields a larger harvest in years to come. I don't harvest from the same area two years in succession.

Roots are an important ingredient to give flavour and body to stocks and soups, and recipes often call for the addition of a carrot or parsnip to a stock. But don't forget the edible roots with medicinal uses, too. Dandelion root is great for the liver and Burdock root will also help to clear the skin and ease the joints.

Roots of all thistles, Common Hogweed, Sweet Cicely and Wild Carrot are edible but need to be gathered from young plants or they are woody and tough. Tubers of Pignut, Silverweed and Marsh Woundwort can be added towards the end of cooking. Bulbs of Wild Garlic, wild leeks and day lilies all provide winter calories.

If you prefer to peel roots, do so before drying them. I just scrub them, aware that many nutrients are concentrated just under the skin. Cut them into pieces and dry them at a temperature of 35 to 50 degrees C. Dehydrated roots have a tendency to go mouldy so they're best stored in paper bags somewhere cool. Mill them to a powder, once dry, to make starches and flours. These augment traditional grains for use in breads, gnocchi, biscuits and baking.

Main foraged species with edible roots useful as flour:

Alexanders ✳ Smyrnium olusatrum	see page 51
Burdock ✳ Arctium lappa and A. minus	see page 60
Dandelion ✳ Taraxacum officinale	see page 61
Pignut ✳ Conopodium majus	see page 61
Marsh Woundwort ✳ Stachys palustris	see page 102
Reedmace ✳ Typha latifolia	see page 128
Silverweed ✳ Potentilla anserina	see page 124
Tuberous Comfrey ✳ Symphytum tuberosum	see page 66
Wild Carrot ✳ Daucus carota	see page 52

Here are some less commonly used species that are worth knowing in case of famine.

Also called Cuckoo-pint, Lords-and-Ladies, or Jack in the Pulpit, the roots of **Arum lily** *Arum maculatum*, known as corms, contain a white, acrid sap. Arum roots are a wholesome food – once roasted and ground into a starchy powder – but they must never be eaten raw. The acridity is removed by roasting or thorough drying but, without heat, it takes from twelve to eighteen months to neutralise. Dig up the corms after the leaves have died back or before the spring growth unfurls. On the Isle of Portland, Dorset, the plants were once so abundant and food so often scarce, that the washed starch – reminiscent of arrowroot – was named Portland Sago due to its popularity with the islanders. The starch was also used to stiffen Elizabethan ruffs and laundry.

The UK is also now host to the introduced species **Dragon Arum** *Dracunculus vulgaris*. Like Arum Lily it is very acrid and if any parts are inadvertently eaten will cause swelling of the mouth and difficulties breathing. The root must be properly processed with heat to render the fine starch safe.

The **Bog Arum** *Calla palustris* is another arum resident in Britain that can be processed this way into a rich and tasty flour. To avoid harmful reactions, all must be processed with great care to destroy the calcium oxalate crystals that cause harmful reactions.

The name **Flowering Rush** *Butomus umbellatus* is deceptive as it is not a rush at all. It's a flowering plant (order *Alismatales*) that likes growing at the edges of ponds and still water. The roots can be dried and ground into a starchy flour.

Nut flours

Nut flours are satisfying to make. Being so much larger than seeds you get more calories for less effort. They also contain healthy oils and fats. We have a variety of nuts in the UK but nut trees are far more fruitful in the south than the colder northern climate. In the south, you find hazelnuts, cobnuts, acorns, walnuts, sweet chestnuts and even almonds. In the north, only hazelnuts and acorns flourish although sweet chestnut can fruit.

Main foraged nuts useful as flour:

Acorns ✳ *Quercus* spp.	see page 156
Sweet Chestnut ✳ *Castanea sativa*	see page 159
Hazelnuts ✳ *Corylus avellana*	see page 155
Walnuts ✳ *Juglans regia*	see page 160
Monkey Puzzle pine nuts ✳ *Araucaria araucana*	see page 174
Beech nuts ✳ *Fagus sylvatica*	see page 150
Sweet Almonds ✳ *Prunus dulcis*	

Making nut flours at home is pretty straightforward. However, the natural oil content of nuts can make it a little tricky if you're not careful. The key is to start with completely dry nuts. Toasting or roasting them lightly can help, which also brings out a richer flavour. Just cool them down before you grind them. Put a small amount into a food processor or blender and pulse in short bursts instead of blending continuously. This prevents heat from building up, which could release the oils and turn your nuts into butter. Sift the powdered nuts through a fine mesh sieve – any larger pieces can go back into the processor for another round. Store nut flours in airtight containers in the fridge or freezer to keep them fresh, as the oil content can make them go rancid at room temperature.

ACORNS

How to process acorns

Acorns *Quercus* spp. can be collected from mid-September, when they start to turn from green to brown, up to November – if the squirrels haven't got there first. As they ripen, they fall on to the ground and can be easily collected into a backpack – easier to carry than in a basket as they are heavy. Reject any that have insect holes in them and remove the cups from the base. Don't store them in their shells too long and allow them to dry out, as they are easier to shell when they are still moist and flexible.

Shelling is best done by inviting friends round for an evening, and getting everyone to join in – many hands make light work. Ideally, the acorns should be fresh enough that their outer skin peels away easily. The discarded shells can be used as a mulch around plants or put on to paths, especially the muddy patches. Or they can be dried and used for kindling or composted with leaves and grass clippings. Acorns are made up of two halves, so chop the peeled nuts across the middle and they'll fall into four quarters. Cut off any bad bits – mould or worm holes. Put the nut pieces into a tub of cold water as soon as they're out of their shells to stop them oxidising.

Leaching acorns

Once shelling is done you can start leaching the chopped nuts. Leaching is the process of soaking the acorns in water to remove the bitter tannins that make your mouth dry up; oak bark was traditionally used to tan leather, giving it its characteristic deep-brown colour and dried-out, leathery feel – a feature you don't want to adopt for your intestines.

The finer you chop the acorns before leaching, the more starch you will get settling out. Acorn starch is not the same as acorn flour or meal. The starch is what gives this gluten-free flour some binding ability. You can collect it separately – for instance, if you wanted to make Korean *dotorimuk* – or reincorporate it with your final flour. To retain the most starch, before leaching, blitz your nut pieces in a blender with some *cold* water until you have a thick meal.

Soak the acorns or acorn meal in a tub or bucket of cold water. (Hot water methods speed up the leaching process so that it happens in hours rather than days, but heat will destroy the starch and darken the flour.) You want at least 50 per cent of your mix to be extra water. The water will go brown as the tannins leach out.

After the first day, loosen any nut skins that didn't come away in the shelling process and fish them out with a straining spoon. (Freezing freshly collected acorns helps the skins to come away with the shells once thawed and cracked, but I rarely have freezer space to do this.) It doesn't matter if some skins remain but too many will darken the flour and make it more bitter, as they are tannin-rich. Change the water once a day until it no longer goes brown. Depending on your acorn species, this can take a week – longer if you forget to change the water daily. This is not a disaster but if you leave your acorns in the same water for too long, or in too warm a place, they will start to ferment, or even sprout, which will affect the flavour of your flour.

If you want to collect the useful acorn starch – which collects as a sediment on the bottom of the tub – it is best to siphon off the water carefully rather than just pouring it out. Or, if you must pour it, do so through cheesecloth or muslin to retain as much of the starch and fats as possible. Most of this will gradually settle on the bottom like thick sticky caramel-coloured house paint that needs to be scraped out with a spatula at the end. I prefer siphoning. I hold the tube just above the water level so it doesn't disturb the starch sediment, and filter out the water at the final rinse through a large cotton cloth jelly bag strainer that prevents any starch from escaping. Draining the acorns or acorn meal gets as much of the water out as possible before it goes into the dryer.

Once the water runs completely clear, the leaching is finished. The chopped acorns or acorn meal will taste bland. It now needs to be dried on fine mesh trays in a dehydrator at 35 degrees C. If you don't have a dehydrator, spread the acorns out on trays in the sun, turning over regularly, or in a very low-heat oven with the door slightly open to release the moisture. Higher temperatures change the taste of the flour.

Once dry, you can store acorn pieces in a brown paper bag or sack in a cool place away from oxidising light. Store dried meal in a jar in a dark cupboard. Meal keeps better for longer than the ground flour, so I make up small batches of flour as I need it.

To make acorn flour, grind the dried pieces or acorn meal in a flour mill. A powerful blender will work for small batches but will need to be sifted for a fine flour. The advantage of a flour mill is that you can change the settings and produce a coarse flour, like a polenta, or a very fine flour, like cornflour.

Leaching shortcuts

We foragers, over time, have come up with some labour-saving ways to process acorns: putting them into baskets and leaving them in a stream for a few weeks; burying them underground in a boggy place and coming back several months or a year later. But the prize for the most ingenious method has to go to my forager friend Lisa, who fills half her toilet cistern with acorns – allowing her to simultaneously save water and leach the acorns. She knows the acorns are ready once the water stops flushing brown and clear water runs through. Of course, be sure only to do this with a clean cistern and no fragrance block.

Acorn nutrition

One or two days spent collecting acorns can provide enough of them to feed a family for the winter. As a rough guide, 100 acorns weigh around 500 grams and will give you 100 grams of flour, providing 500 calories of energy. So if you plan for one acorn per 1 gram of flour, it is easy to calculate how many you need to collect to last the winter.

Pedunculate
Oak leaf

Pedunculate
Oak acorn

Sessile
Oak leaf

Sessile
Oak acorn

OTHER NUT FLOURS

Sweet Chestnut flour

This is made by milling the dried kernels of Sweet Chestnut (page 159) into a slightly grainy, sweet flour. It is easy to make and can be done in different ways.

The first method is to bake the chestnuts before peeling. Score an X on the flat side of the nut's shell with a knife. Put the scored nuts on to a baking sheet and roast them in a preheated oven at 200 degrees C for 20–25 minutes. Remove them from the oven and let them cool until you can handle them easily but they are still warm. The skins should have started to curl back at the X – use this to help you peel the chestnuts. Then chop them roughly.

Alternatively, peel the nuts while they are raw and chop them roughly. Whether you roast them or keep them raw is just a matter of personal preference as there is a slight difference in the taste of the flour.

Either way, once you have chopped the pieces, put them into a dehydrator. Dehydrate them at 40 degrees C until they are so hard you can no longer break them by hand. This can take anywhere from eight to sixteen hours, depending how small you have chopped the nuts.

Once dried, feed the nut pieces through a flour mill, on a coarse setting for polenta or on a fine setting for pastry flour. (You can use a blender for small batches but will have to sift the flour and put larger pieces back in for re-blending. It will not be as fine and the heat of the blender can make the flour a bit oily.) Store the flour in an airtight pouch or jar in a cool, dark place.

Hazelnut flour

You can make an excellent nutty flour from hazelnuts from the Hazel *Corylus avellana* (page 155). Shell and chop the nuts. Leave them in a cool, well-ventilated place for a few days to dry out, turning them twice a day, or dehydrate them at 35 degrees C. Once dried, feed them through a flour mill on a fine setting. They are quite an oily nut so try to just pass them once through the mill.

Walnut flour

Walnuts tend to be too oily to make successful flour at home. Commercial walnut flour is made by grinding the nut-cake residue after the oil has been pressed out of it. It's not impossible to make a coarse meal at home though, if you have access to a Walnut tree (page 160). Just put half a cup of walnuts into a food processor and pulse until they're the consistency of breadcrumbs. If you over-blend them they'll turn into a delicious nut butter instead of meal.

Deliberately making walnut butter at home is very simple, and you only need walnuts. Start with fresh, shelled walnuts. If you lightly toast them in an oven (around 175°C for 8–10 minutes) it is easier to remove the papery skin, which can be a little bitter. Let them cool completely before blending. Put the walnuts into a food processor or high-speed blender and let it run – unlike the short blasts to make flour. Pause occasionally to scrape down the sides. Initially you'll have a dry, crumbly mix, but keep blending for 5 to 10 minutes until the natural oils release and the mix transforms to a smooth, creamy butter.

Orache seed flour

All of the oraches, Fat Hen (see page 42), Good King Henry (see page 43) Sea Purslane *Atriplex portulacoides* and the seaside oraches (see page 45) produce a lot of seed that is easy to gather, but takes quite a bit of processing. Fat Hen, in particular, was an important crop in the Late Bronze Age when large quantities were gathered and threshed. Harvest it just as the seed cases start to turn from green to red, as the bitterness increases the longer you leave it. Inside the seed cases (the chaff), there are tiny black seeds. The chaff is, unfortunately, high in saponins so you have to separate the seed from it or eating it will make you feel queasy.

The minute seed size makes it difficult to work when grinding it for flour. One way is to part-grind it in a mill, on an open setting to crack the seed. A blender will do if you don't have a mill. Then winnow it as much as you can, shaking it and blowing off the chaff. Once you have removed as much chaff as possible, grind it into a rough flour and cook it like a polenta. Diluting it by adding it into nut flours before baking makes it easier to digest.

Some people prefer to wash off the chaff. To do this, put the grain into a bowl of warm water and agitate it, rubbing your hands through the grain. You may notice the soapy saponins forming light bubbles; you can change the water through a sieve to rinse this away. The chaff doesn't easily float to the top but as you stir the mix, it will rise higher than the seed and you can scoop it off. Pour the water off with care, removing the chaff but keeping the black seeds behind. You can then dry the seeds out, making sure they are fully dry before storing them.

Alternatively try soaking them for 24 hours, rinsing them and then sprouting them. Once drained, spread them out on a tray or oven dish, with some moist paper beneath them or a damp tea towel over the top. These can then be cooked or dehydrated and ground into a sprouted flour which is much more digestible.

Cooking the separated seed is straightforward. Simmer it for around 30 minutes in fresh water. It will be crunchy, not as soft as quinoa. The best recipes are those when it is mixed in with another grain, corn or wild rice. Or sauté them with Wild Garlic or wild leeks when making a soup or a stew. Grinding the seed also gives a flour.

Seed or sprouted flours can be used in pancakes, dumplings, biscuits, seed mixes and wild muesli.

Given the amount of work, Fat Hen may seem off-putting but the seed is prolific, keeps well and on a wild food diet a little goes a long way.

Other useful seeds to add to flours for baking and cooking:

Bistort seed * Bistorta officinalis	see page 119
Broad-leaf Dock * Rumex obtusifolius	see page 118
Charlock (wild mustard) * Sinapis arvensis	see page 75
Curly Dock * Rumex crispus	
Fennel, Wild * Foeniculum vulgare	
Hogweed, Common * Heracleum sphondylium	see page 48
Lovage * Levisticum officinal	
Milk Thistle * Silybum marianum	see page 61
Nasturtium * Tropaeolum majus	
Nettle seed * Urtica dioica	see page 130
Plantain * Plantago spp.	see page 112
Poppy * Papaver somniferum and P. rhoeas	
Sweet Cicely * Myrrhis odorata	see page 51
Thistles * Cirsium spp.	see page 61

Basically, anything that you can make into a powder, which also tastes reasonable, can be used to bulk out your wild flours. Foragers are resourceful people and will use everything from ground Dock seed, Pine pollen, Reedmace pollen and Reedmace seed-head fluff to Hazel catkins, and the inner bark of Pine and Birch to survive on. These additions are never usually used as the main flour, as the calorific content is not high enough, but they can add flavour, colour, texture or micronutrients.

CHAPTER 14

Wild Spices

Despite most of our well-known culinary spice seeds coming from relatives in the Apiaceae family – Coriander, Cumin, Caraway, Dill, Fennel, Anise – wild seeds are often overlooked when foraging. However, many can be used to replace shop-bought spices or even, in some cases, add a whole new taste sensation – and they are free.

For example, if you went to a market in Iran and asked for 30 grams of *golpar* you'd be given Persian Hogweed *Heracleum persicum* seed. Like our own Common Hogweed *Heracleum sphondylium*, it tastes like green coriander seed that's been infused in orange oil. Hogweed seed powder (*golpar koobideh*) is a key ingredient in *advieh*, a Persian spice blend similar to the Indian *garam masala*, and sprinkled over bean and lentil dishes to reduce their flatulent effects. Golpar is also often ground with salt to make a seasoning called *golpar namak*.

Incidentally, Wild Rue seeds *Peganum harmala* (Persian: *esfand*) are mixed with golpar seeds, frankincense resin and earth or sand from your garden, and burnt as an incense over hot charcoal to avert the evil eye.

Some wild spice substitutes for your spice rack:

Wild spice conversion chart :

Aniseed	*Green Sweet Cicely* seed * *Myrrhis odorata* *Aniseed Funnel* * *Clitocybe odora*
Black Cumin (Nigella)	*Alexanders* seed * *Smyrnium olusatrum*
Caraway	*Whorled Caraway* * *Trocdaris verticillata*
Cardamon	*Common Hogweed* seed * *Heracleum sphondylium* *Wild Carrot* seed * *Daucus carota*
Celery seed	*Scots Lovage* seed * *Ligusticum scoticum*
Chilli pepper	*Water-pepper*, raw * *Persicaria hydropiper* *Toothwort* root * *Lathraea squamaria* *Dittander (dittany)* * *Lepidium latifolium* also adds some heat, as will some *Russula* mushrooms
Clove	*Wood Avens* root * *Geum urbanum*
Coriander, fresh cut	*Sea Arrowgrass* * *Triglochin maritima* *Spignel* * *Meum athamanticum*
Coriander, seed	*Dried Hogweed* seed * *Heracleum sphondylium* (like coriander with an orange citrus aroma) *Spignel* seed * *Meum athamanticum*
Cumin	*Wild Angelica* seeds * *Angelica sylvestris*
Curry	*Toasted Spignel* seed * *Meum athamanticum* dried *Curry Milkcap* * *Lactarius camphoratus*
Fennel seed	*Wild Fennel* seed * *Foeniculum vulgare*
Fenugreek	*Scots Lovage* seed * *Ligusticum scoticum*
Garlic	Pungent bulbils and bulbs of all of: *Wild Garlic* * *Allium ursinum* *Few-flowered Leek* * *Allium paradoxum* *Three-cornered Leek* * *Allium triquetrum* *Crow Garlic* * *Allium vineale* *Rosy Garlic* * *Allium roseum*

Ginger	*Magnolia* petals * *Magnolia* spp. *Sweet Flag* rhizome * *Acorus calamus*: sweet flavour profile of ginger, cinnamon and nutmeg with a bitter note
Hempseed	*Nettle seed * Urtica dioica*
Horseradish	*Wild Horseradish * Armoracia rusticana*
Lemon, flakes	*Staghorn Sumac * Rhus typhina*
Mustard	*Black Mustard* seed * *Brassica nigra* *Hedge Mustard * Sisymbrium officinale* *Nasturtium* seed * *Tropaeolum majus* *Garlic Mustard* seed * *Alliaria petiolata* young *Black Mustard* pods * *Brassica nigra* young *Wild Radish* pods * *Raphanus raphanistrum*
Parsley	*Cow Parsley * Anthriscus sylvestris* *Ground Elder * Aegopodium podagraria*
Pepper	*Pepper Dulse * Osmudea pinnatifida* *Water-pepper * Persicaria hydropiper* dried, powdered *Toothwort* herb * *Lathraea squamaria* *Peppery Bolete * Chalciporus piperatus*
Rosemary	*Yarrow leaf * Achillea millefolium* *Flowering Currant* blossom * *Ribes sanguineum*
Salt	Any powdered seaweed
Sichuan pepper	*Sneezewort flowers * Achillea ptarmica*
Tarragon	*Rock Samphire * Crithmum maritimum* *Golden Samphire * Limbarda (prev. Inula) crithmoides*
Thyme	*Wild Thyme * Thymus serphylum* *Flowering Currant* blossom * *Ribes sanguineum*
Turmeric	dried, ground *Elecampane* root * *Inula helenium*
Vanilla	*Sweet Woodruff * Galium odoratum*
Wasabi	*Scurvy Grass * Cochlearia officinalis* *Sea Radish * Raphanus maritimus*

Try making your own spice blends. Here is a suggestion.

Wild curry powder

Take ½ teaspoon to 1 teaspoon each of Alexanders seed, Common Hogweed seed, Wild Fennel seed, Scots Lovage seed, dried Wood Avens root, Sea Arrowgrass seed and/or wild Sumac. Grind all the seeds into a powder and mix well. Experiment with different combinations, and write down the quantities so you can replicate a particularly nice mix.

If you want to make a Thai green curry that calls for coconut, consider adding in some Coconut Milkcap mushrooms *Lactarius glyciosmus* or a concentrated extract of Gorse flowers *Ulex europaeus* picked on a warm day.

Not all seasonings are spices. It is worth mentioning capers – the unripened, green flower buds of the Caper bush (*Capparis spinosa* var. *inermis*) – as these add sour-salty piquancy to sauces, mayonnaise and dishes. Many buds, berries and seeds can be macerated in vinegar to use as a substitute. Common pickled alternatives are:

Lesser Celandine buds ❋ *Ranunculus ficaria*
Nasturtium seeds ❋ *Tropaeolum majus*
Elderberries (green unripe) ❋ *Sambucus nigra*
Dandelion buds ❋ *Taraxacum officinale*
Ox-eye Daisy flower buds ❋ *Leucanthemum vulgare*

There are also amazing citrussy alternatives to Lemon, such as Common Sorrel *Rumex acetosa*, Wood Sorrel *Oxalis acetosellaa*, Sea Buckthorn *Hippophae rhamnoides* and even the young tips of European Spruce *Picea abies* and other conifers. Grated Crab Apple, or Flowering Quince fruits in the Chaenomeles family, make a wonderful alternative to lemon juice and zest.

Chocolate

When I was preparing to live only from foraged food in Scotland, I thought there would be three things I'd miss: coffee, chocolate and citrus juice (lemon, lime and orange). I was delighted to realise I could find substitutes for all three. For coffee there's Cleavers (page 127), for citrus juice there's Sea Buckthorn (pages 85–86), and for cocoa there's Linden.

Linden is a collective name for the European Lime trees: the Common Lime *Tilia x europaea*, the Small-leaved Lime *Tilia cordata* and the Large-leaved Lime *Tilia platyphyllos*. Despite the name the fruits do not resemble the tropical citrus lime at all but are hard, round seeds the size of garden peas. These seeds are remarkably like cocoa with a slight hint of coffee. (However, the American Basswood *Tilea americana* is bitter and not a good substitute.)

You can grind the young, green immature seeds, which have the strongest chocolate flavour, into a paste. Pound them up in a pestle and mortar or food processor with a splash of hazelnut oil to make a wild 'Nutella' spread. Adding some powdered, dried Linden flowers adds to the depth of the chocolate flavour. To make this successfully, the seeds need to be very young, still green and you should be able to cut them easily with a knife. The mature seeds are less chocolate-like and more coffee-like.

My favourite way to use them is to roast the seeds and powder them. Then boil a tablespoon in a cupful of hazelnut milk and add a generous tablespoon of honey. This is like drinking liquid praline. The shelf life of dried seeds is not long and the chocolate flavours vanish quickly – so use it or lose it.

CHAPTER 15

Wild Sugar

In the wild, sugar – *when in season* – is most easily found in the form of fruits or honey. Tree saps can also be evaporated to make a sweet syrup (see Chapter 7) but the yields from our native trees are low and time-consuming. Tropical foragers have it much easier as cane, coconut and palm saps can be cooked into hard lumps of unprocessed sugar. As a child, growing up in East Africa, it was a real treat to be given a mouth-melting sweet, dark curl shaved from a jaggery cone – a blend of raw cane juice boiled with palm sap into a hard crystal lump that we called *sukari ngutu* in Swahili. My experience of eating wild food only for a year is that there are very few sources of sugar available to the British or Irish forager. Sadly, it is now so rare to see a wild beehive that even wild honey is hard to come by.

In the first century of the Common Era, sugar was only used for medicinal purposes. Although rich people had access to it in the 16th century, it wasn't until the early 19th century that it became cheap enough to be widely available – due to the discovery in 1747 that sugar could be industrially extracted from sugar beets. At this point,

Britain was consuming half the sugar imported into the whole of Europe and it was inextricably linked with the horrific slave trade and colonisation of other countries on which many of the leading British families built their wealth until the Slavery Abolition Act in Britain in 1833. Global sugar production is now 191 million tons of sugar per year.[28] If you divide that by the world population of 8,045,311,447 (estimated by UNICEF in 2023), that's 23.74 kilograms of sugar per person per year.[29]

Although the recommended daily limit (RDL) for added sugar is 30 grams per person (10.95 kilograms per year), the average Briton gets through two to three times that amount. I would argue that *nowhere* in our history prior to 1800 were we ever able to get our hands on even 30 grams a day. We're paying for it with our health.

Sugar is one of the things that people think they will crave the most if they have to go without. In practice though, we are quickly weaned off it and, on a wild food diet, the cravings go in about seven days as our microbiome changes. What we call a 'sweet tooth' is often the hungry cry of *Candida albicans* resident in our gut (or a blood sugar imbalance from a diet high in carbohydrates).

Sugar has a specific season. Fruit in the summer and autumn; occasional honey in the summer and autumn; and very small amounts of tree sap sugars from December to March. Even eating 30 grams a day is contrary to a wild way of living.

Plants high in sugar

Common Polypody *Polypodium vulgare* is an evergreen fern in the *Polypodiaceae* family that is widespread across the UK and Ireland. It has a saponin compound called osladin in the rhizomes that is some 500 times sweeter than sugar. It's just as well that you only need to use a little as the rhizome can also be somewhat laxative. There is a debate as to whether British Polypody is as sweet as that found in Eastern Europe.[30] It may be that it needs sunshine and soil warmth to develop its full flavour.

Sweet Cicely *Myrrhis odorata* (see page 51) is high in natural sugars and can be cooked with Rhubarb or wild Gooseberries to sweeten them naturally.

Liquorice *Glycyrrhiza glabra* is not generally found wild in the UK except around Pontefract in West Yorkshire. It is a member of the Pea family Fabaceae with a very sweet root. The juice was traditionally heated to evaporate off the water, making a hard block of liquorice juice extract which was then dried and packaged.

Restharrow *Ononis repens* also has roots that taste of liquorice and can be used to make a sweet, liquorice-flavoured drink.

Fruit sugars

Berries are a natural source of sugar, but have a short shelf life so need to be preserved by drying, freezing, canning, pasteurising or preserving them in alcohol.

Dried berries take up the least amount of storage space, stored in kraft pouches, but you will need to gather a lot: 8 kilograms of Bilberries or Elderberries, for example, will yield just 1 kilogram of dried berries. It can take two to three days to dry them in a dehydrator as they are so full of juice. Freeze-drying would be a better method but freeze-dryers are still very expensive.

Fruit juices can be made by pressing (using a juice extractor or cider press), which is suitable for larger fruits like Crab Apple and feral apples. Berry juice is best extracted by putting cleaned berries into a saucepan with just enough water to cover them. Lightly simmer them until they soften, mashing the pulp with a potato masher. Then strain them off through a jelly bag. The juice can either be returned to the stove for further simmering, to concentrate the flavour and the sugar content, or put into bottles and pasteurised.

Making fruit leather from the pulp

Fresh fruit pulp or cooked fruit purées can be used to make tasty, tangy fruity chews. This is also a great use for leftover fruit pulp (strained off after juicing) although it is less sweet, as much of the sugar has gone into the juice. Wild plums, such as ripe Damsons, have enough flesh, when taken off the stone, to pulverise in a blender to make a very fine fruit paste. Spread your paste or pulp out into a thin layer, on greaseproof paper or a silicon sheet. Then put it into a dehydrator or low oven to dry out. I do mine at around 40 degrees C until it is dry and you can peel it off the sheet. The result is called fruit leather and the commercial equivalents are a familiar sight in many schoolchildren's lunch boxes. Cut it into strips or roll the sheets before cutting them to make fruit loops. Store in jars or airtight kraft bags.

Pasteurising

Fruit juices have traditionally been preserved by making cordials and syrups, but both methods require a lot of added sugar, which only became widely available in the UK in the late 1500s. Pasteurising the juices instead allows you to keep bottles all year round without needing to buy a second fridge (although pasteurised juice must be refrigerated once opened) or add any sugar. If, like me, you love the sight of larder shelves groaning with mysterious bottles and jars with handwritten labels, then pasteurising home-made juices is for you.

First, sterilise your bottles by putting clean, glass bottles on a clean baking sheet into an oven, pre-heated to 150 degrees C. Leave them for 15 minutes before removing using oven gloves. It's that simple. To sterilise the lids, boil them for 3 minutes. Fish them out with sterilised metal tongs or a small sieve and put them on clean kitchen paper to dry.

The quickest way to pasteurise fruit juices and herbal infusions is to heat the extracted, filtered juice to over 90 degrees C. Just before it boils at 100 degrees C, pour it carefully into warmed, sterilised bottles, cap them tightly – careful, they are hot – and wrap them in towels to keep them warm. Let them cool very slowly. This method works perfectly well and is a lot easier to do in a domestic kitchen than heating or baking already-filled bottles.

My preferred method, though, is to heat the juice in a stainless-steel pan (fruit acidity reacts with aluminium, so avoid if possible) to the lower temperature of 80 degrees C and then hold the liquid at 80 degree C for 10 minutes. Check your temperature with a jam-maker's thermometer. I prefer a lower heat as it preserves more of the beneficial health properties of juices, even though it requires constant supervision to hold it at temperature. The length of heating time depends on the size of bottle that you plan to fill. As a rule of thumb – and this has worked for all the wild juices I have tried – allow:

10 minutes at 80 degrees
when filling 0.33 centilitre bottles (330 millilitre)

---

15 minutes at 80 degrees
when filling 0.50 centilitre bottles (500 millilitre)

---

20 minutes at 80 degrees
when filling 0.75 centilitre bottles (750 millilitre)

When filling your bottles, use a sterilised Pyrex jug to pour from and a sterilised stainless-steel funnel to pour through. Everything should be as hot as possible, so take care to avoid burns. Fill the bottles to 2 centimetres below the top edge, cap them tightly and wrap tea towels around them to preserve the heat. The aim is to keep them as near to 80 degrees C as possible for the required period of time for the bottle sizes given above. Properly pasteurised juices will keep for at least one, if not two, years as long as the seal is intact and they're kept out of sunlight.

Carbonating drinks

Home carbonation can be done very easily with a soda maker or soda siphon but they do create pressurised canister waste that needs special recycling. You could dilute your home-made wine with fizzy water to make a spritzer. Alternatively – although this will change the flavour a little – try the following experiment.

Mix 2 litres of fruit juice, a herbal infusion or a home-made wine with 240 millilitres of Sea Buckthorn (or lemon) juice, 100 grams of sugar and 2 teaspoons of citric acid. Pour into a tough, plastic family-size (2 litre) fizzy drink bottle (washed out before recycling it). Make sure you have the bottle cap near at hand. Then fold a small piece of stiff paper in half to make a sharp crease. Put 2 teaspoons of bicarbonate of soda onto the paper so it sits in the crease. Now tip the paper and slide the bicarbonate into the bottle mouth. Screw the cap on immediately before it erupts. (For a smaller 500 millilitre bottle, divide the quantities by four.)

Further reading
Sue Azam-Ali, Dr (2008). Fruit juice processing. Accessed online at:
answers.practicalaction.org/our-resources/item/fruit-juice-processing

CHAPTER 16

Wild Drinks

Many wild plants can be used to make a wide variety of drinks. If you've stuck to regular tea and coffee before, you may be surprised at how delicious and satisfying some alternative plants are. After all, modern 'tea' is merely the leaves of *Camellia sinensis* and coffee the roasted bean of *Coffea arabica*. Equally, many other plants than just the Grape *Vitis vinifera* can be used to make wines and the ubiquitous Hops *Humulus lupulus* only became exclusive to beer in 1710, when an Act of Parliament designated it as the only bittering agent allowed in beer. Before then many other wild plants and herbs were used.

Drinks can be simple – a sprig of wild mint, or a handful of Cleavers steeped in cold water overnight, can replace the next day's drinking water. Or you can put a great deal of effort into fermenting country wines or infusing exotic vermouths. However, if you get truly adventurous, remember that while it's not illegal to own a still – for example, to make essential oils – it is illegal to distil alcohol without a licence and paying tax. So stick to elderflower champagne and nettle beer. Cheers! Or sláinte, as we say up north!

Herbal teas

You can make a herbal tea from pretty much any plant as long as it's considered edible and is not toxic or harmful. Remember that most plants have an action on your body. At a normal dose – three cups a day – an everyday tea will provide you with vitamins, minerals, nutrients and balancing compounds. However, some herbs – at three cups a day – can have a strong effect on your body and are really medicinal teas. There can be a fine line between an everyday tea and a medicinal tea, so do learn about their therapeutic effects. If you're not taking a drug that interacts with particular plants, do be encouraged to experiment. By and large, plants are our friends, not our foes.

Infusions

Infusions are used for flowers, leaves and shoots – the more tender parts of the plant – and especially those with an exquisite scent as volatile oils evaporate quickly if boiled. I'd always use the infusion method for lime flowers, clover blossoms, rose petals and elderflowers, for example. Making a herbal infusion is just like making a cup of regular builder's tea. You pour just-boiled water over the plant and let it infuse for 3 minutes before drinking. You need about three times the amount of fresh plant than if dried. So one teaspoon of a cut dried herb per mug or three teaspoons of chopped fresh herb. Generally, the sweeter or more scented you want the tea, the shorter a time you infuse it for. Once you start to infuse something longer than 5 minutes, you will start to get the more bitter chemicals dissolving in it. I always make my infusions in a coffee press. This allows the herbs plenty of space to swirl around in the hot water, but once the plunger is pushed down it is easy to pour. I often add more boiling water once or twice again to extract every last bit of goodness from them. Once you're done with the herbs it is easy to fish them out and put them in the compost.

You'll notice how much better your teas taste, when made this way, than the herbal teabags you can buy, which contain a tiny amount of herb whose natural essential oils have often disappeared during the grinding and filling process.

Cold-water infusions

A cold-water infusion works well with Cleavers (my favourite), Borage (tastes of cucumber), Plantain, Eyebright and culinary herbs such as Mint, Rosemary or Thyme. Put several sprigs of the plant into a jug and pour cold water over them (preferably filtered to lower the chlorine content). Cover the jug. Leave overnight to infuse and use this the next day as your drinking water.

Decoctions

Roots, seeds and bark generally need some persuading to give up their goodness. These are processed by decoction. A decoction means placing the chopped or lightly crushed material (by using a pestle and mortar or rolling pin) into a saucepan of boiling water and simmering for 5–10 minutes, depending on the strength you want. One teaspoon of the roots or seeds per cup of water is sufficient. If a tea is being decocted, it is often easier to make a larger amount than is needed straight away. In this case, strain off the material and cool down the tea, before storing in a fridge. You can either reheat it later or have it as an iced tea.

Wild kombucha

You can turn almost any herbal infusion or decoction into wild kombucha. Make a strong brew and add between 60 and 80 grams of any raw sugar to each litre of warm tea. Then add a SCOBY – a symbiotic culture of bacteria and yeast. You can usually get a piece of this from any friend who makes kombucha or from a health food store. After seven days, filter the now slightly fizzy kombucha off, keeping the SCOBY. Start the process again.

The word *kombucha* actually comes from *kombu-*, the Japanese name for brown kelp and *-cha*, the Japanese for tea. Japanese kombucha is a hot water infusion of the powdered seaweed *Laminaria japonica*. Try this by all means, but restrict it to the occasional small cup as it is extremely high in iodine.

Choosing plants for teas

As well as any culinary herbs that may have escaped from gardens, the following are particularly tasty:

Beech	*Fagus sylvatica*	dried brown leaves	infuse	page 150
Bilberry	*Vaccinium myrtillus*	leaves	infuse	page 89
Birch	*Betula* spp.	ground roasted twigs	infuse	page 151
Bramble	*Rubus fructicosus*	leaves	infuse	page 123
Clovers	*Trifolium repens* and *T. pratense*	flowers	infuse	page 94
Dead-nettles	*Lamium album* and *L. purpureum*	flowers and leaves	infuse	page 101
Elderflower	*Sambucus nigra*	flowers	infuse	page 153
Fennel	*Foeniculum vulgare*	seed	decoct 5 mins	
Ground Ivy	*Glechoma hederacea*	flowers and leaves	infuse	page 102
Hawthorn	*Crataegus* spp.	flowers and leaves	infuse	page 155
Heather	*Erica* and *Calluna* spp.	flowering tops	infuse	page 87
Honey-suckle	*Lonicera periclymenum*	flowers	infuse	
Hops	*Humulus lupulus*	leaves	infuse	page 78
Larch	*Larix decidua*	needles	decoct 5 mins	page 174

Linden	*Tilea* spp.	leaves and flowers	infuse	page 156
Mugwort	*Artemisia vulgaris*	leaves	infuse	page 59
Pineapple-weed	*Matricaria discoides*	flowers and leaves	infuse	page 58
Raspberry, Wild	*Rubus idaeus*	leaves	infuse	page 123
Rose	*Rosa canina* and *R. rugosa*	flowers and hips	infuse	pages 122–23
Rosebay Willowherb	*Chamerion angustifolium*	flowers and leaves	infuse	page 108
Scots Pine	*Pinus sylvestris*	needles	decoct 5 mins	page 174
Sneezewort	*Achillea ptarmica*	flowers and leaves	infuse	page 58
Speedwell	*Veronica officinalis*	aerial parts	infuse	page 112
Spignel	*Meum athamanticum*	leaves	infuse	
Stinging Nettle	*Urtica dioica*	leaves and root	infuse (decoct roots)	page 130
Valerian	*Valeriana officinalis*	flowers, leaves and roots	infuse (decoct roots)	
Water Mint	*Mentha aquatica*	leaves	infuse	page 100
Wood Avens	*Geum urbanum*	root	decoct 5 mins	page 125
Yarrow	*Achillea millefolium*	flowers and leaves	infuse	page 58

Fermented teas

Fermented teas were commonly made from young leaves of Birch, Speedwell, Hawthorn, Wild Strawberry, Bramble and Spignel. One traditional way to process them is to add water, some sugar or honey and let them ferment at room temperature for a few days to a week. The resulting tea can be enjoyed as is or with added flavours like ginger or lemon.

Many leaves can also be fermented in their own juices, such as Rosebay Willowherb (see page 108) which is made into Ivan chai. Scythe the Willowherb at the end of June, just before it flowers. Strip the leaves off and leave them in a heap on a sheet in the sun for a few hours until they start to wilt. Check on them regularly as you do not want them to dry to a crisp but just to go limp. Then bring them inside. Invite some friends around for reinforcements and roll the leaves between the palms of your hands to make wiggly knots. Pack them down firmly into a jam jar and leave for five to seven days. They will start to ferment in their own juices. After a week, take them out and dehydrate or oven-dry them to stop the fermentation – otherwise they go mouldy. This now tastes more like a black tea.

I sometimes go one step further and then put the fermented leaves (in a mesh bag) into the smoker with some burning applewood chips. It's like a fragrant Earl Grey or, with oak woodsmoke, an Assam.

Coffee substitutes

There are several good substitutes for coffee that offer similar benefits without the drawbacks of caffeine. When considering coffee alternatives there are several factors to bear in mind.

Firstly, flavour. Coffee substitutes should have a similar flavour profile to coffee, with a rich and slightly bitter taste. Chicory and Dandelion root, for example, both have a natural bitterness that can mimic the taste of coffee. Coffee substitutes should also have a pleasant aroma, which can be important for the overall sensory experience. It's useful to know that there are health benefits as most of the plants are high in antioxidants and free from, or low in, caffeine.

Acorns make an excellent coffee substitute, especially when mixed with roasted Dandelion root. If you are making acorns into coffee, leave some tannin in when leaching them for a slightly bitter taste. So let the water go pale but don't wash out all the brown colour. Then chop the acorns finely before roasting. A little trial and error is required until you get your perfect 'house blend', especially as different types of oak tree produce acorns with differing tannin strengths.

All coffee-substitute seeds and roots need to be cleaned, chopped and roasted on a baking tray in a hot oven. Remove them when they are nicely brown but not burnt. Store them in an airtight container and grind them when you need to make coffee. When using coffee alternatives I find that you usually need twice as much (by volume) as coffee beans. Ideally use a stovetop percolator, or espresso pot (rather than the weaker drip or cafetière methods), as this makes the best wild coffee. Boil for at least 10 minutes before straining and serving.

With my favourite, Cleavers seeds, toast them in a dry frying pan as they go brown very quickly. You can literally smell the coffee aroma from them as they toast.

Wild coffee plants:

Cleavers	*Galium aparine*	seeds	actually related to coffee
Dandelion	*Taraxacum officinale*	roots	slightly mocha when aged
Hawthorn	*Crataegus monogyna*	roasted seeds	pleasant with spices
Chicory	*Cichorium intybus*	roots	nutty, woodsy
Acorns	*Quercus* spp.	nuts	bitter, malty
Burdock	*Arctium lappa* and *A. minor*	roots	nutty
Juniper	*Juniperus officinalis*	seeds	spicy
Barley	*Hordeum vulgare*	grain	malty
Beech	*Fagus sylvatica*	nuts	fiddly but pleasant
Sow thistle	*Sonchus* spp.	roots	like dandelion
Waterlily˙	*Nymphaea alba*	seeds	roasted

˙a toxic alkaloid (nupharin) occurs in all parts of this plant except the seed

In urban gardens and parks that feature non-native specimen trees, you might also find the following plant substitutes:

Black Locust Tree ✳ *Robinia pseudoacacia* (seeds)
Honey Locust Tree ✳ *Gleditsia triacanthos* (seeds)
Kentucky Coffee Tree ✳ *Gymnocladus dioicus* (seeds)
California Coffeeberry ✳ *Rhamnus californica* (berries)
Carob ✳ *Ceratonia siliqua* (bean pods)

Cleavers

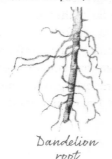

Dandelion root

Acorn

Beech nuts

Wild wine

Making wild wine, or country wines, from foraged ingredients can be a fun and rewarding process. Here are some general steps to follow:

Collect your ingredients: First, you will need to gather your ingredients. Look for fruits, flowers or herbs that are in season and abundant in your area. Some common ingredients for wild wine include berries, apples, plums, elderflowers, dandelions and flowers like honeysuckle or primrose.

Prepare the ingredients: Once you have collected your ingredients, wash them thoroughly and remove any stems, seeds or other unwanted parts. Chop or crush the fruit to release the juice, or bruise herbs to release their oils.

Get your equipment together: It's important to use clean and sterilized equipment throughout the wine-making process to prevent contamination and spoilage. You may also want to use a hydrometer to measure the alcohol content of your wine.

Make a sugar solution: In a large pot, dissolve sugar in warm water to create a sweet solution. The amount of sugar you use will depend on the sweetness of your ingredients and your personal taste. A good rule of thumb is to use about 500 grams of sugar to 5 litres of water.

Add your ingredients: Once the sugar solution has cooled, add your prepared ingredients to a fermenting bucket and pour the solution over them. Then give them a stir.

Ferment the wine: Transfer the mixture to a fermentation vessel, such as a glass demijohn or a food-grade plastic bucket. Add a packet of wine yeast to the mixture and stir well. I often fall back on a basic champagne yeast. Cover the vessel with a clean cloth, lid or bubbler and put it in a cool, dark place to ferment. Stir the mixture daily to aerate it and release any gases.

Rack the wine: After a week or so, transfer the wine to a new demijohn with a bubbler, leaving any sediment behind. This process is called racking and will help to clarify the wine.

Age the wine: Allow the wine to age for several weeks or months, depending on the recipe and your personal preference. The longer you age the wine, the more complex and smooth the flavour will be.

Bottle and enjoy: Once the wine has aged to your liking, transfer it to bottles and cork or cap them. Enjoy your home-made wild wine with friends and family.

Following are some personal favourites.

Red wines:

Bramble berries	*Rubus fructicosus*	a good red wine with a fruity body
Elderberry	*Sambucus nigra*	makes a good red wine, an excellent port and can be fermented with Belgian beer yeast to make an exotic mead

Also: Damson, Bullace, sloes, Blackcurrant, elderberry, Hawthorn berry, Bilberry, Mulberry, Cherry Plum and Bird Cherry.

Rosé wines:

Japanese knotweed spears	*Fallopia japonica*	make a Rhubarb-like pinot that is especially good carbonated and chilled (for its other culinary uses, see page 117)

Also: rosehips, Flowering Currant flowers and Black Elder (the flowers are pink). Willowherb flowers also impart a nice rosé colour but need to be mixed with something else for flavour.

White wines:

Dandelion	*Taraxacum officinale*	use the open flowers to make an excellent white wine. The flower heads must be fully open and removed from the stalk. Don't soak the flowers for more than three days or you'll spoil the flavour
Elderflower	*Sambucus nigra*	the flowers make excellent champagne-style wines and a good mead
Meadowsweet	*Filipendula ulmaria*	the flowers make a good white wine and a good mead. Don't soak them for too long or a note of wet bandages creeps into the flavour

Also: flowers of Cowslip, Primrose, Honeysuckle, Coltsfoot, Gorse, Goldenrod, Linden and Pineappleweed. Crab Apple and Quince also make lovely white wines. For the fruits, chop them up and measure 4.5 litres of water. You need to allow more volume than the flowers as there will be more air gaps between chunks.

How to make a basic flower wine

For a classic flower wine in a standard demijohn you'll need:

3.5 litres of flowers

4.5 litres of water

1.4 kilograms of sugar

rind and juice of two lemons and one orange

a pack of wine yeast

yeast nutrient

450 grams of raisins

Directions:

1 Put the flower heads in a large stainless-steel saucepan, boil the water and pour it on to the flowers. Cover with the lid. Stir every day for three days, keeping it covered in between.

2 After three days, bring to the boil, adding the sugar and citrus rinds, and simmer for an hour. Remove from the heat and add the citrus juices. When the temperature has dropped to 20–21 degrees C, add the yeast and the yeast nutrient. Cover and leave for a further three days.

3 Strain into a demijohn, add the raisins and a fermenting lock (a bubbler) to seal the demijohn. Leave until the wine clears then siphon it into a clean jar, cork and leave for 6 months. Siphon it off into bottles and keep it for a further 6 months to mature to its best.

4 This recipe can be used for all the flower wines. For a sweeter dessert wine, increase the sugar to 1.5 kilograms (stopping fermentation to leave sweetness or you'll end up with a stronger alcohol %); for a dry wine reduce to 1.2 kilograms.

Plants for infusing in mead

Meads were traditionally wines made with diluted honey rather than
sugar. If you want to recreate these ancient drinks you will probably
need to buy honey from a local beekeeper rather than trying to forage
wild honey. All of the flowers that are used to make wine, especially the
white wines, can be infused to give interesting notes to meads. When
steeping any material, taste the mead regularly so as not to spoil the drink
by leaving it in for too long. Remember that volatile plants with aromatic
smells and a high content of essential oils give up their flavours quite
quickly. Once these are exhausted, further steeping just releases other
compounds like the more bitter alkaloids. In general it is better to steep
flowers for a short period, then strain them off and add fresh flowers, to
build up the flavours. I also suggest not making meads too sweet. A dry
mead is much more palatable unless you have a very sweet tooth.

Honeysuckle	*Lonicera periclymenum*	flowers	these make one of the finest meads I've ever tasted
Meadowsweet	*Filipendula ulmaria*	flowers	the original 'mead-is-sweet' flower that also helps to give mead a longer shelf life
Bog Myrtle	*Myrica gale*	leaves and twigs	a few leaves steeped in plain mead impart a pleasant spicy-herb flavour not unlike bay
Oak	*Quercus* spp.	bark and twigs	give a barrel-oaked finish

If you use fruits or fruit juices in your mead then technically it is
a melomel.

Herbal beers and ciders

Herbal beer is made without grain. You can also think of it as a
yeastier version of wild wines. A classic example is nettle beer but
you can substitute many other wild plants.

How to make a basic nettle beer

For nettle beer in a standard demijohn you will need:

500 grams of fresh nettle tops

500 grams of sugar

4.5 litres of water

One lemon, juiced and zested

5 grams of cream of tartar

7 grams of dried ale yeast

Directions:

1 As with wine-making, but particularly important with home brewing, it's important to use clean and sterilised equipment throughout the process to prevent contamination and spoilage.

2 Pick the nettle tops, wearing gloves to avoid being stung. Wash them well in cold water and place them in a large pot.

3 Pour 4.5 litres of boiling water over the nettles and stir well. Cover the pot with a cloth and let it sit for 24 hours.

4 After 24 hours, strain the nettle liquid through a fine mesh sieve into a clean pot. Add the sugar, lemon juice and zest, and cream of tartar to the pot and stir well.

5 Bring the mixture to a boil and then reduce the heat and simmer for about 30 minutes.

6 Remove the pot from the heat and let it cool to room temperature.

7 Once cooled, sprinkle the dried ale yeast over the surface of the liquid and stir well.

8 Cover the pot with a cloth and leave it in a warm place to ferment for two to three days.

9 After two to three days, strain the beer through a fine mesh sieve to remove any sediment.

10 Transfer the beer to clean bottles with swing-top caps, leaving some headspace at the top of each bottle before closing them securely.

11 Allow the beer to condition in the bottles for several days to develop carbonation.

12 Once the beer is carbonated, store it in a cool place and enjoy it chilled.

There are also lots of plants that can be used by brewers of grain-based beers that make a great bittering alternative to hops.

Ground Ivy	*Glechoma hederacea*	reminds me slightly of geranium leaf. Its old name was Ale-hoof and it was used instead of hops as a bittering flavour.
Mugwort	*Artemisia vulgaris*	add to beer as a flavouring and to help preserve it.
Rosebay Willowherb	*Chamerion angustifolium*	fresh leaves make a great ale flavouring.
Juniper	*Juniperus communis*	a common flavouring of liqueurs and spirits (most notably gin) and also used to make juniper beer. This is done in two ways, either by adding the berries as a flavouring or by straining the beer through cut branches of juniper.
Rowan	*Sorbus aucuparia*	in 1664 John Evelyn recommended that 'Ale and Beer Brew'd with these Berries, being ripe, is an incomparable Drink.' He called it the Quick-beam or Quicken tree, which is now thought to be the Wild Mountain Ash, the rowan.
True Service Tree	*Sorbus domestica*	not to be confused with berries of the Wild Service Tree *Sorbus torminalis*. The name 'servise tree' may have come from cerevisiae, meaning fermented beer.

Also try Larch, Pine, Sage and other aromatics instead of Hops.

Sycamore	*Acer pseudoplatanus*	John Evelyn in 1664 said of sycamore sap, 'In some of these sweet *Saps*, one Bushel of *Mault* will afford as good *Ale* as *four* in ordinary *Waters*, even in *March* itself; in others, as good as *two* Bushels; for *this*, preferring the *Sycomor* before any other.'

Ciders are made by fermenting Apple or Crab Apple juice. These don't need extra sugar, just yeast – and often their own wild yeast will be enough, as long as the weather is good and the temperature right. Too hot and other undesirable strains may take over; too cold and the yeast may not kick in before stagnation.

Verjuice, or verjus, originally immature Grape juice, is often pressed by foragers from Crab Apples instead. It is basically a sharp, sour juice that can be used instead of lemon.

Vinegars, in their simplest form, are a by-product of all your winemaking experiments that went wrong. You may notice lots of tiny flies around your brew and you need to strictly keep them out. These are vinegar flies – fruit flies of the family *Drosophilidae* – that carry vinegar-producing bacteria on their feet. If you want to make vinegar deliberately, add some 'mother' unpasteurised vinegar to fruit juice or wine. Then cover and leave it to ferment until you like the taste. Then heat it to stop the fermentation if you wish – although this also kills the beneficial bacteria. If you start with a 5 per cent alcohol, you'll end up with a vinegar around 5 per cent acidity. You can infuse fruit like Wild Raspberry or herbs like Ground Ivy to your base vinegar for salad dressings. When using Elderberries, that must be cooked, add a little brown sugar then bring the vinegar to the boil for 3-5 minutes, to get a lovely elderberry balsamic vinegar.

Shrubs are drinks that mix fruit with vinegar, herbs, sugar or honey. Raspberry with Water Mint Shrub is particularly refreshing.

Caution

Once a bittering agent, Common Clary *Salvia sclarea* is no longer. Herbalist Maud Grieves in 1931 comments 'It was also employed in this country as a substitute for Hops, for sophisticating beer, communicating considerable bitterness and intoxicating property, which produced an effect of insane exhilaration of spirits, succeeded by severe headache.' L'Obel [Flemish physician 1538- 1616] says: 'Some brewers of Ale and Beere doe put it into their drinke to make it more heady, fit to please drunkards, who thereby, according to their several dispositions, become either dead drunke, or foolish drunke, or madde drunke.'

Maud Grieves also remarks about Broom *Cytisus scoparius* that, 'In large doses, Sparteine [a primary compound] causes vomiting and purging, weakens the heart, depresses the nerve cells and lowers the blood pressure and has a strong resemblance to the action of Conine (Hemlock) on the heart.' [31]

Ash Leaf Frenette

Frenette is a mildly alcoholic drink made from fermented ash leaves, which traces its history back to ancient Gaul under the Romans. For more about the Ash tree, see page 149.

Equipment (To make 20 litres. Alcohol content will be around 2 to 5 per cent, averaging 3.5 per cent):
25-litre brewing bucket
Muslin or jelly bag for straining
Sterilised swing-top bottles
Hydrometer (optional)

Ingredients:
Two hundred ash leaves with bitter stalks removed
20 litres of rainwater or soft, de-chlorinated water
1 kilogram of raw cane sugar
25 grams of roasted chicory or roasted dandelion root
2 grams of dried hops (optional)
15 grams of tartaric acid or 25 millilitres of lemon juice
16 grams (two sachets) of baker's or brewer's yeast.
   I recommend Vintner's Harvest Yeast SN9 (Saccharomyces bayanus) which you can get from most winemaking supply shops.

Directions:

1 Put the leaves into a large stockpot and cover them with water (about 2 litres). Bring to the boil and simmer gently for half an hour. Add the chicory or dandelion root and simmer for a further 15 minutes. (If you're using hops, add it 5 minutes after the chicory.) Remove from the heat and set aside to cool.

2 Take 250 millilitres of the hot infusion off and dissolve the tartaric acid into it.

3 When cool, pour the infused liquid into your brewing bucket through a muslin bag to strain it. Compost the leaves.

4 Dissolve the sugar in 500 millilitres of hot water, and the yeast in 250 millilitres of warm water at body temperature (35 degrees C). Add these, with the tartaric acid solution, to the brew bucket and top up to 20 litres with warm water.

5 Leave it to ferment in a dark room, covered with a folded muslin cloth. Each day, skim off any foam that has formed on the top. After 10 days check that the liquid level has not fallen more than 2 centimetres. If necessary add a little more tepid water. Fermentation will last anywhere from 15 to 60 days depending on the room temperature. The warmer the room, the quicker the frenette will ferment. Once it has stopped bubbling, it has stopped fermenting.

6 This can be more accurately worked out if you have a hydrometer. When it reaches 1008/1010 after a slow fermentation, rack it off and bottle it. Cork the bottles and leave them on their sides for two weeks. Do not shake the bottles before serving as there may be a fine yeast deposit.

7 Best served chilled.

Ortilette – nettle beer à la française

Ortilette is a light refreshing fermented drink with a very low alcohol content that nevertheless packs some fizz. Made in a similar way to ash leaf frenette. It is very similar to British nettle beer recipes but it doesn't taste like a hops beer at all.

Liqueurs and Vermouths

Other drinks such as liqueurs can be made by steeping foraged fruits in vodka, gin or whisky with a little sugar. For example: sloe gin, damson gin, bramble whisky, etc. Vermouths are made by steeping bitter herbs such as Mugwort in white wine, often fortified with gin. The art is in knowing how long to leave each herb in for!

Further reading

Pascal Baudar (2018), *The Wildcrafting Brewer: Creating Unique Drinks and Boozy Concoctions from Nature's Ingredients* (Chelsea Green Publishing).

John Wright (2018), *Booze: River Cottage Handbook No. 12.* (Bloomsbury Publishing)

Wild Horses

CHAPTER 17

Wild Household

I try to live as simply as possible. This is partly due to being economical and partly due to wanting to live with as light a footprint as possible on this beloved planet. Here are a few of the ways I try to reduce my environmental impact while adding flavour to life.

Food flavouring essences

It's easy to make food flavouring essences at home to substitute for almond essence and vanilla essence. Here I have used vegetable glycerine or a clear spirit (high-strength vodka) as the base because both help to extract the essential oils. Alcohol is more efficient but glycerine is preferred by people who don't tolerate alcohol well or don't use it for religious or health reasons.

Rowan bud 'almond' essence

Non-alcohol version – slow infusion

Fill a preserving jar half full of finely chopped rowan leaf buds, picked while they are still closed. (Do use proper canning jars like Kilner or Mason as cheaper quality ones may explode under pressure.) Separately, mix vegetable glycerine with filtered water in a ratio of 3:1 glycerine to water. (The weakest you can go while retaining the preservative properties of the glycerine is a ratio of 3:2.) Pour over the rowan leaf buds to the shoulder of the jar. Leave to infuse for up to four weeks, shaking daily. Taste occasionally. Strain into small, sterilised bottles.

Non-alcohol version – quick infusion

Fill a good-quality canning jar half full of closed rowan leaf buds – no need to chop them. For this method, you can use 100 per cent glycerine or a 3:1 ratio glycerine-to-water blend. Fill up the jar with the chosen liquid, leaving 3 centimetres of clear headspace below the jar's rim. Put the lid and ring on loosely – do not tighten them. Place a rack or trivet inside a pressure cooker and add 250 millilitres of water. Stand the jar on the rack and close the lid. Turn the pressure release knob to the locked position if your model requires this. Steam for 30 minutes at the high 15 psi setting. Allow the pressure cooker to cool down until the button releases naturally. When the jars have cooled down but the liquid is still warm, filter through a sieve, gently pressing the leaf buds to squeeze out the liquid. Pour the essence into small, sterilised bottles and label.

Alcohol version

You can use either of the above methods, but with an 80 per cent proof clear spirit instead of glycerine in exactly the same ratios.

Other essences you can make following the methods above include:

Hawthorn 'Almond'	*Crataegus monogyna*	flowers	marzipan, almond
Japanese 'Rose'	*Rosa rugosa*	petals	rose
Sweet Cicely 'Aniseed'	*Myrrhis odorata*	young green seeds	aniseed
Sweet Flag 'Spice'	*Acorus calamus*	rhizome	cinnamon-ginger
Sweet Woodruff 'Vanilla'	*Galium odoratum*	herb	vanilla, tonka bean
Wood Avens 'Clove'	*Geum urbanum*	white lateral roots	clove

Look at the Wild Spice Chart on pages 240–41 to get some more ideas.

Sweet Woodruff   Sweet Cicely   Dog Rose

Leafy larder

Leaves can be used for both cooking and storing food. In the former, they can replace tinfoil – wrap leaves around root vegetables to protect them from the heat when roasting in the coals. A skewered leaf parcel can be held into the flames with reduced scorching of the contents. I remember in Tonga (where my father was working when I was eighteen), going to a feast where everything was cooked underground for several days. Delicate fish in spicy sauces would be folded into banana leaves and placed at the cooler top of the heap to protect them as they cooked. The result was a steaming, fragrant, leaf dish of tenderness.

The antimicrobial properties of many plants can slow down the decay of foodstuffs, which makes leaves ideal for storing and packing. A Finnish fisherman told me that before refrigeration on fishing vessels, they would put to sea with plenty of birch brash (the young twigs) which, sandwiched between the layers of fish, would help keep them fresh until they got back to port. The leaves contain methyl salicylate, which has antimicrobial properties – although in large quantities it is toxic.

The protective power of leaves was known long ago, perhaps as far back as Roman times. In 1597 the herbalist John Gerard advised, 'The report goeth, saith Pliny, that figs do not putrefy at all that are wrapped in the leaves of Mullein: which thing Dioscorides also maketh mention of.' Lovely Mullein has huge, soft, fuzzy leaves so is great for wrapping things in.

Leaves for wrapping food

Leaves that are good for protecting foods during cooking are: Mullein, Burdock, Comfrey, Dock, Horseradish, Mallow, Butterbur and Grapevine. Wrap them around the food you want to bake or roast – whether a fish parcel or a roast potato – and secure it with sharpened birch twigs (or wooden toothpicks or cocktail sticks). Sheets of seaweed are also good for wrapping food, especially Sea Lettuce and Laver.

In Poland, Sweet Flag leaves were traditionally used to line bread ovens during the baking process before cooking loaves of bread.

Tinfoil substitutes

Seaweeds, Burdock leaves, Butterbur leaves and even bought sushi paper can all be used as substitutes for tinfoil.

I'm on a mission to manage without tinfoil when cooking, roasting and baking. Have you ever thought about what goes into that shiny roll of foil paper? First, you have to strip-mine the earth for bauxite rock, for its aluminium ore. This is most likely to happen in Australia, China, Brazil, India and Guinea, but many other tropical countries also produce some bauxite. Strip-mining involves disturbing large land areas, which can include natural and critical habitats, leading to desertification and the loss of species. It also, often, has a huge impact on the indigenous peoples.

Mined bauxite ore is then refined into alumina, which is then smelted into aluminium. The refining process uses sodium hydroxide, under pressure, and creates a highly alkaline residue that is stored in landfill sites and highly alkaline slurry and water run-off, which has to be managed to avoid contaminating the surrounding land and waterways. The smelting process generates solid waste, again destined for landfill, and also, when the chimneys are renewed (every five to seven years), a heap of hazardous waste due to fluoride, cyanide and reactive metal.

Part of the process of extraction involves electrolysis – hugely demanding of energy. The smelting process, in which high temperatures are required to melt the aluminium, use large amounts of fossil fuels with concomitant emissions.

The aluminium is eventually rolled out to make your baking foil. Sprayed with lubricant as it goes through the rollers (food grade lubricant, we're told) and then heated to 340 degrees C for 12 hours. That's quite a fuel bill. And that's before you calculate the energy use of recycling it – assuming it's been washed and put in the right bin, rather than sent to landfill where it will take 400 years to break down.

I've managed without tinfoil for over ten years now, thanks to oven pots with lids; seaweed, leaves or beeswax wraps to cover food; and recycling plastic takeaway boxes to store food in or transport it for lunches, etc. In fact, it's quite hard to imagine now what I could ever have used it for.

Laundry

I'm not great at household chores – there are just too many other more interesting things to do – but clothes have to be washed.

Some plants are high in phytochemicals called saponins. These are soapy molecules that grab onto fat, grease and dirt with one end while the other end is attracted to water. So they pull the dirt off cloth and then sail away on the outgoing tide. Saponin-rich plants only need light agitation in water to release a liquid soap substance that cleans fabric as well as skin and hair.

Conker laundry liquid

The conker seed of the Horse Chestnut tree (not to be confused with Sweet Chestnut) has one of the highest saponin concentrations in European plants. Conkers can be used to make a laundry soap that can even be used in your washing machine instead of the suspect chemicals you buy in the supermarkets. Although concentrated saponins are poisonous to fish and other marine life, it is unlikely that, once diluted by your washing machine, you will do worse with these natural measures than with a chemical product.

Directions:
1 Chop six shelled conkers into small pieces and then blitz them until they are smaller still in a blender.
2 Put them into a large jar.
3 Add 300 millilitres of boiling water, screw on the lid and give them a good shake.
4 Leave overnight.
5 The following day strain the conker 'milk' complete with all its soapy saponins into a jug, before carefully transferring the precious liquid into a bottle. You can discard the pulp.
6 You'll need around 60 millilitres of detergent for each load of washing, so this makes five washes' worth. Just add it to your washing machine as you'd add any commercial laundry liquid. If you live in a hard-water area, you can add a dash of vinegar as a water softener. You can also add a few drops of any essential oil if you like scented laundry.

7   Keep what you don't use in the fridge for up to a week or freeze the rest in ice cube trays before turning them out into bags labelled DO NOT EAT. Keep the stash of laundry cubes in the freezer until you want to use them (and out of reach of children who might mistake them for ice cream). One 'average' ice cube is about 30 millilitres of laundry liquid, so two laundry cubes per wash are needed. Chuck them in the machine on top of your clothes and the hot water will dissolve them.

8   To preserve the liquid without refrigeration, add 1 teaspoon of citric acid to every 500 millilitres of liquid while it is hot and stir well to dissolve it. It may keep in a sealed jar for a year, if you're lucky.

9   Alternatively, pick four conkers and chop them into very small pieces. Then dry them to prevent them going off. Once dry, crush them further into small granular chunks in a blender, then store them in a preserving jar. Every time you are planning a wash, put three or four teaspoons of the grains into a small (300 millilitre) jam jar, half fill the jar with boiling water and leave it for half an hour. Then strain it and put the liquid into your washing machine drawer. Programme the machine as usual and wash those clothes. (The soaked grains can be reused three times before they need to be replaced.)

10 Assuming you do one weekly wash, you need to pick around sixty to a hundred conkers to do your laundry for a year – depending which method you use. If you want to keep unprocessed conkers for a long time, chop them open and dehydrate them to stop them going mouldy.

Soap chunks and powder

If you are in a hurry and have clothes that can withstand a hot wash, chop six medium conkers or four large ones and put the pieces into a mesh bag. Throw these into the washing machine with your clothes. The saponins dissolve best in hot water, so use the liquid for cold and cool energy-saving washes. You will use up more conkers this way though.

If clothes are only lightly soiled, you can also put 4 to 5 teaspoons of granulated conkers into a zipped calico bag and put it straight into a washing machine. The hot water will help to release the saponins and wash the clothes.

Horse Chestnut leaf liquid soap

If you don't have conkers you can also use the leaves of the Horse Chestnut. Bring 1 litre of water to the boil in a large saucepan. Add 100 grams of chopped Horse Chestnut leaves. Simmer for 15 minutes, then take off the hob. Use a stick blender to blitz the leaves in the water. Strain through a mesh bag or sock and keep the liquid. Once the bag has stopped dripping, squeeze it, or put it into a press (tincture or cider press) to extract the last of the soapy liquid. If you're not using it straight away, then add 2 teaspoons of citric acid to 1 litre of liquid soap to preserve it.

Soapwort

You can find Soapwort *Saponaria officinalis* growing wild in parts of the UK, but it is also easily grown as a garden plant. The leaves and stems contain about 5 per cent saponins and the root about 20 per cent. Use 15 grams of dried root (about 3 heaped teaspoons if it's finely chopped) or two generous handfuls of the whole plant to 750 millilitres of hot water. Bring to the boil and simmer for 20 minutes to release the soap.

Horse Chestnut

Plants that contain saponins that can also be used to make soap

Horse Chestnut	*Aesculus hippocastanum*	seed and leaves	native
Soapwort	*Saponaria officinalis*	leaves and roots	native
Common Ivy	*Hedera helix*	leaves	native
Clematis	*Clematis* spp.	leaves and flowers	cultivated
Soapberry	*Sapindus* spp.	berries	foreign
Soapbush (California lilac)	*Ceanothus cuneatus* and spp.	flowers	foreign
Soap Bush	*Miconia crenata syn. Clidemia hirta*	leaves	foreign
Wild Mock Orange	*Philadelphus lewisii*	bark, leaves, flowers	foreign
Soapwood	*Dodonaea viscosa*	seeds	foreign
Soap lily (Amole)	*Chlorogalum pomeridianum*	peeled bulb	foreign
Soap Dogwood	*Noltea africana*	leaves	foreign
Soap Wattle Tree (Australia)	*Acacia holosericea*	green seed pods	foreign
Soap Tree (Australia)	*Alphitonia excelsa*	leaves	foreign
Yucca	*Yucca glauca* and spp.	root (and leaf)	houseplant
Bracken	*Pteridium aquilinum*	rhizome	native
Ragged Robin	*Lychnis flos-cuculi*	whole plant	native
Campions	*Silene* spp.	whole plant	native
Baby's Breath	*Gypsophila paniculata*	roots	cultivated
Soap-bark Tree (Chile)	*Quillaja saponaria*	inner bark	foreign
Buffaloberry	*Shepherdia* spp.	stems and berries	foreign

Please be aware that many plants containing saponins can also be toxic if eaten or drunk.

Washing up

Pot scrubs
For pot scrubs, use coils of Field Horsetail *Equisetum arvense* instead of plastic sponges. They are tough and biodegradable. You can also grow Luffa *Luffa aegyptiaca* plants if you have a greenhouse or a warm balcony with a wall for it to climb up.

Washing-up liquid
You can make a soapy liquid for washing dishes out of Common Ivy *Hedera helix* leaves. Use 10 grams of leaves per 100 millilitres of water. Shred or chop the leaves. If you have a juicer, put them through that but keep all the pulp and put the lot into a saucepan. Add the water and bring to the boil. Simmer for 5 minutes. Strain off the liquid. Add 2 teaspoons of citric acid per litre (1 teaspoon per 500 millilitres) of hot liquid and stir to dissolve. This acts as a preservative (and otherwise you will need to keep it in the fridge).

If you want to thicken the consistency, add 2 teaspoons of guar gum per 500 millilitres and sprinkle it in while whisking (or using a stick blender). Guar gum can't be foraged but Carragheen seaweed can. Add a tight handful of dried carragheen to each litre, cold soak for 20 minutes then boil for 20 minutes. Strain off the Ivy leaves and the seaweed, and store in bottles. Add a preservative if you want to keep it for a long time.

Other soap plants include the imported soap nut *Sapindus* sp. or local conkers *Aesculus hippocastanum*. Boil 10 whole nuts in 1 litre of water. Use 15 if you want it soapier. Strain the liquid through a cloth and bottle it to make a dishwashing liquid. Add vinegar to preserve it at 1:5 parts vinegar to strained liquid by volume or store in the fridge. Alternatively, preserve it by adding 2 teaspoons of citric acid per litre of hot liquid and stir until dissolved.

Put some into a spray bottle to use for wiping down surfaces. (Mix 2:1 parts of soap nut liquid to vinegar to clean stainless steel surfaces or windows.)

Soak dirty jewellery in the washing-up liquid before cleaning it with a soft toothbrush. Then buff with a soft cloth.

Hair dye

Plants have long been used as a rinse to keep your natural hair colour fresh. The following method enhances hair colour rather than dyeing your hair. Decoct a strong tea with your chosen herb, and apply to your hair after conditioning. If you can fill a tub or sink with the rinse and leave your hair to soak in it for a few minutes, all the better. Don't rinse off the herb tea, just air-dry or blow-dry it.

You can also add a strong herbal decoction to an equal part of hair conditioner and leave it in for 5–10 minutes. Do this several times a week to build up the colour as it will fade without regular top-ups.

To brighten blonde hair:
Chamomile or Pineappleweed flowers.
Mullein flowers. Sweet Chestnut bark.

To deepen brunette hair:
Walnut leaves and green husks.
(Strong coffee is a quick hack, too.)

For a reddish-brown hair dye:
Rhubarb root. For a purple tint use Beetroot.

To cover grey in dark or black hair:
Sage – the Mediterranean grandmothers' secret.

To strengthen hair:
Nettle and Horsetail. Both are full of silica.

For stronger results, powdered herbs can be mixed with coconut oil and/or honey to make a paste. This can be left on for much longer and may help to give a deeper colour as a result. This was the way I dyed my hair for years, before I decided to embrace silver.

Home fragrance

Put bunches of dried Sweet Woodruff into empty bud vases for a vanilla-honey-hay scent. I often have a bunch of Sweet Woodruff tucked into the visor of my car.

If you prefer the smell of tangerine and citrus, use Sweet Flag leaves. People in medieval times scattered these rushes on the floor to scent their rooms. Sweet Flag root has insecticidal essential oils, so it probably helped with keeping fleas from the animals at bay, too. You can also weave them into simple mats.

Our ancestors used potpourri and pomanders to scent their homes. If you have a dehydrator, you can dry the petals of any aromatic plant to keep in small pots around the house.

Many synthetic fragrances (even the ones purporting to be 'natural') contain allergens and have been reported to cause problems with breathing, sore eyes, heart palpitations and atrial fibrillation. They are often carcinogenic and are toxic to fish and aquatic life when they leach into the water table from landfill sites. Home-made fragrances are easy to make, cost nothing and are kinder to the environment.

Sweet
Woodruff

Aromatic plants for home fragrance:

Cedar	*Thuja plicata*	needles, bark chips
Douglas Fir	*Pseudotsuga menziesii*	needles, bark chips, resin
Juniper	*Juniperus communis*	needles, berries, wood chips
Mugwort	*Artemisia vulgaris*	leaf
Pineappleweed	*Matricaria discoides*	flowering herb
Rose	*Rosa* spp. especially *Rosa rugosa*	petals
Sweet Flag	*Acorus calamus*	rush, root
Wild Fennel	*Foeniculum vulgare*	seeds
Wild Marjoram	*Origanum vulgare*	leaf
Wood Avens	*Geum urbanum*	root
Wood Sage	*Teucrium* spp.	leaf
Yarrow	*Achillea millefolium*	leaf, flower

Of course, you can also use culinary herbs like lavender, rosemary and sage.

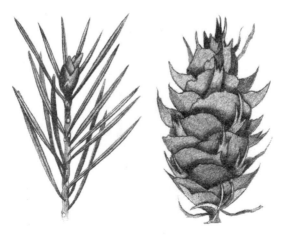

Douglas Fir needle and cone

Final Words

We live in an incredible world. The non-human species that we share this planet with are, each in their own way, intelligent and sentient. Even having studied and loved them for so long now, every day I learn something new – often mind-blowing.

Don't feel disheartened by how much information seems to be required to become a competent forager. The hardest part is taking the first steps. I suggest people start by just taking one new plant a week and learning it well. Once you get going, you will realise that you know an awful lot already and, as you start training your mind, your pace of learning will speed up.

Foraging deepens your connection with yourself and our world in so many ways: culinary, medicinal, physical, intellectual and spiritual. Enjoy the discovery.

Endnotes

1. DEFRA, 2020.
2. Louv, 2013.
3. Goldsworthy, A. (1990). *A Collaboration with Nature*. Harry N. Abrams, Inc.
4. Stark, 2019.
5. Poonia, 2015.
6. Li, 2015.
7. San Andrés Larrea, 2014.
8. Murrell, 1615.
9. De Vincenzi, 2003.
10. Siener, 2013.
11. Visser, 2019.
12. Staniszewski, 2020.
13. Sturtevant, 1919.
14. Wilmot, 2014.
15. Wild, 2020.
16. Alarfaj, 2021.
17. Brodie, 2016.
18. Stout, 2011; Toon, 2022.
19. Bird, 2014.
20. Figueroa et al., 2021.
21. Levandosky, 2021; Frediansyah, 2021.
22. Gerard, 1597.
23. Ibid.
24. Klapp, 2006.
25. Drobnik, 2015.
26. Luczaj, 2012.
27. Luczaj, 2021.
28. Sayle, 2023.
29. UNICEF 2023,
    data.unicef.org/how-many/how-many-people-are-in-the-world
30. Luczaj, 2022.
31. Grieves, 1931.

Acknowledgements

I'd like to thank my literary agent Claire Conrad, my editor Holly Harris and her great team at Simon and Schuster, especially Sophia Akhtar for her patience and attention to detail. Thanks too to designer Doug Kerr for his skill in juggling text and illustrations, and Talya Baldwin whose illustrative talent brings the text to life. I'd like to particularly thank Matthew Rooney for tirelessly proofreading the text from a botanical perspective, and my daughter Caitlin Keddie whose work on the EatWild app challenged me to explore many of my thoughts on wild food further. When I first started teaching foraging it was with the encouragement of John Wright, Joanna Boyce, Jennet Walton, Mark Watson and Romena Huq, and my foraging journey has been made all the richer by my numerous friends from the Association of Foragers.

Index

Page references in *italics* indicate images.

abundance, mindset of 7
access and trespass 19
accidents 16–17
Achillea 33, 56, 58
Achilles 33, 58
acorns (*Quercus* spp.) 150, 160, 231, 232–4, 257, 258, *258*
Acton, Eliza: *Modern Cookery for Private Families* 64
age, foraging and 9
agricultural areas, foraging in 17
Alder Buckthorn (*Frangula alnus*) 140
Alexanders (*Smyrnium olusatrum*) 51, 229, 240, 242
Alkanet (*Alkanna tinctoria*) 32, 66
allergies 17–18, 52, 60
Allioideae 36–9, *36*, *37*, *38*
Alliums 36, *36*, 37, *37*, 38, *38*, 39, 240
Alpine Dock (*Rumex alpinus*) 118
Alpine Sweet-vetch (*Hedysarum alpinum*) 90
Amaranthaceae 40–45, *40*, *41*, *42*, *44*
Amaryllidaceae 36
American Silver Buffalo Berry (*Shepherdia argentea*) 85